PRESENTED TO:

FROM:

Joy *for* Today

Devotional Studies *from* James for Everyday Life

DARYL KRAFT

living oracles

Hayden, Idaho

Joy For Today
Devotional Studies from James—for Everyday Life

Copyright 2017 by Daryl Kraft
Published by Living Oracles, Inc.
Hayden, Idaho 83835
www.livingoracles.com

Cover and interior design by Gearbox
StudioGearbox.com

Printed in China

Living Oracles books are available at special quantity discounts to use as premiums and sales promotions, as book club, Bible study, or edification group selections, or for use in corporate training or incentive programs. For more information, please contact Living Oracles or your local bookstore.

ISBN: 978-1-940706-03-0

20 19 18 17 16 15 14 13 12 11 10 9 8 7 6 5 4 3 2

Colophon is a registered trademark of Living Oracles, Inc.

Unless otherwise indicated, all Scripture quotations cited in this book are taken from *The New American Standard Bible*® ("NASB"®). Copyright 1960, 1962, 1963, 1968, 1971, 1972, 1975, 1977, 1995 by The Lockman Foundation, a Corporation Not for Profit, La Habra, California. Used by permission. All rights reserved (www.Lockman.org).

Verses marked NIV are taken from *The New International Version*® Study Bible, 10th Anniversary Edition, Copyright 1995 by the Zondervan Corporation. Used by permission. All rights reserved.

Verses marked NKJV are taken from the *New King James Version*. Copyright 1982 by Thomas Nelson, Inc. Used by permission. All rights reserved.

Verses marked KJV are taken from the King James Version.

Verses marked TLB are taken from *The Living Bible*. Copyright 1971 by Tyndale House Publishers, Inc., Wheaton, IL. Used by permission. All rights reserved.

Verses marked AMP are taken from *The Amplified Bible*. Copyright 1954, 1958, 1962, 1964, 1965, 1987 by the Lockman Foundation. Used by permission. All rights reserved (www.Lockman.org).

Verses marked NLT are taken from the Holy Bible, New Living Translation. Copyright 1996, 2004 by Tyndale House Publishers, Inc. Wheaton, IL. Used by permission. All rights reserved.

Verses marked IG-ENT are taken from *The Interlinear Greek-English New Testament* 2nd Edition. Copyright 1958, 1959 by Editorial Interlineation Samuel Bagster and Sons Ltd.

Verses marked TEB are taken from *The Everyday Bible*, New Century Version, Copyright 1987 by Worthy Publishing: Fort Worth. Use by permission.

Emphasis of certain words or phrases within Bible quotations have been added by the author for emphasis unless otherwise indicated. Bracketed words within a Bible quotation have been added by the author for clarification unless otherwise indicated.

To *Every* Christian who is
experiencing hardship in their life
and in need of *more joy.*

FOREWORD

Most scholars believe that the book of James was authored by James, the younger half-brother of Jesus and was the earliest written manuscript contained in the New Testament canon. James was a man who witnessed much of the family life Jesus lived while growing up, long before Jesus began His ministry. Although not one of the original twelve disciples, he was an early leader in the Jerusalem church and likely witnessed the Lord's crucifixion, His burial, the empty tomb, resurrection, and ascension. Finally, James witnessed firsthand the full impact of Pentecost and the severe persecution and regional dispersion of Jewish Christians following that eventful day.

James begins his letter with one of the most thought-provoking statements ever made in scripture: *"Consider it all joy ... when you encounter various trials" (James 1:2)*. From the very beginning, James hooks us with a statement that most people find incomprehensible and incompatible—a true paradox. Perhaps if we were the one writing James, we would have used that statement as our conclusion after laying out the elements of our argument incrementally throughout the book. But in God's wisdom James makes this extraordinary declaration immediately, then layer upon layer, proceeds to develop a sequential process by which we can truly experience the reality of joy in our own lives.

James declares that *you* should be experiencing joy in the midst of *all* your problems. Is that your experience? No? Then, according to James, you lack wisdom. What is wisdom? What element of wisdom do you lack that is robbing you of experiencing joy in *every* situation and *every* circumstance, no matter how problematic or stressful? James didn't make this bold statement only to move on to another topic. He sets out this glorious goal for every Christian's life and then systematically shares, with precision, how we can experience God's joy, in real time, in *every* circumstance.

It is clear James knew that the people reading his letter were likely *not* experiencing this kind of joy in their troubles. They were facing severe persecution and death on a daily basis, and they were frightened and stressed. As a gentle pastor, James takes his reader by the hand to travel with him through his letter. He is going to bring a type of clarity and understanding to the reader that increasingly brings them into that joy, right in the middle of a broken world filled with problems and stress.

These daily devotions follow James' journey into joy. Open your Bible and let's begin.

PROBLEMS MAKE US BEAUTIFUL

JAMES 1:1-4

James, a bond-servant of God and of the Lord Jesus Christ, to the twelve tribes who are dispersed abroad: Greetings. [2]Consider it all joy, my brethren, when you encounter various trials, [3]knowing that the testing of your faith produces endurance. [4]And let endurance have its perfect result, so that you may be perfect and complete, lacking in nothing.

DAY 1

Consider it all joy *... when you encounter various trials.*
—JAMES 1:2

Had you been James, what would you have written about? What would you want
the reader to understand before anything else? By inspiration of the Holy Spirit, James chose to convey a message of tremendous comfort in a time of enormous
hardship. He tells us before anything else that the same power that caused Jesus to rise
up from the grave is the same power that uses all of our daily difficulties—everything
we would like to bundle up and ship out of our lives—to grow more of His peace, joy,
patience, and beauty in us throughout our lives. James tells us that Almighty God, far
from being distant and aloof during our darkest trials, is actually near to us and using
these very trials to transform us and bring us into a joyous life in Him.

James, through God's inspiration, knew that trials and problems would be a big
part of our daily life. He knew that we are but sojourners in a dark world, filled with
fallen people, and our own fallen flesh. That's why he begins his letter by making one
of the most paradoxical statements ever made. To paraphrase what he wrote: *Consider
it all joy when you experience lots of problems (James 1:2).*

The world takes the exact opposite view—and considers it awful, not joyful,
when problems occur. By contrast, James challenges us with this thought-provoking
statement. He forces us to ask ourselves: *Do I experience joy in the midst of all my problems?* No? Then the letter James has written is for you. James leads, step by step, to see
the specific elements of wisdom that result in a life full of joy regardless of outward
circumstances. Tomorrow, let's begin our journey with *James 1:1.*

A JOYOUS THOUGHT FOR TODAY:

*These things I have spoken to you so that My joy may be in you,
and **that your joy may be made full.*** —JOHN 15:11

For today, take comfort in the fact that the pain, confusion, worry, and perhaps even
the fear you may be experiencing currently in some trial is *not* God's end for you.
Though you don't see it today, He is bringing you into His joy!

PRAYER

Father, I pray that You would enlighten me
as You did James. Teach me what it means to
have real joy in my heart in the midst of the
daily problems and difficulties so prevalent
in my life. Dear Lord, this seems completely
impossible to me but I have faith in
Your word. Please teach me how this seeming
paradox is possible experientially
in my life. Amen.

DAY 2

James, **a bond-servant** *of God and of the Lord Jesus Christ.*
—JAMES 1:1

J ames begins his letter by introducing himself as a *bond-servant* of God and of the
Christ. This simple introduction provides the first key for understanding how we
experience joy in our own difficulties. Do you see the connection?

James begins, not by claiming a special *position* of authority (as the brother of
Jesus), but rather, a special *relationship* with God Himself. His first utterance is to
declare that he is a *slave* to God and the Lord Jesus Christ. He readily acknowledges
that he is the property of God—that he belongs to God—or to say it yet a third way:
God *owns* him.

What is the implication of this ownership? It means that everything that happens
to him (and to us) is under God's control. God *is* our Good Shepherd and we *are*
His sheep. He *is* caring for us 24/7 and everything is under His watchful eye. He is
sovereign over our lives. And since God is *all* good, which we will see with increasing
clarity throughout the book of James, James is really saying that there is no "net" bad
thing that happens to us because God brings good out of *all* of our difficulties. Today,
discover how comforting it is to truly consider yourself a bond-servant of the Lord—
just like James—where daily and in all of your circumstances you believe and act as a
precious possession owned by God. God will not allow His possessions to be taken
from Him, nor will He allow His work to be thwarted!

A JOYOUS THOUGHT FOR TODAY:

And we know that **God causes all things to work**
together for good *to those who love God, to those who
are called according to His purpose.* —ROMANS 8:28

For today, know that you are owned by God. Yes, bad things happen, often to the
point where it feels impossible to endure. Yet James' comforting word is that you are
not your own master that must figure out how to handle these problems yourself.
When bad things press in on you from this broken world, God will not allow you
to be destroyed or damaged. He is always performing a greater work *in you* than the
destructive forces that press *on you* from your outward circumstances.

ILLUSTRATION *from* GENESIS

Did you know that God illustrated almost everything He is teaching us in the New Testament back in the Old Testament? Way back in Genesis, do you remember Joseph?

His brothers were jealous of him. They wronged him by selling him into slavery for twenty shekels of silver *(Genesis 37:27-28)*, never expecting him to survive the experience. Then they went back and lied to their father about him.

Then, Potiphar's wife tried to take advantage of him, and when he tried to stay moral and pure, she lied to her husband about him *(Genesis 39:19-20)*. So for all of his living right, he still ended up in prison.

I love this story! We can take various times in our own lives and fill in the blanks of that story.

Through all of this, however, we see in Genesis that God was accomplishing His greater purpose. When his brothers sold him into slavery they thought they were doing him harm and that they were going to make money off of him, but God used it all to move him down to Egypt, put him in charge of the food supply, so that in the end, he could be the savior of his own brothers. What a great story.

Why did God record that story for us back in Genesis? Because God is telling us through this story and countless others in scripture that no matter how difficult our daily problems appear to us, we know that God is using that difficulty right now— that stressful thing right now—it didn't fall through the cracks of His loving care for us. We know that He is using it to accomplish His all-good, greater purpose (for us as well as for others).

What great confidence and comfort for us, as children of God, throughout our life.

As for you, you meant evil against me,
but God meant it for good
in order to bring about this present result,
to preserve many people alive.

—GENESIS 50:20

Day 3

*James, **a bond-servant** of God and of the Lord Jesus Christ.*

—James 1:1

In Day 2 we grew to understand that being a bond-servant involves ownership, but there is more to this word than just ownership. The word *bond-slave* is translated from the Greek word *doulos*, meaning "One whose will is swallowed up in the will of another." James begins his letter by telling us that he is in a slave-*relationship* with God, not by his choice but by God's choice, where God's will is continually the prevailing guide in his life. *Philippians 2:13* confirms this truth: *"For it is God who is at work in you, both to will and to work for His good pleasure."*

What does that mean? It means that James is testifying to us the fact that his own life is ordered daily by God! This glorious truth is true of *every* believer as well!

A Joyous Thought for Today:

Since the Lord is directing our steps,
***why try to understand everything** that happens along*
the way? —Proverbs 20:24, TLB

For today, notice the first word of this verse: *Since*. Consider the impact of that single word on the rest of the verse. Our tendency is to incessantly ask "why" things are happening to us in this way or that. We often question God's fairness—how could He allow such a thing to happen to us or someone else? Why do we have to suffer through this [fill in the blank] problem? But this verse cuts through to the truth: *Since the Lord is directing our steps*, why do we try so hard to understand all the "whys" and "wherefores" of a particular difficulty? We are owned by God. He *is* directing our steps. He is *all* good. That is good enough for us!

DAY 4

*To **the twelve tribes** who are dispersed abroad: Greetings.*
—JAMES 1:1

M uch has been written about James' metaphorical use of the term *twelve tribes*—who they were and where (and why) they were dispersed. Since James was an early leader in Jerusalem, most believe that he was writing to his flock of Jewish Christians who had been forcibly driven into the surrounding regions of Jerusalem through severe and life-threatening persecution. These Christians were experiencing enormous difficulties and James wrote to remind them of what was primarily important and give them hope.

While that may be the reason why James wrote this pastoral letter initially, we can trust the inspiration of the Holy Spirit that this letter is also meant to bring God's message of hope and confidence to us as well. We are but an extension of these original twelve tribes who have been dispersed across geography and time, but who all need the encouragement that James offers to each child of God in the midst of trials. It was to these dear Christian brothers and sisters who were facing imprisonment and death on a daily basis, that James wrote his paradoxical words: *"Consider it all joy ... when you encounter various trials" (James 1:2)*, knowing that God would transform their trials to joy.

A JOYOUS THOUGHT FOR TODAY:

*But we all, with unveiled face, beholding as in a mirror the glory of the Lord, **are being transformed** into the same image from glory to glory, just as from the Lord, the Spirit.* —2 CORINTHIANS 3:18

For today, take comfort in the truth that God has inspired His word (like a mirror that reflects the glory of the Lord) with the power to *transform you in the midst of your trials* into a person full of joy and with a *lifestyle of faithing* in God *for everything.*

A QUESTION TO CONSIDER

To truly experience joy when we encounter various trials, we must ask ourselves: *What, exactly, is a trial?* What is James talking about when he uses the term? Use the next page to compose a list of trials in your life and see if you can figure out what the common thread is that defines them as trials.

TRIALS THAT PRODUCE JOY

Trials From a Broken World	Fill In Your Own Trials
Loss of a Job	
Divorce From Spouse	
Auto Accident	
Illness With No Health Insurance	
Cancer	
Heart Attack	
Overwhelming Debt	
Failed Business	
Bankruptcy	
Taking Care of Aging Parents	
Taking Care of Special Needs Child	
Alcoholism (Self/Family Member)	
Raising Grandchild/Grandchildren	
Rebellious Kid(s)	
Car Problems	
Poor Job Review/Other Job Difficulties	
Lack of Job Promotions	
Arrogant and Narcissistic Boss	
Drug Addiction (Self/Family Member)	
Clinical Depression	
Insufficient Finances to Pay Bills	
Rent Being Raised Again	
Kid's College Tuition	
Toilet Won't Drain	
Contentious Neighbors	
Church Gossip Targeting You	
Spousal Infidelity	
Stock Market Losses	
Death of Spouse or Child	

DAY 5

*Consider it all joy ... **when you encounter various trials.***

—JAMES 1:2

For us to understand what the word *trial* means, it is important to look to the immediate context of what James is saying. Verse three continues the thought that James began in verse two (which ends with a comma, not a period). James is saying that we have joy when we have trials because of the testing of our faith.

We will explore the meaning of "testing of our faith" tomorrow, Lord willing. For today, we are asking the question: *What is a trial?*

To answer this question, we need to explore a different perspective. Most often we think of the word "faith" as a noun (a defined object). But for purposes of these verses in James, consider the word "faith" as an action verb that is *exercised* and *put into effect* each time you encounter a trial. With this in mind, a trial (or testing) is any difficulty that causes us to just *faith* in what God's word says! Today, you may be facing a problem that is nothing short of scary. It finally forces you to cry out, *God, I don't know what to do about this awful thing!* A trial is anything in our life that moves us at that moment (or sometime during the day) to live by faith and not by our own sight. A trial is anything that moves us out of our cowering in fleshly fear, stress, worry, depression, and discouragement, and into the active *action of faithing in God and in His word*. In the coming days, I have italicized the word *faith* when it is used as an action verb.

Let's use the next couple of days to consider examples of this truth.

A JOYOUS THOUGHT FOR TODAY:

For in it [the gospel] the righteousness of God is revealed
from faith to faith; *as it is written, '*BUT THE
RIGHTEOUS *man* SHALL **LIVE BY FAITH.**' —ROMANS 1:17

For today, understand that when "faith" is used as an action verb, it has a progressive result. The more you *faith* in God, the more He reveals Himself to you in the midst of your daily trials. What is most troublesome about a current trial you are in? Be comforted that God is using that very trouble to turn your thoughts to Him and renew your faith.

A PERSONAL TESTIMONY

HE IS OUR GREAT SHEPHERD

Around 1962, I borrowed $2,000 from my folks to start a business (which is now over 53 years old). I was just getting off the ground in the third year of operation, when I got slapped with a totally frivolous and unjust lawsuit for $30,000 (factor that up into today's money!). I had no choice but to hire an attorney, go to trial, and eventually settle the dispute for $20,000, which I had to borrow from an Aunt.

I won't bother you with the details of this silly lawsuit; but my attorney told me that the entire case was bogus. People in the office knew it was bogus. Yet, I will tell you—that unjust lawsuit ate at me for years like a malignant ulcer. One thought raced after another in my mind: *Why did God allow this to happen? I just graduated from Bible school. I'm trying to deal rightly with people. I'm already working 12 to 14 hour days just to make a living for my young wife and first child. I'm not trying to cheat anyone. Then someone slaps this lawsuit on me and wants a free ride.* I was intensely angry for years over it.

But in recent years I've had a different perspective. I now see how God used that relatively small lawsuit some 50 years ago to sensitize me to so many things regarding running a business properly, hiring and retaining good employees, giving everyone equal opportunity to advance in the company, and much more. He allowed me to experience what appeared to me to be a huge problem at the time (when my company was grossing only $600 per month) to prepare me for a time when the company would be responsible for handling revenues in the millions each month. As I have grown to see this, the anger in my heart has drained away. I now tell people that I wouldn't change any of that experience from fifty years ago.

We can trust God to care for us. He is our Shepherd and we are His sheep. He has His watchful eye upon us 24/7 and He is converting *every* problem, no matter how horrible it looks to us, into something for our ultimate good.

This is a glorious truth!

DAY 6

*Knowing that **the testing of your faith** produces endurance.*
—James 1:3

Wwhat does *"the testing of your faith"* mean?
Contrary to what many assume, this is *not* a kind of *testing* where we "pass" or "fail" a test (like in school). God is not *testing* our faith to see if it is strong enough. He *never* tests (or tempts) us in this way. God is the One who gave us our faith in the first place! He already knows exactly how strong our faith is. He doesn't need us to pass a *faith* test in order to find out something about us. He knows everything about us already. Scripture tells us that God knew us, through and through, before He even created us.

So, none of my fleshly failures surprise or disappoint Him? I lost my patience today; a word slipped out of my mouth that shouldn't have; I had an immoral thought; (fill in your own experience here). Take a moment to think about what you know about God. God cannot learn. He cannot "learn" because He knows everything already. If He already knows everything, then it is impossible for Him to have expectations (or disappointments) about us. Expectations are only for us humans who can't see the future. We anticipate what will happen in a certain circumstance and expectations result. God sees both the present and the future alike and is not surprised by any of it. He knew our every act before we were born and He loved us anyway.

A Joyous Thought for Today:

*O Lord, You have searched me and known me. ²You know when I sit down and when I rise up; You understand my thought from afar. ³You scrutinize my path and my lying down, and are intimately acquainted with all my ways. ⁴Even before there is a word on my tongue, behold, O Lord, **You know it all.*** —Psalm 139:1-4

For today, understand that God knows all about you already. There is nothing hidden about you that God doesn't know. The *testing* in the context of *James 1:3* means to "exercise" (akin to our modern-day concept of physical exercise) or "to put into effect." So, trials and testing are those things that *exercise* or *put into effect* your *faithing* in God.

DAY 7

*Knowing that the **testing of your faith produces endurance**.*
—JAMES 1:3

A common trial that many face with deep trepidation is the loss of a job with no new job possibilities in sight. This trial may affect you directly or indirectly. If you or your spouse loses a job, you are affected directly. But what if one of your adult children, with their own family to feed, loses their job? Are you unaffected when you learn of it? Of course not; even though this indirectly affects you it still brings its share of anxiety, worry, and concern into your life. It is a trial that God uses to exercise your faith and bring it more powerfully into effect.

Let's be clear about something very important. God does *not* cause you to lose your job, or cause the selfishness of your spouse, or cause the constant rebellion of one of your kids, or some other financial difficulty. The cause of all these things is the broken world we live in. What God DOES do is use each and every one of these trials in your daily circumstances to draw you into a deeper habit of *faithing* in Him for everything. To draw you into a deeper understanding of what it means for the How-Great-Thou-Art God to be *your personal* Shepherd.

A JOYOUS THOUGHT FOR TODAY:

*And my God [not a job] **will supply ALL your needs** according to His riches in glory in Christ Jesus.* —PHILIPPIANS 4:19

For today, take time to dwell intensely on *one word* from *Philippians 4:19*. That word is "ALL." I have capitalized it so you won't miss it. Such a word always heads up an absolute statement. Ask yourself: If scripture promises that God will supply *ALL* my needs, what part of my needs is excluded from this absolute statement? Don't give up too quickly. Try your best to come up with something that is *not* included in this word. Of course, the answer you will eventually reach is obvious: *None* of your needs are excluded from God's supply for you. What the loss of a job does (in terms of being a trial in our lives) is to compel us *to faith* in God's *Philippians 4:19* promise to us.

OUR PROBLEMS

Our problems are NOT

- *Punishment from God*
- *Outside of God's sovereign control and plan*
- *Interruptions or interferences to our otherwise happy life*
- *A test from God that we must "pass" in order to please Him*

Our Problems ARE

- *Used by God to transfer us from the paralysis of wallowing in fear, worry, and anxiety, to actively faithing in*

  – God, our Father

  – Christ, our Good Shepherd

  – Holy Spirit, our Comforter, and the

  – Promises of God for us as revealed in His written word.

- *Used by God to transform all of the brokenness in this world that comes our way to give us (His Children) MORE of His*

  – PEACE

  – PATIENCE

  – JOY

  – TRUST IN GOD

TAKE A MOMENT TO LIST FOUR MORE THINGS GOD GIVES US THROUGH OUR TRIALS AND DIFFICULTIES.

_____   _____

_____   _____

DAY 8

Be anxious for nothing, but in everything by prayer and supplication with thanksgiving let your requests be made known to God. ⁷And the peace of God, which surpasses all comprehension, will guard your hearts and your minds in Christ Jesus.
—PHILIPPIANS 4:6-7

Here is the first time I have used a verse other than in James to begin a daily devotional study. Don't let this confuse you. I will do this frequently throughout this series because it is important for us to see from scripture how beautifully the word of God coheres and communicates the same wonderful truths about God (and us as His children). James is only one chapter in God's great love letter to us, which should be taken as a whole.

Regarding the above verses, I can't count the thousands of times God has used negative circumstances to cause me to reflect back on the first four words of these verses— *"be anxious for nothing"*—to bring me into a peace and joy I could never achieve on my own. These are great verses to memorize or write down on a 3x5 card to carry with you throughout your day. They are full of absolute promises for you *to faith* in. The words "nothing," and "everything," and "all" are all absolute promises from God. These verses are telling us that there is *nothing* for us to worry about in *any* of our trials. God has them *all* under His control and He is working *all* things together for our good.

A JOYOUS THOUGHT FOR TODAY:

Declaring the end from the beginning, and from ancient times things which have not been done, saying, 'My purpose will be established, and I will accomplish all My good pleasure.' —ISAIAH 46:10

For today, meditate on the wisdom from God that there is *nothing* you will ever encounter, nothing you will ever hear or face in this life that you need to be troubled by! Every day, through all of our difficult circumstances, God is accomplishing all of His good purpose for us! Unfortunately, we don't *faith* as much on *EASY* Street as we do on *PROBLEM* Boulevard. This is because of the ego and self-sufficiency we often succumb to from our flesh. This is what James is recognizing in *James 1:2-3.*

A PERSONAL TESTIMONY
When we Lose Control

One of the most painful trials in my own life involved a period of time when I felt I could no longer control a decision one of my adult kids was about to make. It was a decision I thought would bring this child serious consequences, possibly for the rest of their life.

I still clearly remember, as though it were yesterday, the moment the Lord brought me to the place where I could say, "Lord, I can't handle this anymore ... *I'm just trusting You!*

I simply cannot describe the weight I felt lifted from my shoulders at that moment. That particular trial brought me to a place where I was out of options. All I had left was *to faith* in God.

At that moment, the peace of God which surpasses all comprehension, flooded me and began to guard my heart and mind. I couldn't understand it in human terms, but I knew that it was God making good on His promise made to me in Philippians 4:6-7. I was truly set free for the first time to love and support (rather than manipulate) my child, regardless of the decision eventually made.

It is times like this throughout the difficulties of our lives, in work, family, extended families, friends, and ministries we are involved in, all of which we cannot control and we cannot fix, that God is transforming to our good. It is often our difficulties that drive us to live in prayer and talk to the Lord daily. What brings us to pray without ceasing in our daily relationship with the Lord?

Consider it all joy when you encounter various trials!

Day 9

*Knowing that the **testing of your faith produces endurance.***
—James 1:3, NASB

*Knowing this, that the **trying of your faith worketh patience.***
—James 1:3, KJV

Here is a short verse that conveys two big meanings. We will discover the first meaning today. Some translations use the word *endurance* and others, *patience*. The important thing to note, however, is that neither of these qualities is the *goal* for why we experience testing and trials. James isn't telling us that we have all manner of problems just so we can exhibit the quality of being more patient.

James is exhorting us to realize that problems bring us to increasingly trust in the Lord—day after day—after day—after day. Problems lead us faithfully to a *lifestyle of faithing* in the Lord as reflected in what God promises to us through His living written word. No matter what you hear or see in your circumstances, God is in command and working every problem for your good. A fundamental part of that good is His training of your heart and mind to habitually turn to Him and trust in Him for everything. This frees you from being obsessed with worry as you progressively turn more things over to Him who cares for you.

A Joyous Thought for Today:

*For **we walk by faith**, not by sight.*
—2 Corinthians 5:7

For today, ponder the wisdom from God that His goal is not simply to make you more patient, but to build in you day-by-day a *lifestyle of faithing* in Him for *everything*. This is what God is growing in *every* believer: seeing life the way He sees it.

Now that we know that endurance (or patience) is *not* the ultimate goal of the problems we face, tomorrow we will consider the second big meaning from this verse.

DAY 10

Knowing that the testing of your faith produces endurance.
—JAMES 1:3, NASB

James begins verse three with the phrase *knowing that*. What is the meaning of this phrase? James is affirming to the readers of his letter that God is using all of our problems to put into effect a greater degree of *faithing* in Him—to build up in us a *lifestyle of faithing* in God for everything.

We also know that God is bringing good out of all of our problems and difficulties. Just knowing this gives us more patience and faith in the midst of our trials. Why is this so?

Most Christians would agree that God could relieve them of any problem they are presently facing in an instant, without waiting. It is therefore reasonable to conclude that if we *still* have the problem (and for as long as we have it) the very existence of the problem gives us confidence that God has deemed it useful for His purposes—that He is using it to increase our faith. As we will come to appreciate in the coming days:

Greater *Faithing* = Greater Joy!

So, James is telling us to be encouraged in the midst of trials. Our problems may be hard to endure, but they are *not* a punishment from God. On the contrary, they are sourced from the broken world we live in, but God has chosen to use each and every one of them to grow us spiritually *for our good*.

A JOYOUS THOUGHT FOR TODAY:

*For **it is God who is at work in you**, both to will
and to work for His good pleasure.*
—PHILIPPIANS 2:13

For today, are you in the midst of tough times? Know that as long as you are suffering under that circumstance God is using it to work mightily in you for your good!

Day 11

And let endurance have its perfect result, so that you may be perfect
*and complete, **lacking in nothing**.*

—James 1:4

Lacking in nothing is also translated "wanting nothing." A person who is "wanting nothing" is a person who is content and at peace in life. God is bringing us through the difficulties in life until He brings us to a place where we have no more wants or needs but Him. Read how Jeremiah describes a person who is lacking in nothing:

> *Blessed is the man [insert your own name here] who trusts in the Lord and*
> *whose trust is the Lord [for everything]. [8]For he will be like a tree planted by*
> *the water, that extends its roots by a stream and will not fear when the heat*
> *comes [that is, we won't stress in difficult times]; but its leaves will be green [or*
> *we will remain vibrant and healthy when problems hit us], and it will not be*
> *anxious in a year of drought nor cease to yield fruit (Jeremiah 17:7-8).*

Jeremiah likens a person who trusts in the Lord to a great tree planted by the waters of a stream. This person continues to draw a life-giving supply of water from the Lord even when he or she has to live through periods of trials and hard times. Yet the Lord never ceases to yield fruit in that tree, even when the heat comes, in a year of drought.

A Joyous Thought for Today:

> *But whoever drinks of the water that I will give*
> *him shall never thirst; but **the water that I will***
> ***give him will become in him a well of water***
> ***springing up to eternal life.*** —John 4:14

***For today**, be confident that Almighty God has planted you exactly where He wants you planted. And Christ has placed a well of living water within you. Just as the tree in Jeremiah *endures* the outward hardships of the drought because of its supply of water, so Jesus promises to supply you with exactly what you need (and when you need it) in every hardship. Endurance bears fruit by producing a perfect result—that you *lack nothing*!

CONNECTING THE THEOLOGICAL DOTS

What glorious, wonderful, priceless power there is in the cross that makes all of us miserably human folks *flawless* before Him! It is this hope that God gives us *in Christ*.

But the cross, the power that *makes us flawless*, also *transforms every* difficulty, *every* "bad thing" that touches our life, *every* stressful thing in our day, *every* time we feel attacked—*EVERYTHNG*—the cross converts *every* bit of it into *GOOD* for all of God's children. Evil is still evil, but what God does with that evil is truly glorious!

What a powerfully joyous thought! It is hard to wrap our minds around the fact that all the wrong we see with our human sight every day, God is working it all for good as He promises in *Romans 8:28*.

DAY 12

*Riches and honor are with me, enduring wealth and righteousness. [19]My fruit is better than gold, even pure gold, and my yield better than choicest silver. [20]I walk in the way of righteousness [where all believers walk], in the midst of the paths of justice, [21]to endow those who love me with wealth, **that I may fill their treasuries.***

—Proverbs 8:18-21

To *"fill our treasuries"* means that we have no unfulfilled desire. God is faithfully bringing each of us through all of our life's difficulties and challenges. Praise the Lord for this perspective and confidence! He is using *everything* we stress over, *every* concern we have, *every* way we feel attacked by this life's brokenness—to fill our treasuries. It is a comforting thought that James, by inspiration of the Holy Spirit, chose to make this the first message he shared with believers experiencing great persecution and hardships. He knew that as we live our lives sojourning through this broken world we would have all manner of problems and difficulties. But he wanted us to know how privileged we are as heavenly citizens and children of Almighty God. The resurrected Christ would not allow any difficulty to consume us, but would use them all to bring us into greater joy and peace in Him!

A Joyous Thought for Today:

*Grace to you and peace from God our Father and the Lord Jesus Christ. [3]Blessed be the God and Father of our Lord Jesus Christ, the Father of mercies and God of all comfort, [4]who **comforts us in all our affliction** so that we will be able to comfort those who are in any affliction with the comfort with which we ourselves are comforted by God.* —2 Corinthians 1:2-4

For today, abide in the grace, peace, mercies, and comfort which these verses tell you come from God your Father. Can you remember a time that you were able to comfort someone else because you had gone through the same trial before them? One of the great joys in life is bringing real comfort to another person in need.

My Joyous Thoughts

WHEN
WE LACK JOY,
WE LACK
WISDOM

JAMES 1:5

But if any of you lacks wisdom, let him ask of God, who gives to all generously and without reproach, and it will be given to him.

DAY 13

*But **if any of you lacks wisdom,** let him ask of God, who gives to all generously and without reproach, and it will be given to him.*

—JAMES 1:5

Before we go further, let's review where we have come so far. In *James 1:2*, James tells us that when we Christians have many kinds of troubles, we should be full of joy. Is joy your primary experience whenever you find yourself in the midst of trouble? It is apparent that James wrote his letter because of concerns that many Christians tend to forget the reality and power of this joy in the midst of severe hardship. So James tells those who lack joy in their lives the reason for that lack: They lack wisdom.

James 1:5 is key to experiencing God's comfort and joy in our daily challenges, worries, and difficulties. Read this verse again and ask yourself: If I lack joy in the midst of my problems, what does James say that I lack? James makes the simple statement that when we lack joy in the midst of our problems it is because we *lack wisdom*. What does it mean to *lack wisdom?* Let's explore this more deeply from God's word in the coming days.

A JOYOUS THOUGHT FOR TODAY:

*How **blessed** is the man who finds wisdom and the man who gains understanding. [14] For her profit is **better than the profit of silver** and her gain **better than fine gold.** [15] She is **more precious than jewels;** and **nothing you desire compares with her.** [16] **Long life** is in her right hand; in her left hand are **riches and honor.** [17] Her **ways are pleasant ways and all her paths are peace.** [18] She is a **tree of life** to those who take hold of her, and **happy are all who hold her fast.*** —PROVERBS 3:13-18

For today, as you begin your exploration of wisdom and how to lay hold of it, read these six verses from *Proverbs 3*. Consider each metaphor, description, and benefit (all highlighted in bold) that accrue to the person who finds wisdom and understanding. Do you hunger for wisdom as much as these earthly things? James tells us that wisdom is the key to joy, and if we lack wisdom we can ask it of God. Wisdom is the one thing Solomon asked God for when he became king in service to God's people *(1 Kings 3:9).*

PRAYER

Father, I pray that today and in the coming days You will teach me how precious Your wisdom is and how this wisdom is connected to joy in my life. Create in me an enduring hunger to hold fast Your wisdom. Teach me the pleasant ways and peaceful paths of wisdom, that my life will truly be marked by happiness. Amen.

Day 14

But if any of you lacks wisdom.

—James 1:5

This is truly an amazing statement from James. He says if we lack joy—in any day or amidst any problem—then we lack wisdom. By referring to a "lack of wisdom" James is referring to some lack of understanding we have about God. Some lack about God that if we would remember or understand, it would bring great joy no matter the difficulty. Note what James did *not* say:

- If any of you *lacks respect from your spouse*, that's why you have no joy;
- If any of you *lacks obedient children*, that's why you have no joy;
- If any of you *lacks having enough money*, that's why you have no joy;
- If any of you *lacks a comfortable job*, that's why you have no joy!

James tells us that the reason we are not experiencing a vibrant, living joy in our lives is not because of the circumstances we find ourselves in, but because we lack one thing—*wisdom*. So, wisdom is the key to experiencing joy in our difficulties, not a change in our circumstances (or even a solution to our circumstantial problem).

A Joyous Thought for Today:

*For wisdom will enter your heart and **knowledge will be pleasant** to your soul.*
—Proverbs 2:10, NASB

*For wisdom and truth will enter the very center of your being, **filling your life with joy.*** —Proverbs 2:10, TLB

For today, no matter what difficulty you happen to be facing, whether you just lost your job, broke off a special relationship, or were just yelled at by a boss or parent, you can know this direct from the inspired word of God: Wisdom brings JOY to the center of your life! You need not read more to know that there is hope for your worry, fear, and stress in any problem because God is transforming all of it into eventual joy!

DAY 15

Let the word of Christ [God's written and spoken word] richly dwell within you,
with all wisdom *teaching and admonishing one another with psalms and hymns
and spiritual songs, singing with thankfulness in your hearts to God.*
—COLOSSIANS 3:16

What is this wisdom that James is talking about? As we journey with James through his letter we will find that James progressively reveals specific elements of wisdom, that when understood, yield a life of joy in any circumstance (not just during trials). But to appreciate what wisdom is in the context of our trials, we must first see what scripture tells us about wisdom generally.

In *Colossians 3:16*, the words *"with all wisdom"* means "with all enlightenment," or "with all true spiritual understanding." Another way to describe this is "the way that God sees life." That is what wisdom is. If you are faced with a decision, wisdom literally understands the decision from God's perspective—the decision that God would make. Wisdom understands what God wants you to know about Him. This kind of deeper understanding always brings comfort and joy to our life, even in the midst of trials.

A JOYOUS THOUGHT FOR TODAY:

The **fear** *[reverence, respect, worship]* **of the LORD is
the beginning of wisdom, and the** **knowledge of the
Holy One is understanding.**
—PROVERBS 9:10

For today, as God puts in your heart the desire to be filled with the joy that James is speaking of, turn afresh to Him as the source of all wisdom. Just know that *true knowledge of God brings joy*! Be honest and ask yourself whether you believe that there is any wisdom or understanding that you can boast about in yourself apart from God? Consider what the phrase *"knowledge of the Holy One is understanding"* means. Then spend time in prayer, worshipping Him who has promised in *James 1:5* to give you all the wisdom you need, generously and without reproach, to enter into a life of joy in *every* circumstance.

What truths have we thus far learned about God that aids our journey toward joy and peace in every circumstance?

- **Understanding God's Purpose**: God's *purpose* is to use trials to exercise and strengthen our faith so that, little by little, our entire lifestyle becomes one of *faithing* in Him (trials are not God's way of punishing us).

- **Understanding God's Promise**: God's *promise* is that the outcome of all of our difficulties will be good and consistent with *Romans 8:28*.

These two understandings are the first steps on a journey into joy, even in our difficulties. When we lack some knowledge of God, we experience fear, worry, anxiety, and stress.

Day 16

Let the word of Christ [God's written and spoken word] richly dwell within you,
with all wisdom teaching and admonishing one another with psalms and hymns
and spiritual songs, singing with **thankfulness in your hearts to God.**
—Colossians 3:16

I n Day 15 we used *Colossians 3:16* to understand more about wisdom generally. We saw that the words *"with all wisdom"* means "with all enlightenment," or "with all true spiritual understanding." Notice also that this kind of enlightenment produces *"thankfulness in your hearts to God."* So, at the core of wisdom is the knowledge of certain truths about God, not just intellectually *from the head*, but spiritually and emotionally *from the heart*. The more of this wisdom we have the more our hearts overflow with thanksgiving to God. We don't try to remember to thank or praise God, but rather, we cannot contain our praise to Him because true wisdom produces that result in us.

Wisdom is a deep understanding, a special enlightenment that the Holy Spirit gives us to really understand what a verse is saying and what it means. Yes, He will enlighten us as to the original meaning of the text in the context of when it was written, but He will also bring meaning and relevance to us individually in our immediate situation: of whom God is, and who we are as His children. That's what wisdom is. Wisdom is seeing life as God sees it.

A Joyous Thought for Today:

Grace and peace be multiplied to you in the
knowledge of God and of Jesus our Lord; ³*seeing*
that His divine power has granted to us everything
pertaining to life and godliness, **through the true**
knowledge of Him *who called us by His own*
glory and excellence. —2 Peter 1:2-3

For today, let thankfulness abide in your heart to God, who multiplies within you grace, peace and everything pertaining to life *"through the true knowledge of Him."*

DAY 17

For I am God—I only—and there is no other like me ¹⁰*who can tell you what is going to happen. All I say will come to pass, for I do whatever I wish.*
—ISAIAH 46:9B-10, TLB

I was a PK as a kid growing up. You know what a PK is don't you? I don't know what it means in today's Twitter-talk, but in my day it meant a "preacher's kid." Very early in life God revealed His Son in me *(Galatians 1:15-16)* and I became a believer in Jesus as my Lord and Savior. But that didn't mean my childhood days were smooth and without incident. On the contrary, I resisted God to the maximum extent I could without getting into too much trouble from my parents (which was not always successful). I was convinced that I absolutely did not want too much of God. In my young mind, too much God made people dull and boring (and they dressed like nerds). I only wanted enough God to get me into heaven. I was certain that any more than that would ruin my life and spoil all the fun I wanted to have. Thank God, He accomplishes whatever He desires in a person's life even when that person is not cooperative.

I have used this personal example for those of you with children, but it applies equally to a spouse or friend. What do we do when we are faced with a problem concerning a child (and we don't have joy)? The lack of joy is a useful warning sign indicating that we lack wisdom—some understanding about God (from His word) that addresses the situation we are facing. *Isaiah 46:10* is a wonderful promise to us that God *will accomplish* whatever pleases Him. What pleases Him is *all* good for us, His children. He cannot be thwarted *(Job 42:2)*! We need not stress over a particular problem facing our children, spouse, or friend. Especially if we know them to already be a believer, albeit a rebellious one. We know that Christ Himself dwells in them. How comforting is that?

A JOYOUS THOUGHT FOR TODAY:

*For I am confident of this very thing, that **He who began a good work in you will perfect it until the day of Christ Jesus.*** —PHILIPPIANS 1:6

For today, open to this truth as it transforms any gut-wrenching concern in you—into joy. He has done this for me many times. He is doing the same for you.

Day 18

The young lions do lack and suffer hunger; **but they who seek the Lord shall not be in want of any good thing.**
—Psalm 34:10

Opportunities for problems abound in the area of work and business. Are you, or someone you know, discouraged at work? Are you (or they) not being treated with respect? Are you (or they) not being paid fairly? Did you (or they) get overlooked for a job promotion? Should your (or their) boss be awarded the blue ribbon for: "Worst Boss on the Planet?" If you are discouraged, then you lack joy. If you lack joy, then you lack wisdom—a certain understanding concerning God that He wants you to know.

Psalm 34:10 promises us that those who seek the Lord will not be in want of any good thing. The young lion—lean, agile, fast, capable of doing so much in his own effort—nevertheless suffers lack and hunger. But not you! Not you because you have the wisdom to seek the Lord and *faith* in Him for everything.

Are you experiencing an injustice? Perhaps a promised raise has failed to materialize. You wait and wait, but nothing happens. From our human perspective, we would be far away from the description of having "joy" at the moment. But remember, wisdom is how God sees life. And if He sees life that this raise is best for you—you would have gotten it because the Gates of Hell (all the conniving power of Satan) can't prevent it!

A Joyous Thought for Today:

The Lord does what is right and fair for all who
are wronged *by others.*
—Psalm 103:6, TEB

For today, consider these wonderful "wisdoms" (or truths about God)—about His love and provisions for you—they will begin to usher you into periods of joy, and lay the foundation for the progressive development of a *lifestyle of joy* in all circumstances.

Day 19

²³This is the LORD's doing; it is marvelous in our eyes. ²⁴This is the day which the LORD has made; let us rejoice and be glad in it.

—PSALM 118:23-24

Have you ever had a day when absolutely everything seems to go wrong? And I mean *EVERYTHING* that could go wrong, does go wrong! Let's say you promised to get to work early for an important meeting but the neighborhood power to your house went out momentarily during the night and your alarm clock didn't go off. You wake with startled urgency, rush to get ready and out the door, but two miles from the office you get a flat tire. As you pull to the side of the road you suddenly remember loaning your spare tire to your oldest son who hasn't returned it yet (that was two months ago). You abandon your car and after a brisk two-mile, scurrying rush you arrive at the office out of breath and a bit sweaty. The meeting is over, and no one wants to talk to you (it seems). You hunker down at your desk, waiting for the hammer to fall from your boss.

I think you get the picture of the kind of day I'm talking about. From our human perspective, everything is going wrong. James is telling us that if we lack joy at any time during our day, we lack some element of wisdom—a certain understanding about God.

But then in some miraculous way God reminds us of *Psalm 118:23-24* and renews our mind with this verse. This is a day which *HE HAS MADE*. We begin to feel the stress draining away and the joy welling up within us in spite of our circumstances. That is the joy of the Lord!

A JOYOUS THOUGHT FOR TODAY:

'For I know the plans that I have for you,' declares the Lord, 'plans for welfare and not for calamity to give you a future and a hope.' —JEREMIAH 29:11

For today, rejoice and be glad because God is absolutely sovereign over all events of your day and He has a plan for you within this day. Your problems are opportunities for joy by *faithing* in Him. He promises (including using a flat tire for our good) that for those who seek Him they will never lack any good thing (*see* Day 18).

Day 20

*But if any of you lacks wisdom, **let him ask of God**, who gives to all **generously and without reproach**, and it will be given to him.*

—James 1:5

By now, you are probably convinced that you need more of the wisdom James is talking about because there are far too many days of stress and worry in your life and not enough days of pure joy. But how do we get this wisdom (or get more of this wisdom)?

James tells us, in verse five that if we lack wisdom we just need to ask God for it! He does not say to rationalize it out on our own, or seek wisdom from the philosophers of human history, or in the smartest friend we know, or in some human authored self-help book. James' solution is simple: If you lack wisdom—then ask God for it!

What does *ask of God* mean? It means to:

- *Look to God's word* for answers to our daily concerns; or
- *Ask God* to bring a verse to mind that speaks to our concerns; or
- *Text a Christian friend* to share a verse that God puts on their heart for us; or
- *Pray* about what is troubling us; AND
- *Be sensitive* to the Holy Spirit's response in us!

James goes on to assure us that God gives wisdom—*GENEROUSLY* and without reproach! God will give us just the element of wisdom (i.e., the particular understanding about God) we need to produce joy in our life. He imparts joy, peace, and comfort in our difficulties.

A Joyous Thought for Today:

*The **Lord** will accomplish what concerns me;*
Your lovingkindness, O Lord, is everlasting; do not
forsake the works of Your hands. —Psalm 138:8

For today, be comforted by the truth in *Psalm 138:8*, that God is actively caring for all that concerns you. He is not far away. He has not forgotten or abandoned you. He is not punishing you. In His lovingkindness, He is caring for you and all that concerns you throughout this day.

PRAYER

*Dear God, throughout this day, whenever
I don't have joy in my heart, please reveal
to me what I don't know about You,
or what I have forgotten about You—
that will produce joy in me. Overcome
all the fallen feelings from my flesh
and give me joy. Amen.*

Day 21

*Even though I walk through the valley of the shadow of death, **I fear no evil, for You are with me**; Your rod and Your staff, they comfort me.*
—Psalm 23:4

Psalm 23:4 is probably one of the most familiar verses in the entire Bible. But read it again prayerfully to see how consistent it is with the message James is sharing in his letter concerning joy. King David is the author of this Psalm. He is writing about great troubles, how he was walking *"through the valley of the shadow of death"*—evil is all around him and there is no hope apart from God. He was in the midst of trials and circumstances that appeared gravely threatening. What did David do in this dire circumstance? He recited the wisdom of God! He said, *"I fear no evil, for You are with me."* What comforting wisdom this is. God is *always* with us! We are *never* alone. He is not just holding our hand, but He is living *in us*! He is the Creator and we the created.

But you may say: *I'm no King David! I can't experience the Lord in the same way that this extraordinary man did.* Think again! David's sins were many and grave, but he had a heart that sought the Lord. In reality, we are just like David and experience an even more blessed position (*see* "oil" below) to receive God's loving care.

A Joyous Thought for Today:

You prepare a table before me in the presence of my enemies; You have anointed my head with oil; *my cup overflows. ⁶Surely goodness and lovingkindness will follow me all the days of my life, and I will dwell in the house of the LORD forever.* —Psalm 23:5-6

For today, recognize and accept the fact that you are just like David. Like David, have no fear because God has prepared a table for you to receive nourishment from Him in the face of your enemy trials and tribulations. God anointed David's head with "oil" (symbolic of the Holy Spirit), resulting in his cup overflowing, meaning the joy within him is overflowing in the midst of his threatening circumstances. While David had oil poured *on his head*, you have had the Holy Spirit poured *into you!* Notice that God does all the action here. It is not up to you to save yourself. Let God's joy and peace overflow in you today, though your problems may be painful. Declare that God is caring for you!

DAY 22

Who is the man who fears the LORD? He will instruct him in the way he should choose. [13]His soul will abide in prosperity, and his descendants will inherit the land.
—PSALM 25:12-13

These verses are some of the greatest comforts in the midst of my trials. What priceless wisdom is contained in these verses for us! For those who fear the Lord, He promises to do something really special for them throughout their lives. What does *fear the Lord* mean? It doesn't mean to be afraid of God in the way we use the word "fear" in modern times. To "fear" the Lord means to revere, respect, seek out, and worship the Lord. In other words—the person who fears the Lord is *every* Christian believer.

What does God promise He will do for these seekers of Him? Verse twelve says that God *"will instruct him in the way he should choose."* It doesn't say that He *might*, or that He *may* instruct him, but that *He WILL instruct him in the way he should choose.* His soul will abide in prosperity, and his descendants will inherit the land.

A JOYOUS THOUGHT FOR TODAY:

The secret of the LORD is for those who fear Him, and
He will make them know His covenant. —PSALM 25:14

For today, what wonderful wisdom for you to contemplate! Notice that verse fourteen repeats the great promise first given in verse twelve above. The *secret of the Lord* (i.e., God's instruction) is for you who fear Him, and *He WILL make you know His covenant*, meaning His direction for you to follow. Are you in the midst of an important decision that you feel must be decided immediately? Have you prayed to God but He seems to remain silent? Rather than conclude that God is far away or has forgotten you, *KNOW* that He is near and directing you. He will direct you both in terms of direction (*HOW* to act) and timing (*WHEN* to act). If He wants you to do something, He will make you know it. You cannot outwait God. He is never late in giving you the direction He promised you. If you do not have clear direction from Him, be at peace that He has everything under control.

DAY 23

You will make known to me the path of life; in Your presence is fullness of joy; in Your right hand there are pleasures forever.
—PSALM 16:11

The wisdom in this verse is enormously comforting. It promises us that the Lord *will* make known to us the path of life. Does it say He will make known the path of life *only if* we can't figure it out ourselves? No. This verse states an absolute truth about God's character and attitude toward us. He *will* make known to His children the path of life for us to follow. God makes known His path of life (through our entire life) in simple and direct terms. His directions aren't marked by nuance and shrouded in mystery, locked within a conundrum and hidden deep inside an enigma. This may be how we often think about God, but that is a lie. You don't need to be Sherlock Holmes to understand God's simple directions that guide you day-by-day on His path of life.

Just like dumb sheep following their shepherd, we are called by our Great Shepherd to follow Him. Sheep don't need to understand anything. They just follow the presence of their shepherd. Likewise, we can trust in the promises of *Psalm 16:11* that *in His presence is fullness of joy*. As God guides us on His path of life, we remain in His presence and in His hands. It is in this *relationship with God* that we experience fullness of joy and pleasures forever. In *James 1:2*, James tells us that even when this path travels through times of trouble and problems, we still live in God's presence and are full of joy.

A JOYOUS THOUGHT FOR TODAY:

*For **you will go out with joy and be led forth with peace;** the mountains and the hills will break forth into shouts of joy before you, and all the trees of the field will clap their hands.* —ISAIAH 55:12

For today, go out with confident joy. God is leading you forth in peace. He is handling everything for you! Christ refers to you as His sheep. You can trust your Great Shepherd day-by-day to keep you on His path of life. You don't need to worry about what you don't know! You might say *I don't know what to do!* If God wanted you to know more, He would tell you. Pray: *Dear God, you are the Creator and I the created. You are the Potter and I am the clay. You love me and have a plan for me. It looks scary to me but I trust You!*

DAY 24

*Do you not know? Have you not heard? The Everlasting God, the LORD, the Creator of the ends of the earth **does not become weary or tired.** His understanding is inscrutable. ²⁹He gives strength to the weary, and **to him who lacks might He increases power.***
—ISAIAH 40:28-29

I saiah tells us that when we feel weak in our difficulties, when we have worn ourselves out trying to fix, manipulate, or control something, we can always count on God being strong. We can always count on God to be there to strengthen us and increase our power. How often is this true? How often do we feel that we are at the end of our rope? Thank God that His strength doesn't depend on us!

But how do we tap into God's strength and power? Does He provide this strength and power just so we can renew our human efforts to fix, manipulate, or control our circumstances? No, this is not the answer. *Isaiah 40:28* tells us clearly that the Everlasting God-Lord-Creator of the entire earth *"does not become weary or tired."*

If that is true, then what does it tell us when we reach a point of exhaustion in struggling with a particular problem or circumstance in our life or the lives of those around us? It tells us that we have been struggling with the problem *using our own human strength.* We have not been *faithing* in God's strength to handle the matter for our good. The moment we give up and trust Him in the midst of our troubles, we are in a position to experience God's renewal of our strength and power. This is a place of joyous rest.

A JOYOUS THOUGHT FOR TODAY:

Though youths grow weary and tired, and vigorous young men stumble badly, ³¹yet those who wait for the LORD will gain new strength; they will mount up with wings like eagles, they will run and not get tired, they will walk and not become weary. —ISAIAH 40:30-31

For today, you can *always* count on God being strong in any situation! As you wait for the Lord's direction, He will renew your strength.

DAY 25

I will cry to God Most High, **to God who accomplishes all things for me.**
—Psalm 57:2

Here is another verse containing that little word *ALL*. It tells another absolute truth about the character of our God, the Most High. Does it tell us that God *helps us* to accomplish things in our lives? No. This verse tells us in absolute terms that it is God (alone) who accomplishes *ALL* things on our behalf and for our good. There is *nothing* left for us to do. We can *faith* in Him for everything! Isn't that an amazing wisdom? In the midst of your difficulties this week, God will bring this wisdom to you and it will buckle your knees in worship to Him. It will turn your heart in total trust to Him. We can *faith* in the fact that He will make us to know what He wants us to know when He wants us to know it.

As we will see in coming days, He alone is the source of all good things in this world. He alone is the One who accomplishes all things for us during our entire life. So, there is nothing in our trials for us to worry about—ever!

What great, great wisdom is that!

A Joyous Thought for Today:

Thus says the LORD to you, 'Do not fear or be dismayed because of this great multitude, **for the battle is not yours but God's.'** —2 Chronicles 20:15b

Sometimes we find ourselves facing a great multitude of problems. Humanly speaking, we always want to know what to do without waiting. What this really means is that our human flesh doesn't believe that we need God. We may say: *These are my problems. I got myself into them. I already feel guilty about them. I need to fix them. It's up to me!* Our flesh believes we can be our own god. But there is a contrary perspective: *Wisdom* says, "It is not up to you—it is up to God." Scripture is brimming with this truth, promised again and again, but how often do we forget it!

For today, hear the Lord's speaking directly to you: *"Be still, and know that I am God"* (Psalm 46:10a, KJV).

MY JOYOUS THOUGHTS

FAITH = JOY!

JAMES 1:5-8

But if any of you lacks wisdom, let him ask of God, who gives to all generously and without reproach, and it will be given to him. [6]But he must ask in faith without any doubting, for the one who doubts is like the surf of the sea, driven and tossed by the wind. [7]For that man ought not to expect that he will receive anything from the Lord, [8]being a double-minded man, unstable in all his ways.

DAY 26

*But he must **ask in faith without any doubting**, for the one who doubts is like the surf of the sea, driven and tossed by the wind.*

—JAMES 1:6

Let's refresh our memory concerning the context of what James has been talking about since the beginning of his letter. James is writing to Christians and giving them some practical good news. He tells us that we can experience God's joy even during intense human hardship. He tells us that if we are *not* experiencing this joy, it's because we are momentarily lacking some aspect of wisdom (or understanding) about God. We took several days to look at some related scripture to discover that wisdom is found in God's living word given to us. As we look to His inspired word and pray for understanding, God uses these ancient words—containing all of His power—to release us from worry and anxiety and instill joy and praise in our hearts during any circumstance.

Fortunately, when we do lack wisdom, James tells us that we don't have to figure it out on our own but can simply ask God for it—something God gives us generously and without reproach. Why? So we can *reconnect* with the particular wisdom we lack about God for producing joy in our lives at that moment.

Having established this foundational context, let's explore over the next few days what it actually means to *"ask in faith without any doubting."*

A JOYOUS THOUGHT FOR TODAY:

*For the **word of God is living and active** and sharper than any two-edged sword, and piercing as far as the division of soul and spirit, of both joints and marrow, and able to judge the thoughts and intentions of the heart.* —HEBREWS 4:12

For today, take a few moments to consider the absolute uniqueness of God's word, the Bible. Think about how *"living and active"* it is compared to the books and magazines you read. None contain the power of God. None can literally change your life and give you joy from the inside as you read and think about it. Only God's word does that! Now, think about the fact that *every* time you read God's word, whether you know it or not, He is in the process of working the truth of that word into you to give you joy.

A PERSONAL TESTIMONY
A Change of Focus

For decades of my Christian life I took *James 1:6* completely out of context. I thought verse six related to asking God for anything I needed in a particular circumstance: More money, more customers, better employees, a more understanding wife, or obedient children. I didn't understand that James was *not* focused on the external circumstance but on *experiencing joy in the midst of every circumstance*. Of course, when I didn't perceive that God was answering my prayers, I would question whether I had sufficient faith. This often decayed to thoughts about whether I was a Christian at all!

Have you ever had these kinds of thoughts when reading this verse out of context? Now we know that James is talking about asking God for the particular wisdom needed in a specific circumstance that will produce joy in the life of the one praying. This verse is all about giving us practical advice as to how to experience joy in our lives.

DAY 27

*Being a **double-minded man**, unstable in all his ways.*
—JAMES 1:8

James 1:5 tells us that if we lack wisdom we can ask God for it, who gives wisdom to all generously and without reproach. But then in *James 1:6*, he qualifies this statement by stating that the person doing the asking must ask in faith *"without any doubting."* James is really speaking of two objects of our faith here. We will start with the first object today and the second object on Day 32.

The first object James is referring to is *faith in God's word*; or faith in what every word of scripture says.

Notice that James amplifies his use of the word "faith" with a three-word prepositional phrase: *without any doubting. James 1:8* clarifies what doubting means: *"Being a double-minded man, unstable in all his ways."* Double-minded in this verse means "two-souled." This is a descriptive word-picture of a person who comes to the Bible and believes what God's word says ... *for a while* ... but then reverts back to unbelief.

Let's say a person attends a Bible study on *1 Peter 5:7, "casting all your anxiety on Him, because He cares for you."* This verse contains the wonderful wisdom that we can cast *all* of our anxiety—*all* of our stresses, fears, and *everything* that is making our life and mind miserable—on Him because He is truly caring for us. This person believes this word and readily proclaims: "Praise God! I believe He is caring for me!" But then, several hours or days later, as their problems continue, falls back into worrying and stressing once again. This is what it means to be double-minded. It is what robs us of joy.

A JOYOUS THOUGHT FOR TODAY:

*Therefore humble yourselves under the mighty hand of God, that He may exalt you at the proper time, [7]**casting ALL your anxiety on Him**, because He cares for you.*
—1 PETER 5:6-7

For today, ask God throughout your day to make you a single-minded person. It is humbling to admit that you can't control your circumstances, but believe this word of God and cast *ALL* your anxiety on Him—*Faithing* in Him because He cares for you.

PRAYER

Dear God, shine Your light on my heart. Reveal my own tendency toward double-mindedness when reading Your word. Teach me how this double-mindedness cheats me of the joy that James is talking about. I pray, dear Lord, that You will renew my mind and heart. Make me a single-minded person who simply trusts what Your word says without wavering. Place a hunger in my heart for Your word, that I may have available Your living and active wisdom in every circumstance to create joy in my life. Amen.

DAY 28

*For that man **ought not to expect** that he will receive anything from the Lord.*

—JAMES 1:7

B e sure to notice something important: James is not suggesting that if you doubt you are not a Christian. Rather, he is actually talking about *double-minded Christians*. He is pointing out that a Christian, during periods of doubt, *rob themselves* of the Lord's wisdom that produces comfort, joy, and peace in their lives amidst any circumstance they are facing.

It is time for a reality check: Most all Christians would say that we believe in what God's word says, yet we still suffer from stress and worry. That strikes at the heart of what James is sharing with us. We may believe *with our intellect* what God's word says as true, but the stress and anxiety in our life tells a different story. It indicates we momentarily doubt the truth of that word. We may not admit or acknowledge it but we are; otherwise, we wouldn't have stress and worry. I readily admit this in my life.

James 1:6 describes such a person like this: *"for the one who doubts is like the surf of the sea, driven and tossed by the wind."* Think to your own experience. Isn't it true that when we are not anchored in God's word when facing difficulty that our thoughts and feelings get tossed around like being in the wind? We are up one minute and down the next. We are stressed over what to do and feel like we are on an emotional roller coaster! When that anchor of God's word is momentarily pulled up we fall back into believing that it is all up to us to solve the problem before us. James tells us that only faith gets us off of that roller coaster and into God's peace and joy! Tomorrow, let's see what faith is.

A JOYOUS THOUGHT FOR TODAY:

*For in it [the Gospel] the righteousness of God is revealed from faith to faith; as it is written, "BUT **THE RIGHTEOUS man SHALL LIVE BY FAITH**."*

—ROMANS 1:17

For today, ask the Lord to shine His light on your expectations. The gospel is not just for our salvation but for all aspects of our entire life. Do you tend toward being a double-minded person? There is nothing you can do about this in your own effort. Just ask God to anchor you in His word and grow faith and joy in you as a result.

DAY 29

*Now **faith is** the assurance of things hoped for, **the conviction of things not seen.***
—HEBREWS 11:1, NASB

*What is faith? It is the confident assurance that something we want is going to happen. **It is the certainty that what we hope for is waiting for us**, even though we cannot see it up ahead.*
—HEBREWS 11:1, TLB

The writer of Hebrews tells us that faith is the strong confidence that all of God's word is true—and it will prove true—though we can't see how or when right now. Take the promises of *Romans 8:28* for an example. God promises that He is working *all things together for our good*, yet we do not always see this *good* in the middle of great hardship. We have all faced numerous difficulties where we don't see any good that can come out of the problem we face. But we are not God!

Faith is being anchored by God *in His word*, believing it to be true in spite of what we think we see with our human sight. Remember, Paul exhorts us to *live by faith not by sight (2 Corinthians 5:7)*. What does all of this really mean? If you cut through to the core truth, we are talking about how God is sovereign over *all* of life and divinely ordering *everything* according to His will. Faith means that what God's word says—that whatever problem we are facing is *all* in His hands and there is absolutely *nothing* for us to worry about—is true and cannot fail. This gives us joy and peace in the midst of those trials.

A JOYOUS THOUGHT FOR TODAY:

*Heaven and earth will pass away, **but My words will not pass away.*** —LUKE 21:33

For today, prayerfully meditate on what faith is for you. Recognize that faith is not simply a set of doctrines we hold intellectually; but an active *faithing* experience of our heart to lay hold of, and be anchored in, God's word as true regardless of what the outward circumstances look like with our human sight.

DAY 30

*And when Jesus entered Capernaum, a centurion came to Him, imploring Him, ⁶and saying, "Lord, my servant is lying paralyzed at home, fearfully tormented." ⁷Jesus said to him, "I will come and heal him." ⁸But the centurion said, "Lord, I am not worthy for You to come under my roof, but **just say the word**, and my servant will be healed. ⁹For I also am a man under authority, with soldiers under me; and I say to this one, 'Go!' and he goes, and to another, 'Come!' and he comes, and to my slave, 'Do this!' and he does it." ¹⁰Now when Jesus heard this, He marveled and said to those who were following, "Truly I say to you, I have not found **such great faith** with anyone in Israel."*

—MATTHEW 8:5-10

Many of us are familiar with this narrative as a story that illustrates the importance of faith. But what exactly is Jesus referring to when He refers to the centurion's *great faith?* Jesus learns of the centurion's need and volunteers to come to the centurion's house to heal his servant. But the centurion tells Jesus that it is not necessary for Him to come *in person*. If Jesus would only give him a *word*, that would be good enough. According to the centurion's great faith, *God's word was equal to His presence.* For us, this same principle is true in terms of God's inspired word contained in scripture. James is telling us *(James 1:6)* that we experience emotional healing—joy and peace—whenever we believe the scripture we are reading is just like God standing right in front of us and saying it to us!

A JOYOUS THOUGHT FOR TODAY:

All Scripture is inspired [Greek: "God-breathed"] by God and profitable for teaching, for reproof, for correction, for training in righteousness. —2 TIMOTHY 3:16

For today, try on the centurion's great faith like a garment. Take your favorite verse and read it aloud, listening to the words, and believe that the *words being spoken are exactly equal to the presence of God Himself;* to God standing right in front of you and saying it. Does this deepen the meaning of the verse for you?

IMAGINE THIS!

Let's imagine that you are standing in your kitchen, having come in for a drink of water. You are beginning to feel troubled about one of your kids. This child is not walking with the Lord as you would hope for them. Lately, they have grown increasingly disrespectful of everyone in the family.

Suddenly, you hear something behind you and the room fills with a brilliant light. You turn around, then instantly fall to your knees, for none other than God in the person of Jesus Himself is standing before you. His gaze pierces your very soul and fixes all of your attention on Him. Then, in a gentle but commanding voice, He tells you, "Father God did not spare you anything, including His only begotten Son, to care for you and to adopt you into His household. Do you think He would leave anything for you to worry about? I know you love your children but I created them. I love them as much as you do and I am caring for them. I have left nothing for you to worry about. When I leave, seek out My word in *Philippians 4:6-7* and read: *'Be anxious for nothing, but in everything by prayer and supplication with thanksgiving let your requests be made known to God. ⁷And the peace of God, which surpasses all comprehension, will guard your hearts and your minds in Christ Jesus.'* Then turn to *Matthew 7:7-11* and learn how *I love you and your children more than you could ever love them.* Then turn to *Psalm 138:8* and be confident in the fact that I will accomplish what concerns you. I say again: *Be anxious for nothing.*"

The next thing you know, you are prostrate on the ground. When you look up, the Lord is no longer visible to your human sight and the light in the room has returned to normal. You glance at the clock and estimate that the whole visitation from God lasted no more than two minutes.

Now, *all* of your circumstances are *exactly the same* as they were two minutes ago— before God appeared to you—but would you still be filled with stress and worry?

Or would you be overflowing with joy and peace, having your burdens of worry and anxiety lifted off you? Would the scripture spoken to you by God remain dead to you? Would you hunger for even more of God's word from scripture?

DAY 31

*The **mountains melted like wax at the presence of the LORD**, at the presence of the Lord of the whole earth.*

—PSALM 97:5

This verse gives us a deeper dimension to what James is saying. Our fears, worries, and discouragements will *all* "melt like wax" in the presence of the Lord. When we believe that any verse we are reading is equivalent to God standing right in front of us, we are like the centurion officer from Day 30. We equate God's word with His presence. If His words have the power to melt mountains like wax, then they certainly have the power to melt *all* of our stress and worry like wax and replace it with joy and peace. Through it all, God reveals to us that it isn't up to us after all, but totally in His hands. We are inadequate to the task of praising Him enough for His great love and care for us.

Here is an example of what I mean. I had a friend some years ago undergo major surgery. His doctor let him go home the same day. On the way home he started to get very sick and was back in intensive care within a few hours. Upon hearing this, I got very angry at the doctor for releasing my friend too soon. But within a minute I heard the Lord say (as though standing right in front of me): "Daryl, are you still going to *faith* in *Romans 8:28* and trust that I am working *all* things (even a doctor's mistake) together for good?" That instantly pulled the plug on my anger and I was left only with praise to God and prayers for my friend. As His children, we do live by faith, not by sight.

A JOYOUS THOUGHT FOR TODAY:

Your word is a lamp to my feet and a light to my path.
*[107]I am exceedingly afflicted; **revive me, O LORD,***
according to Your word. —PSALM 119:105, 107

For today, do you have worries, concerns, and anxieties looming before you like an insurmountable mountain range? God will melt those mountains like wax at His presence. Even when exceedingly afflicted, God will revive you according to His word. Come to God like the centurion officer, trusting that God's word equals His presence.

Day 32

*But he must **ask in faith without any doubting**, for the one who doubts is like the surf of the sea, driven and tossed by the wind.*

—James 1:6

On Day 27 we discovered that there were two objects of the faith James was speaking about in this verse. We started on Day 27 with the first object: *faith in God's word* (or faith in what every word of scripture says) and today we will look at the second object of the faith in *James 1:6*.

The second object James refers to is *faith that God IS answering our prayers and requests*. Not that He might, or may, or will sometime in the future, but IS currently answering our prayers as we pray them. *James 1:5* says, *"let him ask of God, who gives to all generously and without reproach, and it will be given to him."* The words *"it will be given to him"* mean God's wisdom *will be* given to us at the *very moment* we are asking for it!

In practical terms, of course, we often do not see the answer to our prayers with our human eyes immediately, but that does not mean the prayer has not been answered by God. We also often fret over the notion that somewhere in the Bible it says that *if we ask anything according to His will, He hears us*. Our misunderstanding of this verse leads us to doubt whether we are in God's will for our life. We will look at that verse tomorrow, but for today, *faith* in the fact that your God is a God who answers prayer immediately, generously, without reproach, and without delay.

A Joyous Thought for Today:

*Whatever you ask in My name, that will I do, so that the Father may be glorified in the Son. [14]**If you ask Me anything in My name, I will do it.*** —John 14:13-14

For today, pray to the Lord that He would change your thinking about the timing of *when* He answers your prayers. You may be inclined to think that He only answers prayers in the future, or in eternity, but not immediately. Yet God knows your prayer before you even utter it and has promised to generously, without reproach, answer that prayer instantly. Do you have faith that God *IS* doing that for your good? If not, ask Him for that faith and He will generously give it to you.

DAY 33

*This is the confidence which we have before [literally, "toward"] Him, that, **if we ask anything according to His will, He hears us.** ¹⁵And if we know that He hears us in whatever we ask, we know that we have [present tense, currently, right now] **the requests which we have asked from Him.***

—1 JOHN 5:14-15

O ur human thinking wants to make the meaning of these verses abstract and complicated, but it's not. These verses mean exactly what they say. Asking according to God's will simply means asking according to what scripture says. For example, scripture tells us many times that God will direct our steps *(Proverbs 3:5-6; Psalms 25:9, 12, 14, etc.)*. It doesn't say that He *might* direct our steps (if He feels like it, or we are being good, or we haven't made Him mad recently), but that He *will* direct our steps (an absolute certainty). So, when we ask God to direct us in some difficulty we know with certainty that He is currently ordering our life according to His will. We may not know anything specific to do, but we know that God is sovereign over today's (and every day's) events. To ask in faith without any doubting, according to *James 1:6*, means to believe (and not doubt) that God is sovereign over all events in our life and that His resurrection power will prevail concerning us. He is guiding us as His word promises. Scripture doesn't say that it will always *look* like it or *feel* like it—but only that *HE IS*.

A JOYOUS THOUGHT FOR TODAY:

Man's steps are ordained by the LORD, *how then can man understand his way?* —PROVERBS 20:24

For today, empty your mind of the cacophony of abstract and complicated noises about God clanging around in your thinking. Lay hold of this simple truth from God's word: God answers prayer immediately and is ordaining your steps as you go through this day. Trust that God is caring for you and is sovereign over your life in every circumstance. This will dramatically simplify your life. You no longer need to understand everything going on around you (as if you had to control the outcome) when you are *faithing* in God to care for you and ordain your steps.

Day 34

*But now, O LORD, You are our Father, **we are the clay, and You our potter;** and all of us are the work of Your hand.*
—ISAIAH 64:8

Scripture is full of word-pictures like that given in *Isaiah 64:8*, He is the Potter and we are the clay. God doesn't leave our spiritual growth up to us having to ask Him for it. But He invites us to pray in order to bring us unique peace as we pray for the things in scripture that tells us what He is accomplishing (without fail) in our lives. He knows that through prayer, and what He is already doing, He brings us into abundant joy!

For example, have you ever struggled with disappointment concerning your Christian life? For decades I struggled with this mightily. We shouldn't be failing as much as we do with anger or immoral thoughts. Husbands think they are not the spiritual leader they should be for the family. Wives think they are not as good a wife and mother as they should be. On and on these thoughts can multiply. But both John (Day 33) and James tell us that as we just ask God to make us the Christians He wills for us to be, we have the absolute confidence that *He IS* making us that way (because we are asking according to His will as reflected in scripture). In reality, we are actually asking for what God says He is *already doing* in our life, even when we are *not* asking Him to do it! Remember what we read on Day 17: *"For I am confident of this very thing, that He who began a good work in you will perfect it until the day of Christ Jesus" (Philippians 1:6).* Paul was *confident* that God has begun the work and He (not us) will complete it.

A JOYOUS THOUGHT FOR TODAY:

*For **we are His workmanship,** created in Christ Jesus*
for good works, which God prepared beforehand so
that we would walk in them. —EPHESIANS 2:10

For today, don't gloss over this word-picture of *God as our Potter*. Take time to consider its implications. Ask yourself: *What can the clay do for itself? Can it sculpt itself in any way? Can it even marshal the energy to jump onto the Potter's wheel in its own effort?* What God is telling you is humbling but true: you are *His* workmanship, *not your own*. You are but clay and can do nothing in your own effort. The good news is this frees you to trust in God for everything, which leads you to joy and peace even in the most difficult times.

PRAYER

*Dear God, Your words are often too great to
contemplate. They just leave us speechless to
realize that You love us this much. That You
chose to redeem each one of us and bless
us with Your eternal life, which includes
providing Your word as Your presence. You
know how often we fall back into worry, stress,
and fear as we see things with our human
sight. Yet, over these last several days, You
have reminded us that Your words NEVER
FAIL. Your word is what is true. What we see
is not eternal, but what You have written is.
We just thank You and praise You!
In Jesus name, Amen.*

THE JOY OF
BEING
INSIGNIFICANT

JAMES 1:9-12

But the brother of humble circumstances is to glory in his high position; [10]and the rich man is to glory in his humiliation, because like flowering grass he will pass away. [11]For the sun rises with a scorching wind and withers the grass; and its flower falls off and the beauty of its appearance is destroyed; so too the rich man in the midst of his pursuits will fade away. [12]Blessed is a man who perseveres under trial; for once he has been approved, he will receive the crown of life which the Lord has promised to those who love Him.

DAY 35

*But the **brother of humble circumstances** is to **glory** in his **high position**.*
—JAMES 1:9

J ames continues his discussion of having joy in the midst of every circumstance by addressing what he knew would be a common complaint: *If only I had more of this or that, I would be happy*. Or *if I just had a little more money, or a little more financial freedom, I would be happier*. But James tells us that this is not true. He will tell us over the next few days that it doesn't matter if you are rich or poor; God is caring for every one of His children the same out of His abundance of goodness *(Psalm 23:6)*. He begins in verse nine with those of humble circumstances.

The word *brother* makes it clear that James is referring to Christians. And *humble circumstances* refers to those with modest means, perhaps living from paycheck to paycheck (or without a paycheck at all). The word *humble* also refers to those in positions of little or no recognition, power, or authority in this life. James specifically identifies this group of Christians, the poor and the "nobodies" in this life, to experience *great joy*. He says that they are to *glory* (meaning, "to be overjoyed") in their *high position. High position,* according to James, is the position God chose to give the poor and those less educated over most rich and elite people in the world to be: *recipients* of His eternal life, *beneficiaries* of God's grace, joy, wisdom, and contentment in this life, and *residents* of heaven as our everlasting home!

A JOYOUS THOUGHT FOR TODAY:

*Listen, my beloved brethren: did not God **choose the poor of this world to be rich in faith and heirs of the kingdom** which He promised to those who love Him?*
—JAMES 2:5

For today, are you struggling right now financially? Do you feel alone and forgotten? Take a moment to consider what James is saying from a heavenly perspective. God chose you *by name* before the foundation of the world *(Ephesians 1:4)* so He could *make you rich in Him!* Today, lift your eyes off your "poorness" and look to His "richness." Take time to pray and offer all glory, joy, and praise to God for His abundant and loving gift to you.

Day 36

Blessed is a man who perseveres under trial; for once he has been approved, he will receive the crown of life which the Lord has promised to those who love Him.
—James 1:12

For today, we skip from verse nine to twelve in order to follow James' discussion concerning the poor. We will return to verse ten and eleven later to learn what James has to say about the rich among us. Verse twelve can sound onerous and burdensome, particularly with the use of words and phrases like *perseveres* and *"once he has been approved."* But remember, God's good news word is *never* burdensome when properly understood *(1 John 5:3)*. Let's break this verse down into its four major phrases, which we will cover over the next four days. Today, we look at the phrase: *"Blessed is a man."*

Blessed in the context of what James is saying means a profound and deep inner joy—a joy that specifically comes from realizing that we've been chosen by God to be recipients of His forgiveness, grace, mercy, daily care and direction, and eternal life! So, we are *blessed* because we belong to God *FOREVER!* That is what the first phrase in this verse is saying. We are *blessed* beyond any earthly wisdom, any earthly amount of money, any earthly amount of power or authority, any earthly amount of recognition or notoriety, because *God chose us to be His children.* And to be His children means He is our How-Great-Thou-Art Shepherd and we are His sheep. He is caring for us 24/7— today, tomorrow, and throughout eternity. What could be equivalent to this? How much earthly wealth could be equivalent to being a child of God and cared for by Him?

A JOYOUS THOUGHT FOR TODAY:

*Blessed be the God and Father of our Lord Jesus Christ, who has **blessed us** with every spiritual blessing in the heavenly places in Christ, ⁴just as He **chose us in Him** before the foundation of the world, that we would be holy and blameless before Him.* —Ephesians 1:3-4

For today, take a searching inventory of what you value. Can you imagine any earthly thing, any amount of money, any prestige that you would exchange for being a child of God and cared for by Him? If not, let your heart overflow with praise to Him.

DAY 37

*Blessed is a man who **perseveres under trial**; for once he has been approved, he will receive the crown of life which the Lord has promised to those who love Him.*
—JAMES 1:12

Perseveres under trial sounds rather unpleasant at first glance, but remember the context of what James is talking about. He has been telling us how to have joy in the midst of trials. He has told us that by understanding *God's purpose* (He uses trials to strengthen our faith into a *lifestyle of faithing* in Him) and *God's promise* (that He will work all things together for our good), He grows in us the habit of trusting God with everything—specifically for the wisdom and understanding we lack (or have temporarily forgotten) about Him in the midst of a particular trial that will produce joy in us. It is God's power in His word, just as though He were standing right in front of us talking to us, which produces joy in every circumstance.

With this in mind, *perseveres under trial* is more insight from the same context, and refers to our continuing to trust the Lord in our difficulties. "Persevering" is not something we humanly work hard at doing, like some heavy burden—but rather, the habit (or lifestyle) of *"casting all your anxiety on Him, because He cares for you" (1 Peter 5:7).* It is a quality that the Holy Spirit is growing in every believer's life as He progressively causes us to turn everything over to Him in faith!

A JOYOUS THOUGHT FOR TODAY:

And not only this, but we also exult in our tribulations,
*knowing that **tribulation brings about perseverance**;*
⁴and perseverance, proven character; and proven character,
hope; ⁵and hope does not disappoint, because the love of
God has been poured out within our hearts through the
Holy Spirit who was given to us. —ROMANS 5:3-5

For today, recognize that perseverance is not a burdensome task for you to bear upon your own human shoulders, but a quality of character that the Holy Spirit is building within you as He is bringing you to increasingly *faith* in God for everything.

DAY 38

*Blessed is a man who perseveres under trial; for once he has **been approved**, he will receive the crown of life which the Lord has promised to those who love Him.*
—JAMES 1:12

Remember, James is writing his letter to Christians. The phrase *been approved* comes from the Greek word *dokimos*, meaning "genuine" or "authentic." It is not approval *from God* that is being discussed here. God has already approved, chosen, and adopted His children into His household. God needs no further evidence of who His authentic children are *(John 17:6)*. What James is talking about here *relates to us*; how the process of turning to God and trusting Him in our trials—authenticates and gives evidence *to US*—that we have eternal life and that Jesus Christ lives in us!

What does turning to God in the midst of our trials authenticate (or evidence) to us? It gives evidence that we are children of God. If we were *not* a child of God we would *not seek after God at all*. It is *only* God's Holy Spirit that works in us to turn us to Him. Here is a practical example of this. Have you ever done (or thought) something sinful that makes you uncomfortable, ashamed, or disappointed? Do you hate it when this happens? Think about why you hate these sinful thoughts and conduct so much. If you were not chosen by God as one of His children, these thoughts and actions would not bother you. The very fact that they do bother you *authenticates* that you *ARE* a child of God in truth and is *evidence* that you have Jesus Christ dwelling in you. It is Christ's new nature within you that makes you uncomfortable when you sin. This discomfort is not sourced from your human flesh. Your flesh can never overcome itself.

A JOYOUS THOUGHT FOR TODAY:

*THERE IS NONE WHO UNDERSTANDS, **THERE IS NONE WHO SEEKS FOR GOD.*** —ROMANS 3:11

For Today, look back in your life at the number of times you have turned to God in your trials. Rather than become disappointed in yourself for lack of spiritual growth when you sin, recognize that the discomfort you feel is God's Holy Spirit working in you. It is His process of authenticating *to you* that you are a child of God. By the very fact that you turn to God at all is evidence that you have Christ Jesus living in you!

DAY 39

*Blessed is a man who perseveres under trial; for once he has been approved, he will receive the **crown of life** which the Lord has promised to those who love Him.*
—JAMES 1:12

Now we come to the fourth phrase in this wonderful verse. At first glance, this verse is often interpreted as referring to some future time in heaven when we *"receive the crown of life."* But just as the "approval" mentioned in the verse does not refer to an approval from God, so too, this *crown of life* is not referencing "eternal life" in heaven. This *crown of life* refers to experiencing Christ's life in *our* life *right now*. *Crown* means "reward" and *life,* as used here, doesn't refer to the "eternal" aspect of our New Life (since every believer already has that), but refers to experiencing the *quality of Christ's life* in our daily living. What a wonderful reward this is!

So, taking the four phrases together from this verse, James is telling us how blessed is the person who goes through life continually trusting God for everything. Not only do we grow ever more confident in our salvation and God's moment-by-moment care for us, but the Holy Spirit increasingly causes us to share in the experience of Christ's life within. We experience *His peace* (not earthly peace, but peace that passes all understanding as in *Philippians 4:7*); and *His joy* (not joy that comes only from positive circumstances, but the joy that comes from confidence that God is sovereign over *all* our circumstances). All of this is what it means to be blessed. All of this is why James tells us that every believer struggling from paycheck to paycheck, and having no power or authority in this world, are to glory greatly in their *high position* (Day 35).

A JOYOUS THOUGHT FOR TODAY:

The LORD will give strength to His people; the LORD will bless His people with peace. —PSALM 29:11

For Today, wear your *crown of life* with joy. Recognize how blessed you are to have been CHOSEN BY GOD to turn to Him for everything. You now have evidence that you are a child of God and are truly saved. Pray that the Holy Spirit will bless you with more experiences of Christ's qualities of peace, joy, patience, and compassion throughout your today.

PRAYER

*Father, I often reach a breaking point in the midst of my trials when I think, "I have no other option but to trust in You." Dear God, may I never think or say this again. Please remind me of what James is saying, that it is my highest position and privilege to be able to turn to You, call upon You, and trust in You daily **with everything.** I Praise You for this evidence of my salvation and adoption into Your household. Grant me today a portion of Your Son's quality of life in my life, that I may truly experience His joy, peace, patience, and compassion in the midst of my trials. Amen.*

Day 40

*And the rich man is to **glory in his humiliation**, because like flowering grass he will pass away.*
—James 1:10, NASB

*But the **one who is rich** should take pride in his **low position**, because he will pass away like a wild flower.*
—James 1:10, NIV

Some Bible commentators believe that the *rich man* refers to a non-Christian, wealthy person, but this does not fit the context of James' letter to Christians. In verse nine he encourages the *"brother of humble circumstances"* to glory in his *high position*. Then in verse ten he encourages the *rich man* (the *NIV* translates *"one who is rich"*) to glory in his *low position*. James is telling the few Christians who were not poor how they may also experience true joy in the same way the poor do. It seems rather unlikely that James would encourage an unsaved person to glory in their trials (for what purpose?).

Don't get distracted by trying to quantify when a person becomes rich. This does not matter to James. No matter how rich, we all (like flowering grass) fade soon enough. His point is that rich Christians should glory in whatever low positions, or trials, they have—just like the poor do. It is only through these times of humiliation, during low positions and trials, when we grow in trusting the Lord and experiencing His joy, peace, and contentment. So, whether a person is rich or poor (or in between) God is using *all* of our low positions to accomplish His good will in our life. One person's low position may be different from another person's low position, but God uses it all for our good.

A JOYOUS THOUGHT FOR TODAY:

*Open the gates to everyone, for **all may enter in** who love the Lord. ³He will keep in perfect peace all those who trust in Him, whose thoughts turn often to the Lord!* —ISAIAH 26:2-3, TLB

For Today, thank God for exactly the estate you are in. God has you exactly where He purposes for you to be. He has promised to use your trials to bring Christ's joy and peace into your life in abundance.

A PERSONAL TESTIMONY
EMBRACING THE LOW POSITION

When Sherryl and I got married over 52 years ago, we bought our first bed from the *Goodwill* for $10.00 because that is all we could afford. I won't even attempt to describe the condition of that bed, but we hauled it back to our small apartment and cleaned it up as best we could. After a few days, our backs hurt so much (and we kept rolling into each other) that we bought a sheet of plywood to fit between the mattress and box springs so it wouldn't sag so much. Let's just say we were rich in love but very poorly furnished.

Thirty years later, our finances weren't quite as tight. I wouldn't say we were rich, but we were not so poor either. It was about this time when I was faced with a great "humiliation" (to use James' word). I suddenly learned that I needed an emergency angioplasty! I had a severe heart condition that could take my life if not treated quickly. This was a cruel and humiliating circumstance for me because I suffered from a paralyzing phobic fear of hospitals at the time. I feared death more than anything and this medical procedure would require a four-day stay in a hospital! I got faint just thinking about it. It was the reason I held to an obsessive exercise program, thinking I could keep myself healthy (and out of the hospital) through my own effort.

Following that angioplasty (and quadruple bypass surgery fifteen years later), I still go to the doctor's office every ninety days to get my cholesterol and blood pressure checked—all of which are *low positions* for me. But through it all, God has removed that phobic fear of hospitals and the sick; and any fear of death from my heart. He made me realize that I am not in control of my health—HE IS! I still exercise, but do so because I enjoy it and it gives me time to commune with God and meditate on His word.

Today, God knew that He would call Sherryl and me to a ministry of visiting many dear saints during times of illness in the hospital. He used those early and ongoing trials, those *low positions of humiliation* in my life to prepare me for that ministry with my wife. I can honestly say now, that I am as comfortable encouraging and praying with a sick friend in the hospital than I am relaxing in my favorite chair at home.

My Joyous Thoughts

I'M THE REASON FOR ALL MY UNHAPPINESS

JAMES 1:13-16

Let no one say when he is tempted, "I am being tempted by God"; for God cannot be tempted by evil, and He Himself does not tempt anyone. [14]But each one is tempted when he is carried away and enticed by his own lust. [15]Then when lust has conceived, it gives birth to sin; and when sin is accomplished, it brings forth death. [16]Do not be deceived, my beloved brethren.

DAY 41

Let no one say when he is tempted, "I am being tempted by God"; for God cannot be tempted by evil, and He Himself does not tempt anyone.
—JAMES 1:13

So far James has been sharing with us *how* to experience joy in our trials by simply *faithing* in the Lord throughout our day. As He draws us to trust Him, we grow in His joy and peace because we increasingly remain focused on the fact that He is in control of all things, we are in his hands, He is working all things together for our good, and He will accomplish all His good purpose for us.

Now James moves on to explain the *source* of any unhappiness that we still may feel in our difficulties. He first tells us that whenever we experience anything other than joy—we should *never* blame God. The source of our problems is *never* God's fault. This is a very important clarity to begin with if we are to truly understand our difficulties. I can't tell you the number of people I have counselled who finally confess when you drill down to the core of what is really troubling them: "I'm angry at God and blame Him for this problem!" But James tells us that God is *never the source* of our problems—*something else is*. Over the next few days we will learn the true source of *all* of our problems.

A JOYOUS THOUGHT FOR TODAY:

No temptation has overtaken you but such as is common to man; and God is faithful, who will not allow you to be tempted beyond what you are able, but with the temptation will provide the way of escape also, so that you will be able to endure it. —1 CORINTHIANS 10:13

For Today, be encouraged that while temptation is a common affliction of every human being, it is *never* sourced from God. Have you ever been angry at God for something, or blamed Him for a particular circumstance, perhaps believing that He was punishing you personally? A clear understanding of this truth is the beginning of wisdom. It releases you from destructive misconceptions and unnecessary fear of God (your *loving* Father). It frees you to turn to Him without reservation in the midst of your trials, knowing that He is *never* the source of the troubles you face. He is *always* the source of healing, *never* affliction. And He will bring you to increasing relief through this study.

Many years ago I saw a great illustration of the spiritual principles embedded in *James 1:13* in a way that I have never forgotten. A teacher set before his audience a glass jar filled with what looked like pure water (except there was a hardly noticeable thin layer of silty mud settled on the bottom of the jar), and a lid secured on top. He told us to consider the glass jar as representing us.

Then he demonstrated what happens to us when troubles come along to "shake us" out of our comfortable living. As he shook the jar, the silty mud exploded from its dormant state and clouded the entire fluid, filling the jar with a turbid muddy mess.

The teacher surmised that the jar might complain to God, who obviously allowed the jar to be shaken by circumstances, concerning the muddy and unhappy result, but God might answer, "I may have allowed the shaking, but I didn't put the mud in you."

This illustration clarifies both the source of the mud (temptation and sin is sourced entirely in us) and also why God cannot be tempted. He cannot be tempted because He has no "mud" in Him capable of tempting Him! This is why you can shake Jesus all you want, mock Him, slander Him, even crucify Him, and never produce any feelings of anger, resentment, worry, or vindictiveness from Him.

Since He has nothing but pure water in Him, He has no "evil" in Him. He cannot attract anyone else to evil (to be angry, critical, vindictive, to do harm, or an injustice, etc.) because to do any of these things is evil in and of itself.

Day 42

*Let no one say when he is tempted, "I am being tempted by God"; for God cannot be tempted by evil, and **He Himself does not tempt anyone.***

—James 1:13

It is apparent that some (perhaps many) people in James' day were just like those of us today who react to their troubles by blaming God for them and their unhappiness. What an encouragement to us that in the first chapter of the first pastoral letter written after Christ's death, burial, resurrection, and ascension, James is inspired by God to assure us that when we are facing problems, we need never even consider blaming God for it. That is a wonderful and *absolute* truth direct from God's word. Scripture tells us two things emphatically: God cannot be tempted by evil; and God Himself does not tempt anyone.

The phrase *"God cannot be tempted by evil"* means that He can't be tempted to feel, think, say, or do anything contrary to His righteous nature because He has no evil (or unrighteousness) in Him. He has no moral depravity (mud) in any form that can draw evil from Him because there is no muddy evil in Him in the first place. No human has been shaken by circumstances more than Christ, yet He remained entirely without sin.

A Joyous Thought for Today:

*For we do not have a high priest who cannot sympathize with our weaknesses, **but One who has been tempted in all things as we are, yet without sin.*** —Hebrews 4:15

For Today, don't make the mistake of thinking that just because God cannot be tempted by evil He doesn't understand and sympathize with your weaknesses and sins. To be *"tempted in all things as we are"* means He has felt the same things we have felt. He has felt rejection, betrayal, injustice, and countless people treating Him unkindly. The difference is that while these things often trigger sin in us, He endured them all without sin. He never stressed out, worried, or became resentful, fearful, or vindictive. Having this truth in mind, offer worshipful thanksgiving in your heart that this is the very Christ who now lives His life *in you!*—And He will increasingly manifest *in you* His peace, His wisdom, and His comfort in your difficulties.

DAY 43

*To declare that the LORD is upright; He is my rock, and **there is no unrighteousness in Him.***
—PSALM 92:15, NASB

*This honors the Lord and exhibits his faithful care. He is my shelter. **There is nothing but goodness in him!***
—PSALM 92:15, TLB

I once spoke to a young man in his thirties who was fearful of praying to God because his wife had a degenerative back condition causing her much pain. The young man confessed that he would sometimes get impatient over the whole thing, but didn't want to pray for more patience believing that God would injure his own back in order to teach him more patience. It is sad to speak with many Christians who hold similar (and completely false) concepts about God. But scripture tells us unequivocally that there is *"nothing but goodness in Him."* Every way that God takes care of us on a daily basis is out of His total goodness! We can confidently trust Him forever and for everything.

"But look at this problem I'm facing!" you might say. We all experience troubles because we are human and live in a broken and depraved world. But all of God's children have something wonderful going on *within* them at the same time. God is progressively converting us from people of sight *to* people of faith. We often want God to hasten this process so our faith is bigger than what we see. But He is renewing our minds in His timing to trust that what His word says is true, not what we see.

A JOYOUS THOUGHT FOR TODAY:

*O taste and see that **the LORD is good**; how blessed is the man who takes refuge in Him!* —PSALM 34:8

***For Today**,* if you remember anything from this entire book, remember this absolute truth from God's word—*There is nothing but goodness in God!* There is no dirt in Him. He is never the source of unhappiness. Take shelter under His wings. Pray that He remove every doubt in your mind about this wonderful truth. He will only bring goodness to you. He will only affect your life in a way that causes you, in time, to praise Him.

DAY 44

But each one is tempted when he is carried away and enticed by his own lust.
¹⁶Do not be deceived, my beloved brethren.
—JAMES 1:14, 16

I f God never makes us unhappy, where does our unhappiness come from? James tells us that WE are the reason for *all* of our unhappiness! Not God, not any circumstance, not anyone else, just US. To believe otherwise, according to James, is to be deceived and without hope of experiencing any true happiness.

It is worth reminding ourselves again of the context of James' writing. Only a few verses after he has told us to *consider it all joy if you encounter various trials* (verse two), he is saying that if we are not praising the Lord in the midst of our difficulties it is because we have been *carried away by our own lust* (verse fourteen). It is our own lust that tempts us, or *carries us away to evil*. It is our own lust that is the source of *all* of our stress, anger, discouragement, and unhappiness!

I pray God would deeply work this truth from His word into us. Our difficult finances are not the reason for our stress. Our job is not the reason for our unhappiness. The disrespectful way our spouse treats us, our kid's behavior, or our relatives' attitudes are all not the reason for our lack of joy. It is solely a matter of our own lust. Tomorrow, Lord willing, we will bring definition to what *lust* refers to, but for today understand the actual mechanics of sin that James is talking about. It is not sourced from God, but our own lust. This understanding is necessary if we are to avoid being deceived.

A JOYOUS THOUGHT FOR TODAY:

*Therefore **there is now no condemnation for those***
***who are in Christ Jesus.** ²For the law of the Spirit*
of life in Christ Jesus has set you free from the law of
sin and of death. —ROMANS 8:1-2

For Today, do not condemn yourself for being the source of sin and unhappiness. God does not condemn you. Rather, rejoice that God's word is progressively setting you free from deception—to live a life of joy and happiness in any situation. God is doing it. He is shaping your life, as a potter shapes the clay, to experience *His* peace and joy!

DAY 45

*For all that is in the world, the **lust of the flesh** and the **lust of the eyes** and the*
*boastful **pride of life**, is not from the Father, but is from the world.*
—1 JOHN 2:16

This verse describes the three main categories of lust. Lust (of flesh and eyes) and pride, the leftover remnants of our fallen human nature, refer to what our flesh wants only for itself. This is the exact opposite of wanting God's will. Our selfish flesh wants *more* pleasure, *more* material things, *easier* finances, *less* problems and inconveniences, and of course, *more* glory and time for our self! James is telling us that our unhappiness daily comes from what our flesh wants. God has His daily will for our lives that brings peace, joy, and happiness. When we assert our own will to please only ourselves, we end up unhappy because we always stand in opposition to God. It is that simple.

Look again (with new perspective) at a verse we have read before. *Proverbs 20:24 (TLB)* reads: *"Since the Lord is directing our steps, why try to understand everything that happens along the way?"* Why question, and stress along the way? God has given us many examples of this truth: He is the Potter, we are the (incapable-of-doing-anything-for-ourselves) clay; He is the How-Great-Thou-Art Shepherd and we are His (dumb) sheep. But our flesh doesn't want to trust God. By contrast, Christ had no dirt in Him. The only thing He said to the Father was *"Thy will be done."* The only thing our flesh can dependably produce is unhappiness and misery in our life.

A JOYOUS THOUGHT FOR TODAY:

Though he give you [allows you to experience] the bread
of adversity and water of affliction, yet he will be with
you to teach you—with your own eyes you will see your
Teacher. [21]And if you leave God's paths and go astray,
you will hear a voice behind you say, "No, this is the
way; walk here." —ISAIAH 30:20-21, TLB

For Today, be confident that no matter how far afield your flesh takes you, God is still there calling you back to *walk here.* Thank God that He has made *you* to hear His voice and follow Him. *Thank Him that He doesn't require you to hold on to Him, but He holds on to you!* This is the true path of joy and happiness in all circumstances.

DAY 46

*But each one is tempted when he is carried away and **enticed by his own lust**. ¹⁵Then when lust has conceived, it **gives birth to sin**; and when sin is accomplished, it brings forth death.*

—JAMES 1:14-15

Each of us is tempted (or made unhappy) when we are *enticed by our own lust*. *Enticed* is an interesting word in the Greek that connotes the way a hunter baits his trap to draw in his prey for the kill. James tells us that all of our "fleshly" desires— or all that we want for ourselves—is a "baited trap" set within us, ready to spring at any time to catch us. Verse fifteen tells us what our "flesh trap" catches us in: *"when lust has conceived, it gives birth to sin."* Or to say it another way, when our fleshly desires meet some form of inconvenience, our flesh trap springs into action and catches us in sinful feelings, comments, and actions.

For example, our "flesh" wants to be *treated with kindness*. So when our boss or a spouse does or says something we perceive to be unkind, our flesh-trap springs and catches us in feelings of resentment and making unkind remarks back. Our "flesh" also *wants what it wants*. This explains why we can come directly from church, go to the nearest restaurant, and react resentfully and rudely to the server who didn't bring our lunch just the way we ordered it! How about when we plan a lovely day of activities with our friends or family (forgetting that God is ordering our day)? When those "fleshly" plans are interrupted we feel impatient and upset because "our plans" set a trap for us.

A JOYOUS THOUGHT FOR TODAY:

For the wages of sin is death, but the free gift of
*God is **eternal life** [which is Christ's life in you now]*
in Christ Jesus our Lord. —ROMANS 6:23

For Today, consider events from your own life when your "flesh" trap has sprung (and how cunning the enemy is in your flesh), but don't stop there. Give thanks to God that He did not leave you with the wages of your own fleshly sin, but gave you the free gift of eternal life, which includes His Holy Spirit's continual work in you. Read again *Philippians 2:13, "For it is God who is at work in you, both to will and to work for His good pleasure."*

DAY 47

*Then when lust has conceived, it gives birth to sin; and **when sin is accomplished, it brings forth death.***

—JAMES 1:15

N otice the systematic development of what James is showing us: when *lust* is conceived, it gives birth to *sin*, and when *sin* is accomplished, it brings forth *death*. Lust, sin, death—none of which comes from God, but all of it sourced in us. Ultimately, all of this comes from *"your adversary, the devil, who prowls around in your flesh, like a roaring lion, seeking someone to devour" (1 Peter 5:8).* While he cannot devour your salvation, which is forever secure in Christ, he is hungry to devour a piece of your joy and happiness through "trapped-in" bitterness, anger, discouragement, and worry. He loves for us to forget that God *is* ordering our day. He loves for us to forget God's promises from scripture. He loves for us to take our focus off of (even for a few moments), *"fixing our eyes on Jesus, the author and perfecter of [your] faith" (Hebrews 12:2)*; or your focus off of your How-Great-Thou-Art Shepherd who has you under His watchful care 24/7. He loves all of these things so he can trigger your "flesh trap" and devour your joy.

The phrase *"when sin is accomplished it brings forth death"* does not mean that we lose our salvation (which the next verse makes clear, *see* Day 48). The phrase means that the *result* of our fleshly attitudes, actions, and comments is always painful and destructive to ourself *and* to others around us! Our "flesh" wants to have a *problem-free life*, so when we have problems at work or at home, our "flesh trap" springs and we are caught again in unkind feelings, remarks, and maybe even actions! This is what is accomplished by sin. It produces all manner of unhappiness in our lives.

A JOYOUS THOUGHT FOR TODAY:

*You are from God, little children, and have overcome them; because **greater is He who is in you** than he who is in the world.* —1 JOHN 4:4

For Today, what a good time for God to display His immense loving care for you! *First*, God knows your enemy better than you do; *second*, His wisdom is life-transforming while your enemy's deception is not; and *third*, His power to defeat your enemy is greater than the enemy's power to defeat you. *Praise God for His greater life in you!*

DAY 48

Do not be deceived, my beloved brethren.
—JAMES 1:16

This verse makes it clear that the "death" spoken of in verse fifteen (Day 47) is not referring to the loss of our salvation. When James is exhorting us to "*not be deceived,*" he is speaking to "*my beloved brethren.*" James is encouraging us to never think that anyone else, or anything else, is the source of our unhappiness. He wants us to own the fact that WE are the sole source of our unhappiness. When we are so mad at our boss, spouse, kids, or a friend that we can't see straight, *we are being deceived!* When our How-Great-Thou-Art Shepherd—who is the source of peace and joy— turns our focus back to Him it transforms our life. At the speed of thought, He frees us from our painful self-trap!

A JOYOUS THOUGHT FOR TODAY:

*Search **me**, O God, and know **my** heart; try **me**
and know **my** anxious thoughts; [24]and see if there
be any hurtful way **in me, and lead me in the**
everlasting way.* —PSALM 139:23-24

For Today, take time to pray *Psalm 139:23-24* to the Lord. Pray to Him to "search *me*," not "search my spouse, or my kids, or my boss," but *just ME!* Ask the Lord to show you where there is any desire in you other than for Him to manifest more of His life, joy, and peace in you. Pray that He will lead *you* in the everlasting way, and then praise Him that He is doing so. As John declared to his disciples upon seeing Jesus—"*He must increase, but I must decrease*" (*John 3:30*)—this is the path of freedom from your "flesh trap." Simply wanting God's will more than your own, and recognizing that His will is prevailing in ALL of your circumstances, sets you free from every painful (and destructive) thing you want for yourself. What a glorious thought! We cannot free ourselves. Our flesh will never defeat itself. Only God has the power to do this— AND HE DOES—again, and again, and again! How great is His mercy toward us?

CONNECTING THE THEOLOGICAL DOTS

Recognizing *how* our flesh works is not a negative thing. It should give us a greater understanding of what it means to be blessed, to be saved, and to live in the joy of our salvation. As we consider the flesh-trap, we must always remember that the flesh can never put down and defeat the flesh. This lack of understanding is a source of great frustration for many Christians. They are painfully aware of their struggles with self-ishness or lust for material things, yet they remain hopeful that *they* can make themselves better in their own effort (or with *some* help from God).

But here is the glorious truth: God *chose* you and me—to put our human clay on His potter's wheel—to shape us according to His will in a way that makes us increasingly joyful in any circumstance. This redemptive act by God is already complete. Yet, He progressively and continually, day after day, over the course of our lives, defeats the fleshly ugliness in us. There is nothing for us to boast in after all. Our boast is only in God and His mercy for us. Many Christians struggle to understand this in full measure. They think, as I did for decades, that salvation is only a future event, a "ticket to get into heaven," without realizing the incredible salvation *process* going on *every day of their lives* through the circumstances affecting them. This is how we are *being saved every day*!

So, what is really going on here? There is only good and evil in life. Evil is everything apart from God. And since God is all good, evil is everything contrary to what is truly good. Evil is contrary to true peace, true joy, and true happiness. Our flesh is saturated with evil, but God's Spirit *in us* is all good. This means, in practical terms, that the more of God we experience, the less of our flesh we experience at the same time. The more God draws us to pray, the more He sensitizes us to the Spirit's leading within; and the more He leads us to read His word, the more good we experience instead of our flesh.

He is the One growing His peace in us and progressively transforming us. This is why Paul said in *2 Corinthians 3:18* that we *"are being transformed into the same image [as Christ] from glory to glory, just as from the Lord, the Spirit."* And in *Ephesians 2:10*: *"For we are [continuously, day after day] His workmanship ...."* He lives more and more in us and puts down our flesh—so we can live more and more in His joy and happiness in all circumstances. To realize that God is doing *all of this in me*—and He doesn't expect me to do any of it for myself—is glorious joy!

My Joyous Thoughts

HOW
GOOD IS GOD?

JAMES 1:17-18

[17]Every good thing given and every perfect gift is from above, coming down from the Father of lights, with whom there is no variation or shifting shadow. [18]In the exercise of His will He brought us forth by the word of truth, so that we would be a kind of first fruits among His creatures.

HOW GOOD IS GOD?

If you were having lunch with someone and they asked you the question: How Good is God? What would you answer? Would your answer be as short as "I don't know," or would it take several minutes for you to detail and describe the goodness of God as you've experienced Him in your own life? The world doesn't believe God is good at all. Many do not believe He exists. Many more believe He is the source of much of the world's conflicts and is responsible for much of the problems the world faces today.

Over the next few days, we are going to listen to James tell us that not only is God good, but His goodness far exceeds what most Christians think. God is so good, in fact, that the English language is wholly inadequate to share the magnitude of His goodness toward us, nor is there any hope that we can, with human intellect, grasp His goodness in theological terms. The level of *experiential knowledge* of God's goodness that I am talking about only comes through God's personal revelation. Pray earnestly in these coming days that He would grant you, by His mercy and grace, a true glimpse of His unfathomable goodness and how impactful His goodness is on your daily life, throughout your life.

Let's briefly recall what James has already told us. In *James 1:2* he tells us to consider it all joy when we encounter various trials, or when we have lots of problems we should be joyful. What a paradoxical statement this is! But he didn't stop there. He said if we don't have joy, then we lack (or have temporarily forgotten) some aspect of wisdom about God that is keeping us from experiencing the joy God intends for us to have in the midst of any difficulty.

Over the last several days we have been looking at one of these wisdoms: That ***we are the source of all of our unhappiness***. It is the lust of *our flesh* (or all that we want for ourself) that makes us unhappy. In the coming days we will see another one of these life-changing wisdoms: That ***God is all good!*** Rather than try to blame God for our problems we will learn from James that the more we know God, the more of His goodness we experience.

DAY 49

Every good thing given and every perfect gift is from above, coming down from the Father of lights, with whom there is no variation or shifting shadow.
—JAMES 1:17

For the first forty years of my life, my image of God was the "club and hug Guy." He was the stern sovereign who was ready to club me with one hand and hug me with the other. I heard plenty of sermons about God's love, but I could never quite get comfortable with the "hug" because my mind would always flash back to the "club" ready to strike me at the least provocation. I was tormented by the fear during my high school and college days, that if I had a certain immoral thought enter my mind more than once within a few minutes, the next bolt of lightning might have my name on it.

We will never experience a passion and joy for God while holding to this false and delusional concept of God. But the more the Lord grows an increasing understanding of His goodness, particularly of His love being *unconditional* toward us, the more passion and joy we experience for Him. This is the next "wisdom" that James is summarizing for us in verse seventeen: "*Every good thing given and every perfect gift is from above.*" James is telling us that *ALL* that is good is from God! Or think of it another way, *EVERY* true good comes from God! *Every good thing ... is from above. Every* is one of those absolute words. Can you think of anything good, truly good, which does *not* come from God?

A JOYOUS THOUGHT FOR TODAY:

There is no fear in love; but perfect love casts out fear, because fear involves punishment, and the one who fears is not perfected in love. —1 JOHN 4:18

For Today, examine your concept of God. Does it involve a stern God ready to strike you with a club (or some other form of punishment) at your slightest misbehavior? Pray to God to slay this false concept of Him in your heart, and resurrect the eternal truth of these verses. He is the source of *all* good. *Faith* (believe) in Him, as your sovereign God, to bring *all good* to your life. He has BOTH arms around you, hugging you, and protecting you more than you could ever imagine. He never treats you according to what you (or any of us) deserve, but always according to His mercy and goodness.

PRAYER

Dear God, I know that my thoughts concerning You are often clouded and vague. I have mixed understandings of You, and often I am fearful that You are ready and willing to punish me and are just waiting for any action on my part that displeases You. Please reveal to me over these next few days, from Your word, how You are 100% good and how You have nothing but good for me. Overcome every fallen idea from my flesh concerning who You really are and how consistent is Your goodness toward me. Amen.

DAY 50

*Every good thing given and every perfect gift **is from above**, coming down from the Father of lights, with whom there is no variation or shifting shadow.*
—James 1:17

How often we have been taught that "God is good" (which is certainly true), but have we ever considered what it means for *God to be ALL that is good?* Or to think of it in another way: that there is NO good in this life *apart* from God? When James tells us that every good thing is from above, what does he mean? He means that the only *true good* in this life is God's working in, and on behalf of, our life! The only *true good* is experiencing God's daily care for us—His peace, joy, unconditional love—bringing fulfillment, contentment, and wisdom into our hearts in the midst of our daily living.

But what about all the fun and enjoyable things I like to do that aren't sinful? How about hunting and fishing to bring food home for my family; or going shopping to buy food and clothing to care for them? And how about my dog (he's about as close to unconditional love as you can get next to God Himself)? Yes, all of these things are good—*but temporal.* And no matter how fun and good these temporary things are, they don't last. By contrast, the good that comes from God—*LASTS!*

A JOYOUS THOUGHT FOR TODAY:

*These things I have spoken to you so that **My joy** may be in you, and that your joy may be made full.*
—John 15:11

For Today, dwell on the fact that Jesus Himself is speaking to you in this verse; that His joy (how good is that?) may be in you and that your joy may be made full (not temporal and fleeting, but full all the time). Jesus is providing His spoken word to you today so the joy you experience will not come merely from temporary circumstances but from God, the source of *all true and lasting good* in your life. Ask Him to fill you up with His goodness today and give you the eyes to see what form that goodness takes in your life. In truth, His goodness is granted to us in BOTH temporal and eternal blessings, all of which are sourced from God.

DAY 51

For the LORD gives wisdom; from His mouth come knowledge and understanding.
⁹Then you will discern righteousness and justice and equity and every good course.
—PROVERBS 2:6, 9, NASB

For the Lord grants wisdom! His every word is a treasure of knowledge and
understanding. ⁹He shows how to distinguish right from wrong, how to find the
right decision every time.
—PROVERBS 2:6, 9, TLB

According to Solomon, the *"every good thing"* from God, as referenced in *James 1:17*, is not limited only to temporal and eternal "things" from God (Day 50), but literally includes every *good decision* we make related to our family, work, and finances in daily life. How do we communicate better with our parents, spouse, or kids? How do we resolve conflicts at home or work? How do we know whether to take that new job or stay where we are? Or whether we should put our kids in private or public schools (or home school them)? Every good decision comes through God's leading from His word.

This is the wisdom that cannot be duplicated anywhere in the world. Look at the so-called wisdom of this world. All of us can see what is happening. Half of the planet is on fire. It hates, manipulates, and lies. It is unjust, unkind, and disrespectful. All of this comes from the world's wisdom. The world says this is how you get things done, how you "fix" things. None of this produces good decisions. *Only God's word does that!*

A JOYOUS THOUGHT FOR TODAY:

How blessed are the people who know the joyful sound! O
*LORD, **they walk in the light of Your countenance.***
*¹⁶In Your name they rejoice **all the day,** and by Your*
righteousness they are exalted. —PSALM 89:15-16

For Today, rejoice in the fact that God has called you to hear His joyful sound! He has given you ears to hear His voice as He draws you to read His word and leads you in every good decision. It is not up to you, but rather, it is *HIS countenance* wherein you walk, *HIS name* wherein you rejoice, and *HIS righteousness* wherein you are exalted.

Day 52

Every good thing given and every perfect gift is from above, coming down from the
*Father of lights, **with whom there is no variation or shifting shadow.***
—James 1:17

James gives us yet another peace-inducing, joy-releasing truth about God in this verse. James has already told us that: (1) God *is* good, *and* (2) He is *all* that is good, but James doesn't stop there. In the latter half of this verse he tells us an even more magnificent truth about God—that He is *consistently* good! God doesn't hug us one day, and slap us around the next! He is never anything other than *good* toward us! Verse seventeen tells us that *"there is no variation or shifting shadow"* with God. As the earth rotates around the sun, we observe the shadows on earth shift and move as the sun radiates its light generously upon the earth. James tells us that God is the *"Father of lights"*—He is the source of *all* light—His goodness *never* shifts or changes toward us!

But we sometimes say "God has been good to me today (or this week)" and what we mean by this is we didn't have as many problems, or our spouse treated us better, or our kids made the basketball or soccer squad, or we didn't owe as much in taxes, or got an "A" on an exam, or we made a big sale at work, or got a new job. But this statement *denies* the truth expressed in *James 1:17* and reinforces the lie that somehow God's goodness *does* change. This lie keeps us from trusting Him in everything because deep down we fear that some of what He does to us won't make us happy.

A Joyous Thought for Today:

Oh give thanks to the Lord, *for **He is good,** for His*
*lovingkindness is **everlasting** [or His good toward us*
is always and forever]. —Psalm 107:1

For Today, prayerfully let this understanding of *God's consistent goodness* sink in for a moment and it will blow to smithereens every false notion the enemy has ever lied to you about God. In truth, He always (and forever) has both arms around you in a loving embrace of absolute protection and provides nothing but goodness for you. *No matter how much you fail, His loving you never fails.*

DAY 53

*To declare that the LORD is upright; He is my rock, and **there is no unrighteousness in Him.***
—PSALM 92:15, NASB

*This honors the Lord and exhibits his faithful care. **He is my shelter. There is nothing but goodness in him!***
—PSALM 92:15, TLB

We have considered *God's goodness* for several days. Time to review: *How good is God?*

If He answers all of our prayers only with goodness (so we never need to fear praying to Him about anything): *How good is God?*

If He is sovereignly and lovingly caring for us 24/7 simply out of His goodness, even though we may not recognize it at times: *How good is He?*

And if there is never a reason to fear anything in regards to our relationship with God because, as *Psalm 92:15* declares, *there is nothing but goodness in Him: How good is He?*

A JOYOUS THOUGHT FOR TODAY:

> ***How great is Your goodness,*** *which You have stored up for those who fear [revere, worship] You, which You have wrought for those who take refuge in You, before the sons of men!* [20]*You hide them in the secret place of Your presence from the conspiracies of man; You keep them secretly in a **shelter** from the strife of tongues.* —PSALM 31:19-20

For Today, continue to contemplate the goodness of God. As you read over *Psalms 92* and *31*, note that the Lord is referenced as *a shelter.* Have you ever thought of Him as your secret shelter, your hiding place, or your safe place? Pray these Psalms to God from the bottom of your heart: *"Dear Lord, I declare that **you are upright** and **there is no unrighteousness in You. You are my rock** and **my shelter** where I can **hide** and **take refuge.** Now I know that **there is nothing but goodness in You;** and, O Lord, **how great is Your goodness for me!** In all the difficulties I experience, I thank you for the confidence that you are **hiding me in the secret place of Your presence.** Thank You, Lord. Amen."*

DAY 54

In the exercise of His will He brought us forth by the word of truth, so that we would be a kind of first fruits among His creatures.

—JAMES 1:18

If there ever was a world-class example of God's goodness, this verse is it. Let's examine this verse over the next few days, layer by layer, to understand the joyous message that James is sharing with us.

Let's begin with what "God's goodness" is *NOT*. The dark and depraved world we live in is based entirely upon our *human performance* for acceptance and success: work hard, meet *expectations*, and receive reward; or make a mistake and suffer the consequences.

Many Christians falsely assume that this *worldly* principle applies to God's kingdom. They believe that their relationship with God depends on how well they meet His *expectations* for them (which they often fail). This is why many Christians think of God as the "club and hug" guy—hugging us one moment and punishing us the next.

But the stunning reality is that in God's kingdom *we* have *nothing* to do with how God treats us! God has *no expectations* for us. He already knows that we are dead in our sins without Him. James tells us that our salvation *begins* and *continues* for all eternity, *solely* because of God's choice! The phrase, *"In the exercise of His will,"* teaches this: *God alone* willed to unite you and me to Himself!

A JOYOUS THOUGHT FOR TODAY:

For God, who said, "Light shall shine out of darkness,"
is the One who has shone in our hearts to give the Light
of the knowledge of the glory of God in the face of Christ.
⁷But we have this treasure in earthen vessels, so that
the surpassing greatness of the power will be of God
and not from ourselves. —2 CORINTHIANS 4:6-7

For Today, dwell on this simple truth: you didn't choose God—God chose you! Do you feel unworthy of His choice? You are—we all are—because we are but dust. But God chose to make you an earthen vessel to contain the glory of His Son. He expects nothing from you. God simply, from your clay pot, chose to reflect His glory!

DAY 55

In the exercise of His will He brought us forth by the word of truth, so that we would be a kind of first fruits among His creatures.

—JAMES 1:18

Before we were ever born, God simply decided to include us in His new creation by the sole exercise of *His will*. He wasn't compelled to do it. He wasn't needy or lonely and somehow had to do it. He chose to demonstrate His great love for us *unconditionally*, out of pure goodness, by an exercise of *His* will. Often a Christian will exclaim, "Are you saying that He doesn't *expect* anything from me? Really?" I say, "That's right. That is what *unconditional* love is." We don't earn our way into God's family or new creation.

This brings us closer to another dimension of God's goodness, which I pray He will show each of us in a life-changing way. Answer this question: Who did God *choose* to show His love and mercy to? *Ephesians 2:4-5* tells us: "*But God, being rich in mercy, because of His great love with which He loved us, ⁵even when we were dead in our transgressions, made us alive together with Christ (by grace you have been saved)."* Whom did God *choose* to give His love to? He chose US! Did we deserve it in any way? No, our condition was encased in *death*. Dead people can't do anything for themselves, yet that is precisely who God chose: a people who had *no* merit to deserve anything from Him.

This loving action by God is the very definition of mercy: *unmerited favor*. Now we know that God is good; that all good is from God; and that He is *consistently* AND *unconditionally* good. God is rich in mercy toward us who deserve nothing from Him.

A JOYOUS THOUGHT FOR TODAY:

And raised us up with Him, and seated us with Him in the heavenly places in Christ Jesus, ⁷so that in the ages to come He might show the surpassing riches of His grace in kindness toward us in Christ Jesus. —EPHESIANS 2:6-7

For Today, pray/read—with a thankful heart—the single sentence spanning *Ephesians 2:4-7* to learn *why* God chose you. Not so you might work hard to please Him. Note that every verb in the sentence describes an action taken by God, none by you: *so that ... He might show the surpassing riches of His grace in kindness toward [you] in Christ Jesus.*

DAY 56

In the exercise of His will He brought us forth by the word of truth, so that we would be a kind of first fruits among His creatures.
—JAMES 1:18

I n human terms, we utterly lack a conceptual point of reference in Christian life about God's goodness. It is so far beyond our human comprehension that it is difficult even to begin to grasp. When I ask a group of Christians whether *God is good*, all of them will readily agree. When I ask them whether *God is always good*, they usually hesitate a bit in their response, pausing a moment before answering yes. Ask yourself these two questions and see if you pause before answering the second. Why are these answers important? They are important because they bring us to the heart of God's goodness.

Yes, God *is* good, and *all* that is good, and *consistently* and *unconditionally* good, but what does "God's goodness" mean? Most Christians answer that question with "God saved me and gave me the gift of eternal life." I ask, "How is that good?" They usually respond with something like, "I get to go to heaven when I die." Of course, that is true, but God's goodness is not restricted only to that glorious fact. The core of God's goodness radiates from the essence of who God is: From His *great love* He chose us out of *mercy* (which means *unmerited favor*). This means He *never* treats us in response to what we deserve, but always in a manner according to His loving will—something we never earn and don't deserve. Because He is unchanging, His goodness applies not only to a future heaven, but equally relates to a 24/7 salvation in our daily life here on earth.

A JOYOUS THOUGHT FOR TODAY:

But as many as received Him, to them He gave the right to become children of God, even to those who believe in His name, [13]who were born, not of blood nor of the will of the flesh nor of the will of man, but of God. —JOHN 1:12-13

For Today, pray to God for His enlightenment to see that when you were dead and in darkness, God gifted you with the belief to receive His Son and become His child. After reading these verses in John, thank God that it was not your family bloodline, or anything you decided (or will of man), but only God's will that saved you!

DAY 57

In the exercise of His will He brought us forth by the word of truth, so that we would be a kind of first fruits among His creatures.

—JAMES 1:18

Remain in prayer as we go deeper into the reality of God's goodness. A true revelation of His goodness is a wisdom that James considers foundational if we are to personally experience joy in the midst of our trials and difficulties.

We didn't deserve to be chosen by God, but He did it. We didn't deserve Christ leaving His rightful place in the heavens to humble himself even to the point of death on a cross to pay the price for our sins, but He did it. We didn't deserve to be clothed in Christ's righteousness, but He did it. We didn't deserve the gift of belief given to us by God and His Holy Spirit dwelling in our earthen vessels, but He did it. And we don't deserve His 24/7, moment by moment, ongoing and continuous, loving, guiding, nurturing, and protecting care for us as His children, but He does it!

This is but a tiny glimpse of God's goodness for us. When we begin to understand God's goodness and how He faithfully directs His goodness toward us in every situation, we lose our fear of Him as a source of punishment. He becomes what He is in truth: our loving heavenly Father who is working all things together for our good.

A JOYOUS THOUGHT FOR TODAY:

What then shall we say to these things? **If God is for us, who is against us?** *[32]He who did not spare His own Son, but delivered Him over for us all, how will He not also with Him freely give us all things?* —ROMANS 8:31-32

For Today, take a moment to marvel at the practical impact of God's goodness in your life. If God saved you just by an exercise of *His will*, no one (including yourself) can thwart His will and rob you of that salvation. If in His infinite goodness, He did not spare His own Son to save you; how much encouragement does that give you to trust Him with your life and all your daily problems? He has committed to freely give you all things good for your life right now! Pray to God to show this truth to you, not just intellectually in your head, but experientially in your heart.

CONNECTING THE THEOLOGICAL DOTS:

Let's take a moment to clarify an important distinction from scripture. Many Christians believe, when they are facing hardships or serious trials, that God is punishing them. They are locked into the worldly notion of *performance* (Day 54) and believe that God has certain *expectations* of them, which if they fail to meet, God will punish them for it.

This is not scriptural. There is no verse in the New Testament which states, or even suggests, that God punishes any of His children. Don't take my word for it, sit down with your Bible and an exhaustive concordance and take as long as you need to search out the truth of this statement. God does not punish His children, pure and simple.

In fact, *1 John 4:18* declares the opposite: *"There is no fear in love; but perfect love casts out fear,* **because fear involves punishment***, and the one who fears is not perfected in love."* (Day 49) ***"God is love"*** *(1 John 4:8)*. In God's perfect love there is no room for punishment based on your performance.

What scripture refers to is not punishment, but *discipline*. *Hebrews 12:4*, quoting the Old Testament, tells us that *"whom the Lord loves He disciplines."* And *Hebrews 12:11* states that, *"All discipline for the moment **seems not to be joyful**, but sorrowful; yet to those who have been **trained by it, afterwards it yields the peaceful fruit of righteousness."***

In reality, the discipline mentioned by the author of Hebrews is the same dynamic going on with James when he says to *"consider it all joy ... when you encounter various trials" (James 1:2).* Such trials produce endurance and endurance perfects and completes you until you lack nothing. What scripture calls "discipline" is really God's *"Romans 8:28 process"* of working all things together for our good. God uses the hardships caused by this broken, corrupt, and fallen world to train, shape, renew, and transform us into the image of His Son. This is what Biblical "discipline" is referring to.

This is why, in all my Christian life, I have never heard a Christian tell me that they would prefer to give up what the Lord matured in them during a certain hardship, and avoid going through the hardship in the first place. This includes people who have lost their own children. I personally, would not exchange a single hardship in my life for what God gained in me as a result of that hardship. Take a moment to consider past hardships in your life. Would you give up any of them for what God established in you through those hardships?

DAY 58

*In the exercise of His will **He brought us forth** by the word of truth, so that we would be a kind of first fruits among His creatures.*
—JAMES 1:18

James makes God's goodness even clearer in the next four words of verse eighteen when he says: *"He brought us forth."* This phrase refers to God's creative action of bringing forth Christ's eternal life in us. This is our *new life* in Christ, the *new creation* that God has made us a part of *in Christ!* This phrase is the capstone of God's goodness.

What defines God's goodness is not that He passively put a "gift" of salvation out there in the universe so we could come along later, find it, and choose to accept or reject it based on what we want to do (a common Christian teaching). His goodness is far bigger and more active than that. His goodness is not defined by what we want or don't want. Take the Apostle Paul. If there was anyone on the planet who did NOT want anything to do with Christ, it was Paul. But God's goodness is not defined by what Paul wanted. *It is defined by what God wanted.* Look at Paul's testimony of his own salvation in *Galatians 1:15-16: "**But when God**, who had set me apart even from my mother's womb and called me through His grace, **was pleased to reveal His Son in me**."* According to Paul, all the action words were God's, not Paul's. Purely out of God's goodness, God didn't *offer* to save Paul (and us); He actually *DID* save Paul (and us) for His glory!

A JOYOUS THOUGHT FOR TODAY:

*Just as **He chose us** in Him before the foundation of the world, that we would be holy and blameless before Him. In love ⁵He predestined us to adoption as sons through Jesus Christ to Himself, **according to the kind intention of His will**, ⁶to the praise of the glory of His grace, which He freely bestowed on us in the Beloved.* —EPHESIANS 1:4-6

For Today, dwell on this simple truth: God decided before you were ever born to *choose you* to be reconciled to Him. Christ accomplished this loving reconciliation to God on your behalf. He even gave you the saving faith to believe this glorious fact. This is your reality. Meditate on how God, out of His goodness, uses your trials to grow *in you* His joy, peace, kindness, etc.; and progressively create in you His new creation *in Christ!*

DAY 59

*In the exercise of His will He brought us forth **by the word of truth**, so that we would be a kind of first fruits among His creatures.*

—JAMES 1:18

James, in verse eighteen, goes on to tell us *how* God brought us forth: *by the word of truth*. The phrase, *"word of truth"* refers to the special enlightenment God brings to our hearts to understand (and believe) that Jesus is God's gift of eternal life to us. The context of this verse points to and flows from God's goodness discussed in verse seventeen.

Let's add more richness to what James is saying. In *2 Corinthians 4:6*, Paul says: *"For God, who said, 'Light shall shine out of darkness,' is the One who has shone in our hearts to give the Light of the knowledge of the glory of God in the face of Christ."* The context for Paul's comment is his discussion of salvation and the gospel. He makes reference to God's initial creation *(Genesis 1:3)* where God simply spoke the word, *"Let there be light"* and light flooded the darkness. Paul tells us that this is exactly what God has done in our hearts. He has spoken light (the *word of truth*) in our hearts to enlighten the darkness within us. It is in this context *(from Day 58)* that Paul refers to us as reconciled to God *through Christ*, and as His new creation *in Christ (2 Corinthians 5:17-18)*.

A JOYOUS THOUGHT FOR TODAY:

But when God, *who had set me apart even from my mother's womb and called me through His grace,* **was pleased** [16]*to reveal His Son IN ME.* —GALATIANS 1:15-16

For Today, take time to ponder Paul's personal testimony of his own salvation experience and compare it to your own. Paul said that his salvation occurred *"when God ... was pleased to reveal His Son in me."* Paul's testimony was not that God revealed His Son TO Paul, but rather, that God revealed His Son IN Paul. Paul is saying that God's goodness far exceeds giving Paul a *choice* to be saved. God's goodness means He *acted* to save Paul (purely out of the exercise of His will)! Is this not like your own experience, when God put His Spirit within you to give you understanding of (and belief in) His Son Jesus, your Savior? What joy there is in the fact that our salvation does not depend on *our goodness*, but only on *God's goodness* (and Christ's perfection)!

DAY 60

In the exercise of His will He brought us forth by the word of truth, **so that we would be a kind of first fruits among His creatures.**
—JAMES 1:18

W hy did God bring this *word of truth* (this light, this understanding) into our hearts? So we Christians *"would be a kind of first fruits among His creatures."* The phrase *"first fruits"* means *"a sample of what He created to be consecrated to Himself"* (*James 1:18, AMP*). God's new creation involves more than just Christians. It involves the renewal of all of His original creation until God reveals His new heaven and new earth in the last days *(Revelation 21:1)*. We are but the *first fruits*, wrought in Christ, to the glory of God.

Does being part of God's first fruits give us something to boast of in ourselves? Not at all! Our only boast is in the Lord *(1 Corinthians 1:31)* for we were all chosen solely by God's will and saved only through His divine enlightenment. The Apostle Paul, after telling us that God is shining His *"Light of the knowledge of the glory of God"* in our hearts (Day 59, *2 Corinthians 4:6*), tells us in the very next verse the truth of our sojourn on earth: *"But we have this treasure in earthen vessels, so that the surpassing greatness of the power will be of God and not from ourselves."* How good is God? That in spite of our ugly flesh in our human clay pots, He chose to redeem us to Himself anyway!

A JOYOUS THOUGHT FOR TODAY:

Now all these things are from God, who reconciled us to Himself through Christ and gave us the ministry of reconciliation, [19]namely, that **God was in Christ reconciling the world to Himself, not counting their trespasses against them, and He has committed to us the word of reconciliation.** —2 CORINTHIANS 5:18-19

For Today, give praise to God for His unfathomable goodness! Can you possibly comprehend it? Why would God take your earthen vessel and choose to put His glory (His Son) *in you*? What have you done to deserve that? You were dead before God *(Ephesians 2:5)*! Yet, you are now a *first fruit*—an "exhibit A" to the rest of creation—that God is renewing all of it in the same way day by day. *You* are blessed among all of God's creation. How big (or small) are your troubles compared to this? *Count it all joy!*

HOW GOOD IS GOD?

We started this section by asking *How Good is God?* What have you concluded?

If God just willed, out of His goodness, to reveal to us (the most undeserving of all of His creation), that Christ is God's gift of eternal life to us ... *How good is He?*

If God also gave us the *word of truth* which shines His light in our hearts that we might have enlightenment of Christ and saving belief in Him ... *How good is He?*

If God chose us just as we are, without a requirement for us to change anything about ourselves first in order to receive this gift ... *How good is He?*

If every way He treats us—and answers our prayers—is not based on what we deserve, but out of His immense goodness ... *How good is He?*

If God is working *every* trial and tribulation that comes our way from this broken and fallen world together for our good ... *How good is He?*

If He just willed to come live in us (through the power of the Holy Spirit) so we can experience His lasting peace, joy, fulfillment, direction, and daily care for our life ... *How good is He?*

Having said all of this, here is the GREATEST evidence of God's goodness to me: I once didn't want too much of God. I was afraid that He would take the fun out of my life. He, however, had a greater love for me. He gave me all of the above in spite of my lack of desire or care for Him. He grew an amazing joy and love for Him in my nothing clay pot.

So, how would I explain God's goodness? By now you know my answer: *I can't with human language*, but by God's loving mercy and grace, He allows me to experience it more and more each day. Thank you, Lord!

PRAYER OF JASON

AGE: 9

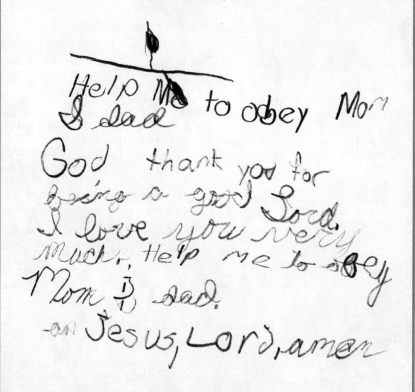

Help Me to obey Mom
I dad
God thank you for
being a good Lord
I love you very
much, Help me to obey
Mom & dad.
on Jesus, Lord, amen

God is good. Thank Him for His goodness!

*Be anxious for nothing, but in everything by
prayer and supplication **with thanksgiving** let
your requests be made known to God.*

—Philippians 4:6

FREEDOM
FROM ANGER

JAMES 1:19-20

This you know, my beloved brethren. But everyone must be quick to hear, slow to speak and slow to anger; [20]for the anger of man does not achieve the righteousness of God.

DAY 61

*For the **anger** of man **does not achieve the righteousness of God.***
—JAMES 1:20

I f we keep in mind the context of verses nineteen and twenty, we recognize that James is honing in on the difficulties we experience in life in more detail. In verses one through twelve he referred to life's difficulties in general, then in verses thirteen through sixteen he shared how *our flesh* responds to these difficulties. Now, in verses nineteen and twenty, James is singling out just one of our fleshly responses: *anger.*

We get angry at all manner of things. We get angry at our spouse when he or she is unkind or disrespectful to us. We get angry at the driver who cuts in front of us, or at the store clerk who was rude to us, or the doctor's office for not returning our call, or the soccer coach for not playing our son or daughter enough. We get angry at our kids for not doing what we say, or for making life difficult for us. We can even get angry at God for allowing some difficulty to intrude in our life.

Over the next few days, pray that God will give you the understanding for what James is telling us about anger, and how anger from our flesh *destroys* God's peace and joy within us. It destroys the *joy* that James speaks of in his letter: *Consider it all joy ... when you have lots of problems.* The phrase *"does not achieve the righteousness of God"* means that anger never accomplishes *God's good (joyous) purpose* for our life; *AND* it *never* accomplishes *any good thing* in the person we are angry at. In fact, since anger *never* achieves the righteousness of God it *always* tears down and destroys life—it separates friend from friend, parents from child, husband from wife—it destroys relationships.

A JOYOUS THOUGHT FOR TODAY:

*Let all bitterness and wrath **and anger** and clamor and slander **be put away from you,** along with all malice.* —EPHESIANS 4:31

For Today, pray for God to remove any anger in your life. Pray for Him to remind you that He is sovereign over all of your life; so there is nothing to be angry about. This truth is the beginning of healing for you!

IS ANGER WRONG?

The topic of anger is one of the more misunderstood and controversial subjects among Christians today. Here are a few examples of how we justify our anger to ourselves and to others:

- Some time ago, I was invited to speak at a leadership seminar on the topic of anger. In the middle of my talk, a Christian businessman interrupted me and said, "What do you mean, Daryl, God gave us our emotions and *anger* is one of them. So, how can our anger be wrong?"

- Several years ago, one of my daughters called me. She was confused over hearing her pastor say in his Sunday sermon that anger was okay, "because Jesus got mad in the temple."

- Additionally, I have heard some Christians say that our anger is okay: IF we are patient for a period of time BEFORE we get angry, since *James 1:19* says to be "***slow*** to anger."

What is the common error being committed in these three examples? Each takes one true element from scripture and then "logically" reasons to a *wrong* conclusion, based on that *one* element of true scripture. Good Bible study avoids making an assumption based on a solitary fact or isolated phrase from a single verse. Scripture tells us a lot of things that can be taken superficially as meaning one thing, but really means the opposite when carefully considered in context; and in association with cross-references, Greek word studies, and other verses from God's word to explain God's word.

Absent this careful study, the flesh will always explain the isolated phrase or verse in a superficial manner that allows the flesh to feel okay about itself: "I held back for an hour before I blew up, so I was okay because I was *slow to anger*." The flesh is always looking for ways to justify the flesh. It is always looking for interpretations of scripture that allow it to feel comfortable even while living an unrighteous life. As our flesh cares for itself, it keeps us unhappy and void of experiencing the joy that God desires for us.

The true message from scripture frees us from anger and causes us to live daily in joy and praise to God.

DAY 62

*For the **anger of man** does not achieve the righteousness of God.*
—JAMES 1:20

If anger is wrong and destructive to life, and if anger will eat away at us like a cancer to keep us miserable as long as we try to justify our anger toward others, then how do we reconcile anger being wrong with scripture verses about Jesus getting mad in the temple *(Matthew 21:12-13)*?

James 1:20 makes this distinction clear. James tells us that the *anger of man* does not achieve the righteousness of God. The word "man" refers to our "flesh" or "self." Do you remember the example on page 75 of the glass jar filled with what looked like pure water (except there was a hardly noticeable thin layer of silty mud settled on the bottom of the jar)? That dirt is the flesh I am talking about now. James is saying that the anger that stems from that dirt in us is never sourced from God. It is the anger we feel when *we* are mistreated, or when *we* don't get our way, or someone offends *us*, or an injustice is done to *us*.

Jesus' anger in the temple was because of the money changers disrespect toward God the Father, NOT toward Himself. Jesus came to earth to forgive sin, heal the sick, feed the hungry, and bring peace to a world that had no peace. Yet they mocked Him, beat Him, ridiculed Him, and finally crucified Him. Did He lash out in anger, saying, "I can't wait to get back at you for this!"? No. We all remember the response Jesus had to all of this mistreatment: *"Father, forgive them for they do not know what they are doing" (Luke 23:34).* There is a vast difference between the anger *of man* and the anger *of God*; and James tells us that there is wisdom that leads to joy and peace when we stop conflating the two.

A JOYOUS THOUGHT FOR TODAY:

*But now you also, **put them all aside**: anger, wrath, malice, slander, and abusive speech from your mouth.*
—COLOSSIANS 3:8

For Today, think back and consider which form of anger you have displayed for most of your life. Be thankful to God that He is freeing you from your flesh's destructive anger by first purging you of all deception and justification concerning it. This is the true wisdom which leads to true peace and joy!

A PERSONAL TESTIMONY

THE CORROSIVE EFFECTS OF ANGER

I still remember an event from decades ago concerning anger that still feels like it happened yesterday.

The family was in our kitchen back when we lived in Anaheim, California. My oldest son at the time was about sixteen. What started as a mild disagreement, soon escalated into a heated discussion. I don't even remember what the argument was about now, but I still remember the raw anger and unrestrained emotions. The mood grew ominous, and emotions on both sides were increasingly unrestrained, until I could tell that my son was on the verge of exploding in rage against me (and I was certainly on the verge of exploding in rage against him). Together, we could hardly contain ourselves.

Then something stunning happened to me. It felt like the Lord appeared in my mind and said, "Daryl, I am saying this out of love for you—what is all of this anger in your discussion accomplishing?" I froze with that question echoing in my mind. *Our arguing was getting increasingly tense; accusatory, and pointed; but what was it accomplishing?* I was quiet for more than a minute looking at my son. In that moment I realized the only thing the anger was accomplishing was erecting a wall between us that could do lasting harm to our relationship.

When I finally spoke, it was a humbling experience, but I knew I needed to explain to my son the powerful message God had just delivered to my mind. I wanted him to be a witness to what I was about to tell him. After explaining what happened, I said to my son, "I will *never* argue with you again. You will *never* see this anger in me again. I love you too much for this to *ever* happen again."

This was the Lord showing me how destructive anger is in our lives. That anger, not only was not accomplishing what *I* wanted—to make my son understand—but it was separating us further apart and increasingly making us enemies.

This change was all due to the grace of God. For half of my life I was torn-up inside by the corrosive effects of anger toward people who I perceived had wronged me. But God brought His bright, transforming light into my life that day to show me how destructive our human anger really is. Even today, when someone wants to argue, I just back off quietly because anger always destroys relationships (and our peace and joy from God).

DAY 63

*This you know, my beloved brethren. But everyone must be quick to hear, slow to speak and **slow to anger.***
—JAMES 1:19

Now that we know how destructive anger can be, let's step back to the last three words of verse nineteen: *slow to anger.* To be *slow to anger* doesn't mean to be patient for a period of time before we blow our stacks. To be *slow to anger,* whenever we feel any unhappiness about anything, means to get on our knees in our hearts before the Lord and be sure that the anger we are feeling is from God's Spirit, not our human self. Is it anger toward an "evil" done against God, or against us? Pause, and ask, "Lord, is this about You or about me? Is this anger from You against sin; or is it coming from my flesh because *I* have been inconvenienced or disrespected?"

God will answer this prayer and bring clarity to your heart. One thing is certain, if we release anger from our flesh, it destroys! It destroys families, homes, and relationships. In over forty years of counseling couples, I can't tell you the number of people who have told me they can no longer live with the anger of their spouse, either directed at them or at their kids. I can't tell you the number of people who have shared with me the pain they still feel from an angry comment made to them from years ago.

Thank God, that beginning in verse nineteen, and continuing through the remainder of the chapter, James tells us how to experience freedom from all the evils in our life, including the evil of anger. Tomorrow, we will begin this path to freedom with James.

A JOYOUS THOUGHT FOR TODAY:

*My flesh and my heart may fail, but **God is the strength of my heart** and my portion forever.* —PSALM 73:26

For Today, thank God that He is your strength, and that He has not left you to be deceived by your anger or left you to be continuously pained by the angry comments made by others to you. He is molding and transforming you to be like Him—free of anger and full of His peace and joy. Thank Him ... and thank Him again.

DAY 64

*This you know, my beloved brethren. But everyone must **be quick to hear,***
slow to speak and slow to anger.

—JAMES 1:19

The phrase *"be quick to hear"* is often taught to mean that we should be good listeners and not talk too much. But James makes clear in the verses that follow that He is talking about being quick to hear *what God's word says.* Look at the context. In verse twenty-two, James tells us to *"prove yourselves doers of the word."* In verse twenty-three he says, *"if anyone is a hearer of the word"* which makes direct reference to hearing God's word. God actively speaks His word into our hearts from scripture today *(2 Corinthians 3:3).*

So, how does "hearing God's word" remove anger? The answer to that question traces back to the source of the anger *(see* Day 62). Anger sourced from the flesh is not from God, but is based on a temporary belief in the *sovereignty of man.* We believe that what another person does to us, or says concerning us, or thinks about us, controls our happiness. "Hearing God's word" breaks this ensnaring belief that puts sovereignty in man. God's word causes us to believe in the *sovereignty of God*: in the eternal truth that all good comes from Him *(James 1:17),* that He is working all things together for our good *(Romans 8:28),* that no man can thwart any of His good purposes for us *(Job 42:2),* and that He is our Great Shepherd who continually leads us to green pastures and still waters *(Psalm 23:2).* Hearing these words from God evaporates our anger!

A JOYOUS THOUGHT FOR TODAY:

*I know that **You can do all things,** and that **no***
purpose of Yours can be thwarted. —JOB 42:2

For Today, dwell on the *sovereignty of God* over your life. Dwell on the fact that God's word tells you that God can do *all* things, and that He is working *all* things together for *your good*, and that *nothing* can thwart what He purposes *for you*. Job 42:2 tells you that nothing man does *to* you, or doesn't do *for* you, can keep you from the joy, peace, wisdom, and every other good thing God has purposed for you! Hold your focus on these scriptural truths the next time you feel mistreated and see how that changes your anger to peace, joy, and praise to God.

DAY 65

*This you know, my beloved brethren. But everyone must **be quick to hear**,
slow to speak and slow to anger.*

—JAMES 1:19

J ames doesn't say only that we need to "hear" God's words, but that we should be
quick to hear His words. The phrase *quick to hear* is a relative term that contrasts with
being *slow* to hear. Have you ever been watching TV when a message of some breaking
news begins to scroll across the reader board on the bottom of the screen? That scroll-
ing message is intended to give you up-to-the-moment information about something
important. James is telling us that when we are *slow to hear* God's words, or slow to
see verses from God's word on the "reader board" of our mind or in our heart, we will
continue to feel and react angrily toward everything in life which our flesh doesn't like.

Before we know it, we are angry. Our flesh has already changed our belief momentarily *from* the sovereignty of God *to* the sovereignty of man. We think the injustice being done to us is permanent, but God intervenes and says *no, I am going to work
this all out for your good.* You have likely already experienced this. Have you been in the
middle of a perplexing problem where you are troubled about this and worried about
that? Then God brings you His word, *"Be still, and know that I am God."* You may
not know where the verse is located in the Bible but you remember reading it *(Psalm
46:10a, KJV)*. He speaks to your mind that *He is being God*. You start to feel your
shoulders relax. This happens because the power of God's eternal life *inhabits* those
words (and all scripture). When He brings them freshly to mind, it changes our focus
from man being sovereign to our heavenly Father being sovereign.

A JOYOUS THOUGHT FOR TODAY:

*The young lions do lack and suffer hunger; **but
they who seek the LORD shall not be in want of
any good thing.*** —PSALM 34:10

For Today, meditate on the image of the young lions in *Psalm 34*. In earthly terms, they
are at the height of their predatory power, yet at times suffer and lack what they need.
But not you! God is never tardy with you; He brings to you precisely what you need,
exactly when you need it, every day. He is working all things together for *your good*!

DAY 66

*This you know, my beloved brethren. But everyone must **be quick to hear**,*
slow to speak and slow to anger.
—JAMES 1:19

Let's say someone falsely accuses us, or treats us unfairly, in a certain situation. James encourages us, right in the midst of the situation, to quickly listen to the truth contained in verses from God's word. I'll use *Psalm 103:6 (Everyday Bible)* as an example. It says: *"The Lord does what is right and fair for all who are wronged by others."*

By quickly hearing those words, they create an effective shortcut to freedom from anger. Only God's word has the power to do this. Everything outside of God is destructive. Look at what is happening in this world without God—it is destroying itself with anger, selfishness, and rage.

God has a different plan for us. Being *"quick to hear"* means to have God's word *continually* "flowing through our veins" so that verses appear quickly on our "reader board" in the midst of whatever would otherwise make us angry. This is precisely what God was referring to when He spoke to Joshua: *"This book of the law [or God's word] shall not depart from your mouth, but you shall meditate on it day and night" (Joshua 1:8).* This is why I keep verses taped to various places at home, at work, and in my car. I can only testify to you that I was once the angriest man I knew. I couldn't help myself. But I've experienced God's word being *more* powerful.

A JOYOUS THOUGHT FOR TODAY:

Let the word of Christ richly dwell within you, with
all wisdom teaching and admonishing one another with
psalms and hymns and spiritual songs, singing with
thankfulness in your hearts to God. —COLOSSIANS 3:16

For Today, to let the *"word of Christ richly dwell within you"* means to have verses as familiar in your heart and mind as the family photos you have in your home. Pray that God will bring fresh meaning to you as you live your day and reflect regularly on these verses. Feel the calming effect the word of God has on your heart and mind. You won't be able to contain your praise to God.

A TALE OF TWO FAMILIES:

I know of a Christian couple who to this day, after decades of struggling with anger, still blames a past employer because they believe "he cheated them out of God's best for them." Those words are not mine but their own description of the reason for their long-standing anger. How has this anger benefited them? It has only robbed them of the joy and peace God has for them right now. As Paul shared in *Philippians 4:12*, *"I know how to get along with humble means, and I also know how to live in prosperity; in any and every circumstance I have learned the secret of being filled and going hungry, both of having abundance and suffering need."*

What joy and peace this couple would experience if just one verse, *Job 42:2*, became a fresh word from God to them: *"I know that You can do all things, and that no purpose of Yours can be thwarted."* They would finally realize, after decades of anger, that their old boss is not more powerful than God. God is achieving precisely the purpose He has for them and used their old boss to advance, rather than hinder, His purpose.

Contrast this couple with another one. I first met the young man (he was not yet married) over forty years ago during my first missionary journey to India. We traveled together across India where I spoke in many villages to many small gatherings. Over those days, I had the opportunity to observe this young man. He lived in humble conditions that I can hardly describe. He grew up in an orphanage, with no father or mother. He had *no* worldly possessions or earthly means. He wore sandals (or no shoes) and cast-off clothes by others. Later, he got married—an arranged marriage through another missionary which brought his young wife to him—who is now going through extreme health problems.

Yet, he still writes (now by email) to tell me how blessed his family is by God. How God has cared for them and provides for their every need. It brings tears to my eyes to read his emails because he is one who literally has nothing, yet wants nothing more than what he receives from God's hand, in Christ Jesus his Lord.

What is the distinction between these two families? One believes in the sovereignty of man and the other in the sovereignty of God. One has God's word flowing in his veins and other does not. One has only anger, the other God's peace and joy!

DAY 67

This you know, my beloved brethren. But everyone must be quick to hear,
__slow to speak__ and slow to anger.

—JAMES 1:19

The phrase *slow to speak* in this verse means taking the time necessary to con-template our thoughts (and word tones) before the Lord, making sure that what we are about to say is coming from God's Spirit in us and not from our flesh. Do you remember the "flesh trap" that springs into action and catches us in sinful feelings, comments, or actions (Day 46)? The counter-wisdom to our *flesh trap* is being *slow to speak*.

Let's say I am beginning to feel uptight or stressful about something. That is a big red flag for me to know that my *flesh trap* is getting ready to spring. If I speak out of this stressful place, my words will likely be destructive to whomever I am speaking to. This sometimes happens to me in the middle of a conversation with my kids or wife; and they will notice that I have paused from the conversation. Rather than try to "save face" by making an excuse, I tell them honestly: "I am feeling uptight right now and need to stop this conversation for a little bit so I can talk to God." In reality, what better thing could you demonstrate to your children or spouse (or to other Christian friends)?

This is what James means by being *slow to speak*. There is wisdom in stepping away from a stressful conversation to *listen* to God's word. Being *slow to speak* is a great wisdom that reliably dissipates anger, and leads to peace and joy.

A JOYOUS THOUGHT FOR TODAY:

We are destroying speculations and every lofty thing
raised up against the knowledge of God, and we
are __taking every thought captive to the obedience__
__of Christ.__ —2 CORINTHIANS 10:5

For Today, as you engage others in conversation, especially when you have feelings such as stress, impatience, worry, fear, or resentment, take what you are about to say *captive* by carrying it to the Lord. You may be slower to speak, but it will never be de-structive; and what you end up saying will always be encouraging, and helpful to the listener *(Ephesians 4:29)*.

Day 68

*The **heart of the righteous ponders how to answer**, but the mouth of the wicked pours out evil things.*

—Proverbs 15:28

As we are *slow to speak*, but *ponder* what we are about to say in light of God's word, it is amazing how God's truth from scripture changes our conversation. It actually changes *everything!* *"For the word of God is living and active and sharper than any two-edged sword, and piercing as far as the division of soul and spirit, of both joints and marrow, and able to judge the thoughts and intentions of the heart.* ¹³*And there is no creature hidden from His sight, but all things are open and laid bare to the eyes of Him with whom we have to do"* (Hebrews 4:12-13).

As we are *slow to speak*, but *quick to listen*, God's word is active in us; not only changing the words we might subsequently speak, but also our heart's intent from which our words will ultimately flow. This is an important wisdom to grasp; for when we are *slow to speak* and *quick to listen* to God's word, the transforming power is not merely in the selection of new words to say (or a different tone to say them in), but in the purification of our heart. God's word cuts to the "heart" of the matter, literally, by piercing and discerning the thoughts and intentions *of our heart.* As His word heals and purifies *our heart*, the words we were about to say change automatically. We no longer have a desire to say what we intended to say while we were in a stressed or angry place.

A Joyous Thought for Today:

Acquaint now thyself with Him [referring to God],
and be at peace; thereby good will come to you.
—Job 22:21, NKJV

For Today, there is no need for you to try to apply God's word to your life (that is God's work to bring you into conformity with His word). Just read it with a *desire* for God to make what His word is saying true in your life. Job tells us that as we continue to do this, it dissipates anger and every other evil thing that God's enemies would use to destroy us. At the same time, continue to acquaint yourself with God through His word. He will grow in you His *true fulfillment*, peace, joy, and contentment. You will only have praise to Him!

A SPECIAL WORD TO THE READER...

The next series of devotionals relating to *James 1:21-25* (Days 69-76) are going to reveal a liberating truth that will, as God prepares your heart to understand it, *completely revolutionize* how you look at the Bible ... *forever*!

I often encourage people to take out their Bibles, turn to *Genesis 1:1*, and write just above that first verse "Dear ____ (fill in your own first name)"; then turn to *Revelation 22:21* and write just below that last verse "Love, God." This graphically demonstrates that scripture is really a personal love letter from God to each of us. We might all think to ourselves, *that sounds wonderful*, and start writing those notations in our Bibles. But then we read *James 1:21-25*, and puzzled frowns settle on our faces. Upon our first quick reading, out of context with the entire letter, these verses appear to be nothing more than a series of commands and exhortations that seem to put us under more and more bondage to get our acts together and start working harder for God. This doesn't sound like any love letter we have ever read (nor want to read).

Here's the catch. These five verses in James, like many in scripture, can be grossly misinterpreted if they are read too quickly. To fully understand what James is saying, I encourage you to take your time and read each verse carefully. To help you, I have defined words and subdivided verses into their component phrases in order to carefully discuss how each word and phrase relate to other words and phrases in context. Regardless of what I do, however, it is only the work of the Holy Spirit in your heart that can (and will) enlighten you concerning the liberating truth contained in these verses; a truth that, once understood, will confirm (without doubt) that scripture is, indeed, the greatest love letter you have ever read; and create in you a hunger for God's word unlike anything you have ever experienced before.

MY JOYOUS THOUGHTS

SOFT WAX HEART

JAMES 1:21-25

Therefore, putting aside all filthiness and all that remains of wickedness, in humility receive the word implanted, which is able to save your souls. [22]But prove yourselves doers of the word, and not merely hearers who delude themselves. [23]For if anyone is a hearer of the word and not a doer, he is like a man who looks at his natural face in a mirror; [24]for once he has looked at himself and gone away, he has immediately forgotten what kind of person he was. [25]But one who looks intently at the perfect law, the law of liberty, and abides by it, not having become a forgetful hearer but an effectual doer, this man will be blessed in what he does.

DAY 69

*But the **path of the righteous** is like the light of dawn, that **shines brighter and brighter** until the full day.*

—Proverbs 4:18

In *James 1:21-25*, James acknowledges something that was true in his time and is still true throughout Christianity today. Why do some believers appear perpetually troubled, while others seem to be increasingly sensitive to the Lord's leading and genuinely experiencing more of God's peace, joy, wisdom, and conviction in their lives? Over the next several days, James will explain the primary reason for why this is so.

However, to understand James fully, we need to understand a fundamental principle revealed in *Proverbs 4:18*: *"But the path of the righteous is like the light of dawn, that shines brighter and brighter until the full day."* God has placed *every* Christian on this *"path of the righteous."* This path is *"like the light of dawn"* because God causes our relationship with Him to grow *"brighter and brighter"* as He continues the good work He began in us *(Philippians 1:6)*.

James is next going to tell us how God *uses His word* to move us along this ever-brightening path. For decades, I saw the Bible as a scary collection of restrictions primarily designed to make me afraid of God and take the fun out of life. But now, and I say this with *all* glory to Him and not a single boast for myself, God has drawn me to a place where His word is the *Bread of Life* for my spiritual well-being. Just as God has provided food, water, and air to support our physical life, His word is the spiritual sustenance that brings increasing understanding, wisdom, peace, and joy to our lives.

A JOYOUS THOUGHT FOR TODAY:

*But He answered and said, "It is written, 'MAN SHALL NOT LIVE ON BREAD ALONE, **BUT ON EVERY WORD THAT PROCEEDS OUT OF THE MOUTH OF GOD.**'"*

—MATTHEW 4:4

For Today, God has made you righteous in Christ *(1 Corinthians 1:30)*. He has placed you on His ever-brightening *"path of the righteous."* You need not compare yourself to anyone else. You are on His *path* precisely where God wants you to be. He will continue to nourish you along this *path* as He grows within you a hunger for His word.

GOD'S EVER-BRIGHTENING PATH
OF THE RIGHTEOUS

Have you ever read a section of scripture and had no idea what it was talking about, but later, read it again and it made a bit more sense? Or have you listened to a friend discuss a verse and realized that he or she was seeing more in that verse than you have seen? If that has ever happened to you, don't be disappointed in yourself. God has you *exactly* where He wants you to be at this point in your Christian life. You can be confident that in God's wisdom and timing, He will teach you all that He wants you to know *(John 14:26; Philippians 1:6, 2:13)*.

Proverbs 4:18 assures us that God has placed every one of His children (young to old physically, brand new to ancient in Christian experience, immature to mature in spiritual understanding) on His *ever-brightening path of the righteous*. God ministers to all of His children, regardless of their differences, through His word. This speaks to how truly unique the word of God is because it can guide, protect, and nourish both the youngest and oldest Christian, precisely in their present circumstances.

Early in my Christian life I tried to live by what God's word said (granted, I did so more out of fear of God than understanding His love for me). The word, in that regard, served primarily as a tutor and protector with outward rules, in the same way it protected the Israelites before the coming of Christ. It did keep me away from a lot of harm, and gave me a general understanding of God and my salvation. God was accomplishing His purpose in my life *at* that time, *for* that time. However, as God drew me deeper into His word over the years, I grew to realize that the Holy Spirit was imprinting on my heart the very things that God had written in His word. The word of God was no longer a set of rules that I must struggle to live by, but a love letter of promises which God was bringing into reality in my life through His word.

This is why Paul, in *Romans 14*, encourages us not to judge others by what we understand the Bible to be saying, based on where *we are today* on God's ever-brightening path, but trust God to move *every other believer* along His path as well *(Philippians 1:6)*. We are *all* on *His path of the righteous!*

PRAYER

Dear God, bring memories back to my mind over these next few days, from my own life as a Christian, to show me how You have been faithfully leading me along this path of the righteous. I pray that through these memories, You will increase my confidence in the fact that You will continue to faithfully guide me on this path until glory. Reveal to me how You have changed my attitudes and grown my spiritual understanding over these years. Enlighten me to this fundamental joyous truth, because as You do, it causes me to trust You all the more with my future life. Amen.

DAY 70

Therefore, **putting aside** *all filthiness and* **all that remains of wickedness,** *in humility* **receive the word implanted,** *which is able to save your souls.*

—JAMES 1:21

The word *wickedness* in this verse is a term James uses to cover all manner of human ugliness. It includes the *anger* (Days 61-68), *critical tongue* (Days 77-78), and *judgmental spirit* (Days 85-90) James discusses in his letter, but is not limited to those examples.

If we are not careful, we can quickly read the first phrase in this verse and think it is exhorting us personally to try harder to "put aside" all of this human ugliness through our own effort. But this is not what the verse is saying. Its message is much more liberating. The next phrase, *"in humility receive the word implanted"* gives us the answer. This second phrase begins with a preposition *in* which shows the relationship with the first phrase. How is all wickedness put aside? By the word of God *which has been implanted in us* (Christ in us)! We are not being called to reach for our own bootstraps and work harder, but in humility, to receive the word already implanted.

The words *in humility* mean to recognize that we can't change ourselves. We are totally incapable of accomplishing any Godliness on our own. We are totally dependent on the Lord to manifest His life in us. Notice, that James doesn't tell us *to apply* the word, but only *to receive* it; meaning to take it to heart and meditate on it. The *word implanted* is what contains the power to put aside every wickedness and human ugliness in us.

A JOYOUS THOUGHT FOR TODAY:

Your word I have treasured in my heart, *that I may* *not sin against You.* —PSALM 119:11

For Today, notice the similar pattern in *Psalm 119:11* and *James 1:21*. God does not call you, by your own effort, to put aside wickedness and not to sin against Him; but rather, to *treasure His word in your heart*. It is the *word* who is at work in you, not your own self-effort. May the truth and freedom contained in these verses bring unspeakable joy to your life. As you value God's word—God changes your life!

DAY 71

Therefore, putting aside all filthiness and all that remains of wickedness, in humility **receive the word implanted,** *which is able to save your souls.*
—JAMES 1:21

Today, let's look deeper into the word *receive*. James used this Greek word to convey a wonderful image. During his day, when a keeper of an important document wanted to secure it against being tampered with, he would roll the document into a scroll and bind it tightly with a leather strap into a firm knot. He would then dollop some warm wax over the leather knot and press a seal into the warm wax that uniquely identified him. The warm wax would take on the exact replica of the seal's image being pressed into it by the keeper. The Greek word James used for *receive the word* is the same word used to describe how that warm wax took on the image of the keeper's seal.

James is exhorting us to receive God's word with a heart like soft, warm wax desiring only for God to imprint His word into our hearts as we read it. As we discussed yesterday (Day 70) this is God's provision for us. The power is in His word for putting aside all filthiness and wickedness (such as worry, anger, and stress) in our life.

The next word, *implanted,* makes this image even more compelling. The word *implanted* refers to Christ who has been implanted in us. Paul refers to *"Christ in you, the hope of glory" (Colossians 1:27).* James is not saying that we need to receive Christ again, but simply to be sensitive to Christ as the *word implanted* in our heart. As our heart is soft wax toward Christ and His word—God changes us from within.

A JOYOUS THOUGHT FOR TODAY:

Being manifested that **you are a letter of Christ,** *cared for by us, written not with ink but with the Spirit of the living God, not on tablets of stone but on* **tablets of human hearts.** —2 CORINTHIANS 3:3

For Today, give thanks to God that He is softening your heart *(Philippians 2:13)* to be increasingly receptive to His transforming word, which is Christ implanted in you. He is daily shaping your clay for His glory and for your peace and joy.

DAY 72

*Therefore, putting aside all filthiness and all that remains of wickedness, in humility receive the word implanted, **which is able to save your souls**.*

—JAMES 1:21

I f the life of Christ *implanted* in us is *able to save our souls*, then it is certainly powerful enough to conform our lives daily to what God's word says. If the life of Christ is powerful enough to redeem us from Satan's clutches through His shed blood, and bring understanding and a saving-belief in Christ into our heart, it is certainly powerful enough to also evict the stress, worry, and anger out of our lives and bring God's unity into all of our relationships with others.

Yet, I often hear Christians conclude from this verse (and others) that it is *our responsibility* to be good Christians. If this is true, then wouldn't that mean we have some "good" in us? But Paul tells us: *"For I know that **nothing good** dwells in me, that is, in my flesh; for the willing is present in me, but the doing of the good is not" (Romans 7:18)*. The truth is this: without the working of Christ in us we do not possess the power (in our self) to soften our own hearts toward God. The path that leads to wisdom is the example of the potter and clay given to us in *Isaiah 64:8* and again by Paul in *Romans 9:21*. The potter sculpts the clay (which can do nothing for itself) into exactly what pleases Him *(Philippians 2:13)*.

This is the wisdom which produces freedom and joy. God has placed us on *His path of the righteous*. We may live for a while believing that the Bible is a fearful thing and full of restrictions; but eventually, over the course of our lives, the Lord brings us to share Solomon's love for God's word, that it is sweet as honey in our mouth *(Psalm 119:103)*.

A JOYOUS THOUGHT FOR TODAY:

*But now, O LORD, You are our Father, **we are the clay, and You our potter;** and all of us are the work of Your hand.* —ISAIAH 64:8

For Today, rejoice in the Lord that you are just clay in the potter's hand. Consider whether the clay can soften itself. When you answer no, praise and thank the Lord that He is sculpting you—as it pleases Him. He is doing it all. All praise goes to Him!

DAY 73

*But **prove yourselves doers of the word**, and not merely hearers **who delude themselves.***

—JAMES 1:22

Here is another verse that superficially appears to be telling us that we have to pull on our own bootstraps and try to make ourselves better Christians. In reality, it is saying the opposite. The word *prove* in this verse means to give *evidence of* something. James is conveying that as we just humbly receive the word implanted (which James discussed in the previous verse), our lives will increasingly *evidence* (or prove) that Christ is living in us. There is nothing for us to accomplish on our own or in our own self-effort.

James is sharing with us a powerful wisdom that leads to joy and peace. As our hearts (like soft wax) deeply desire for God to change our life according to whatever verse we are reading—He imprints the reality of that verse into us. This is what it means to be a *doer of the word.* Contrast this with being *"hearers who delude themselves."* The word *delude* means to *deceive.* It refers to anyone who deceives themselves into thinking that they can receive God's word merely through passive osmosis. They might attend church, sing the praise songs, listen to sermons, but *not yet* approach the word of God with a soft-wax, receptive heart. By God's mercy and grace, and in His timing, He will use the power in His word, even in the hearer's life, to move him or her from *hearer* to *doer.*

A JOYOUS THOUGHT FOR TODAY:

*For our **gospel did not come to you in word only,** but also in **power** and in the **Holy Spirit** and with full conviction; just as you know what kind of men **we proved to be** among you for your sake.* — 1 THESSALONIANS 1:5

For Today, consider Paul's message to the Thessalonians. He did not expect them to believe the gospel based only on his words. Paul was confident that the gospel was also being continually *proved* to them through his life. You can be as confident as Paul, that God is not only preparing your heart to receive His word implanted; but He is also revealing the truth of His gospel to others by expressing/proving it through your life.

DAY 74

*For if anyone is a **hearer of the word and not a doer**, he is like a man who **looks at his natural face in a mirror;** ²⁴for once he has looked at himself and gone away, he has immediately forgotten what kind of person he was.*

—JAMES 1:23-24

I n these verses, James continues to drill deeper into the difference between a *hearer* and *doer* of the word (or a Christian experiencing the peace, joy, and comfort of the word and one who is not). Yesterday (Day 73), we saw that a *doer of the word* is one who approaches God's word with a deep desire and prayer in their heart for God to change their life according to whatever verse they are reading. They are not trying to apply God's word to their life, but rather, praying for God to conform their life to His word. James is confident that this is *exactly* what happens every time we approach the word of God with a soft heart. God does, in fact, change us (whether we are aware of it at the time or not). What else should we expect from a word that is *living* and *active* and *sharper* than any two-edged sword? It *pierces* us, *divides* soulish from spiritual things, *judges* the thoughts and intents of our heart, and *exposes* our innermost thoughts to the penetrating gaze of Christ *(Hebrews 4:12-13)*. This is a personal and deeply impactful process. No one walks away unaffected when they read the word of God in this way.

By contrast, the *"hearer of the word"* looks at the word as briefly as though looking in a mirror. They look at the flaws in their face and see moles, wrinkles, blemishes, etc., but as soon as they walk away from the mirror they forget what they saw. This brief, ritualistic consideration of the word has little lasting impact on them.

A JOYOUS THOUGHT FOR TODAY:

*He is clothed with a robe dipped in blood, and His name is called **The Word of God.*** —REVELATION 19:13

For Today, meditate on this life-changing truth: that *"The word of God"* is not merely black ink on white paper, but the person of Christ Jesus, the living God. Thank Him that He lives in you and has chosen to conform your life to His life through His word. Pray that God will cause you to sense the power that raised Jesus from the dead in every verse of scripture.

DAY 75

*But one who **looks intently at the perfect law**, the law of liberty, and abides by it,*
not having become a forgetful hearer but an effectual doer, this man will be blessed
in what he does.

—JAMES 1:25

In contrast to being a *hearer* only, who looks and immediately forgets, the *doer* of the word *looks intently* at the perfect law (God's word). The word *intently* means to look with penetrating absorption. It is the same Greek word used to describe how John looked into the empty tomb for Jesus to see whether He was there *(John 20:5)*. Imagine the intensity in which John looked into that tomb for His Lord! To look intently includes a sense of passionate inquiry into God's word, both to *understand* and to *experience* it! It includes a deeply held desire that the verse being read becomes new life to the person reading it. It is an earnest desire for the word to become more and more our true identity: who we are, what we feel, how we see life, and how we act.

To look *intently* at God's word does not require that you know Greek, or be a graduate from some theological seminary. A brand new believer can look intently at the word in the same way as a believer who has been a Christian for decades (in fact, it may be easier for the new believer). To look *intently* is simply a matter of desire and focus. It is looking to experience God's life through His word. It desires for God to conform your life to His word, not you attempting to conform God's word to your life.

A JOYOUS THOUGHT FOR TODAY:

Keep my commandments and live, and my teaching
*[referring to God's word] **as the apple of your eye***
[or what you desire most!]. —PROVERBS 7:2

For Today, as you read God's word, pray that He will grant you a soft heart and conform your life to the verses you are reading. Then trust that God is using every word you read to transform you into the very image of His Son. He is accomplishing His will in your life at His pace *(Philippians 1:6)*. You are on God's ever-brightening path of the righteous. You can't fall off, wander off, or even get behind. Praise Him for putting you (and maintaining you) on His path!

IF GOD IS DOING IT ALL...

I am often asked a question about how God's working in us *(Philippians 2:13)* relates to all of the commands and exhortations given to us in His word. The question goes something like this: If God is doing it all, without our effort to help, then why does His word contain so many commands and exhortations for us to live by? If you think about it for a moment the answer becomes obvious based on what James has already told us.

If God has placed us on His ever-brightening *path of the righteous* (Day 69), and is softening our hearts to be conformed to the image of His Son (the Word of God); then why would he write to us in His word to accomplish all of this? It is easier to grasp this truth by example. Let's say God desires that we not be anxious but turn all of our worries, cares, and anxiety over to Him in prayer. How would He achieve this work in us? Remember our discussion of the Greek word *receive* in *James 1:21* (Day 71) as conveying the meaning of a seal being imprinted identically into soft wax. God softens our hearts to make them receptive to His word, then inspires His word to say, *"Be anxious for nothing, but in everything by prayer and supplication with thanksgiving let your requests be made known to God" (Philippians 4:6);* and *"Therefore humble yourselves under the mighty hand of God, that He may exalt you at the proper time, casting all your anxiety on Him, because He cares for you" (1 Peter 5:6-7).* **The Holy Spirit then writes these words on the tablets of our soft, receptive hearts** *(2 Corinthians 3:3); creating an imprint that changes us.* Over the course of our lives, we become a reflection of what His word says.

Every child of God has been placed on His path of the righteous, but many think we are still responsible to do something for God. *Philippians 4:6* and *1 Peter 5:6-7* sound like commands and exhortations that we are responsible to live by. Gradually, however, we discover that it is impossible to comply with these verses on our own. God gently brings us to a place where we come to Him humbly and pray that *He* would produce the reality of these verses in us. We begin to read verses not as commands and restrictions, but as *promises and guarantees* of what *God is doing* as part of His transforming work in *us* into the image of His Son. This is why Paul could say, *"For I am confident of this very thing, that He who began a good work in you will perfect it until the day of Christ Jesus" (Philippians 1:6).*

DAY 76

*But the man who **looks intently** into the perfect law [God's word] **that gives freedom,** and continues to do this, not forgetting what he has heard, but doing it—he will be blessed in what he does.*

—JAMES 1:25, NIV

James concludes this section by assuring us that the path to being blessed with joy in every circumstance is to continue to look intently into the word of God that gives freedom. The *Amplified Bible* translates the clause "*continues to do this*" into "*perseveres in looking into it.*" Do you want to experience freedom from stress, anxiety, worry, guilt, shame, anger, selfishness, lust, hate, to name a few of the bondages our flesh regularly tries to enslave us with? Then turn to God's word. Ask Him to soften your heart to the imprint of His word on your heart and He will do it.

The *Living Bible* reads "*But if anyone keeps looking steadily into God's law [God's word] for free men, he will not only remember it but he will do what it says, and God will greatly bless him in everything he does.*" God has given His law (word) *for free men and women*, not for restriction and bondage. The way to remain free from fleshly entanglements is to remain in God's word. He will write that word on our hearts as we read it. He will use that word to change us from within and bring it to our memory precisely when we need it. Without our even being aware of it, our lives begin to reflect what the word says. God is making us *doers* of the word, not hearers only.

A JOYOUS THOUGHT FOR TODAY:

*For this reason we also constantly thank God that when you **received the word of God** which you heard from us, you accepted it not as the word of men, but for what it really is, the word of God, **which also performs its work in you who believe.*** —1 THESSALONIANS 2:13

For Today, desire for God to make you like soft wax and imprint His word on the tablets of your heart, gradually transforming you into the very promises and guarantees stated in the word that you are reading. God's word never fails to succeed at what He sent it to accomplish in you *(Isaiah 55:11)*. Praise the Lord for His transforming word!

OUR SPIRITUAL BAROMETER (OUR MOUTH)

JAMES 1:26-27

If anyone thinks himself to be religious, and yet does not bridle his tongue but deceives his own heart, this man's religion is worthless. [27]Pure and undefiled religion in the sight of our God and Father is this: to visit orphans and widows in their distress, and to keep oneself unstained by the world.

DAY 77

*If anyone thinks himself to be religious, and yet **does not bridle his tongue** but deceives his own heart, this man's religion is worthless.*

—JAMES 1:26

W̱e are coming to the end of the first chapter of James. We began the chapter with James telling us to consider it all joy when we encounter various problems (verse two). He offered this as sort of a "reality check" of our spiritual condition. If we lack joy in the midst of our problems, James tells us it is because we lack (or have temporarily forgotten) a relevant wisdom about God (verse five) that would bring joy to our life.

James is now giving us another "reality check," a practical wisdom that will act as a spiritual barometer concerning whether we are living God's *true* religion (or truly experiencing God's life in us). The first thing James mentions is the condition of our tongue. He has already hit on this topic in verse nineteen when he exhorted us to be slow to speak (Day 67).

Why does James use our tongue as the barometer revealing our true spiritual condition? Because our tongue exposes the true intentions of our heart. Further, he says the words we say have a direct impact on others and will either lift them up or wound them. Just as importantly, those same words have a profound effect on us. Over the next few days, James will share three essential elements of *true* religion and how we can expect it to manifest itself in our daily living.

A JOYOUS THOUGHT FOR TODAY:

*For, 'THE ONE WHO DESIRES LIFE, TO LOVE AND **SEE***
GOOD DAYS, MUST KEEP HIS TONGUE FROM EVIL
AND HIS LIPS FROM SPEAKING DECEIT.' —1 PETER 3:10

For Today, ask God to open your heart concerning how you speak to others. Read *1 Peter 3:10* throughout your day, desiring for God to imprint it on your heart and conform your life to what it says. Watch for how sensitive God makes you to what you say to others. Then, watch your joy increase!

Day 78

*If anyone thinks himself to be religious, and yet **does not bridle his tongue** but deceives his own heart, **this man's religion is worthless.***

—James 1:26

In Days 69-76 we saw how God's word (not our own effort) changes us. Here is a good example of this spiritual truth. As God draws us to His word, His word makes our conversation refreshing to others. Someone who does not bridle his tongue is simply someone who does not have God's word controlling his or her conversation. James will have more to say about the tongue in chapter three (Days 98-107), but for now he is giving us a barometer to test how much God's word is affecting our life.

James tells us bluntly that if our tongue is not yet bridled (or controlled by God's word) *our religion is worthless*! The word *worthless* does *not* mean that we are not saved. It means that no matter how much we go to church and sing the praise songs, donate money to help others, or communicate the gospel; we are (at the same time) tearing people down (or corrupting them) with our tongue through critical words or gossip. Our rotting words negate the good done for no gain (it all becomes *worthless*). So, James tells us that the first thing to expect God's word to change, as He imprints it deeper in our hearts, is to make our spoken conversations never hurtful, but refreshing to others.

A JOYOUS THOUGHT FOR TODAY:

*Let **no unwholesome word** proceed from your mouth,*
but only such a word as is good for edification
*according to the need of the moment, so that it will **give**
grace to those who hear.* —EPHESIANS 4:29

For Today, ask God to make you mindful of all the words you speak. Ask Him to keep you mindful that *unwholesome* (which means rotten) words will rot (or corrupt) both you and the hearer; and that God has a much more joyous life *for* you (and more uplifting life for others *through* you). Pray these verses back to God, simply desiring that He conform your life to what they say.

PRAYER

*Dear God, throughout these next days,
make me aware of the words I speak to others.
Show me how and when I tear others down
rather than build them up. I pray that You
would search my heart and remove any
hurtful thing that resides there. Do not let me
wander from Your word implanted in me.
I pray that not only would Your word build
me up, but also those I speak to during
my every day. Amen.*

DAY 79

*The upright speak **what is helpful**; the wicked speak rebellion.*

—PROVERBS 10:32, TLB

*Some people like to make cutting remarks, but the words of the wise **soothe and heal.***

—PROVERBS 12:18, TLB

God's word is full of verses concerning our tongue and how it serves as a barometer of what is in our heart. Proverbs is particularly good at giving us the stark contrast between what a wise person does compared to what a foolish person does. The technical term for this written technique is called "antithetical parallelism," which juxtaposes and contrasts the way of wisdom and the way of folly.

What does a wise (or godly) person do? What does a fool do? Proverbs is a book of instruction from God to us (His children) to teach us to *think biblically* according to His covenant with us. *Thinking biblically* is not something we do naturally in our own effort, but is a result of reading God's word with a desire that He imprint it on our hearts. As God's word increasingly fills our heart and renews our mind—helpful, healing, and soothing speech to others is the result.

A JOYOUS THOUGHT FOR TODAY:

*The **heart of the righteous ponders** how to answer*
[to make sure the words we are about to say are helpful and
an encouragement to the listener], but the mouth of
the wicked pours out evil things [or says things that hurt
and destroy]. —PROVERBS 15:28

For Today, ponder whether the words you are about to say to another person will be helpful and encouraging to them. To ponder means to pause for a moment. In that moment, ask God to direct you in what to say that will soothe and heal. It is better to say nothing than to tear down, which damages both you and the listener. God is bringing you to greater joy.

A PERSONAL TESTIMONY
COMPLAINING WORDS DESTROY

Early in my marriage, I was not aware that all of my complaining words to my wife were destroying her. "Why didn't you pick-up my shirts at the laundry?" "Oh, you fixed this for dinner, I wanted that." I didn't see that all of this hurtful speech was damaging our marriage and came from my selfish and self-centered heart.

One day (after yet another snide remark), she burst into tears and said, "Daryl, I just wish I could die so you could be free to marry someone who could make you happy!"

I was stunned! I stammered a response, "I've said other words to you. I've told you a thousand times how beautiful you are and how much I love you." "Yes," she said, "but you've done so amidst a constant stream of criticism!"

As I considered what my wife had said, the very person I loved the most in this world, I realized that the selfish things I often said were so filled with poison that it made her want to die! *And all of it came from MY mouth*! As I turned over my anguish to God, He brought me to these verses in *Psalm 139: 23-24*, which continue to live with me to this day:

> *Search me, O God, and **know my heart**;*
> *try me and know my anxious thoughts;*
> *²⁴and see if there be **any hurtful way in me**,*
> *and lead **ME** in the everlasting way.*

As my wife and I have counseled couples over the years, we have seen that their problems often began with a negative comment said by one or the other spouse. In one case, the wife broke into tears, crying out something the husband had said from twenty years before (*"I wish I had never married you!"*). Another young woman was asked why she continually dated "losers" and she said "Well, my mother always told me I was no good ...."

None of us can truly understand how great the power is in the words we say to others, either to hurt and destroy, or to lift up and heal. We can only pray that God will make us increasingly sensitive to *every word* we say.

DAY 80

*The advice [or talk] of a wise man [someone who speaks Christ's words] refreshes **like water from a mountain spring**. Those accepting it become aware of the pitfalls on ahead.*
—PROVERBS 13:14, TLB

This verse brings back one of my fondest memories of youth. Each summer, our family would go camping high in the mountains in California. We could look up and see the snowpack and right beside our campsite was a crystal clear, bubbling stream of ice cold water. There was nothing I loved doing more on a hot day than borrowing the old tin cup my mother used for cooking, and going down to plunge that cup deep into the stream for a long drink of ice-cold water!

Solomon is telling us that when our spouse, children, friends, and co-workers drink in our words—if they truly are Christ's words manifest in us—they will feel like they just dipped their tin cup into that ice cold mountain stream and took a refreshing drink!

But how does our conversation become refreshing regardless of what problems we may be confronting, or what circumstances happen to be pressing in on us? It begins by asking God to stamp the truth of this verse deeply into our life. Make that your prayer for the next week. Tomorrow, we will pause to consider a practical example of how God changes us through His word.

A JOYOUS THOUGHT FOR TODAY:

*The **law** of the LORD is **perfect, restoring the soul;** the testimony of the LORD is sure, **making wise** the simple.*
*⁸The **precepts** of the LORD are **right, rejoicing the heart;** the **commandment** of the LORD is **pure,** enlightening the eyes.* —PSALM 19:7-8

For Today, rejoice in how active and effectual God's word is. The words "law," "testimony," "precepts," and "commandment" are all synonyms for *God's word*. It is perfect, sure, right, and pure, and restores our soul, makes us wise, and enlightens our eyes. It causes our heart to rejoice, and it makes all our conversation healing and uplifting. Praise God for drawing *YOU* to His glorious word!

DAY 81

*But **by His** [God's] doing you are in Christ Jesus, who became to us wisdom from God, and **righteousness** [or flawless in God's eyes] and sanctification, and redemption.*

—1 CORINTHIANS 1:30

A dear friend of mine some time ago confided in me that he had a "hot button" which would always trigger his anger. Whenever someone would criticize his character, he would immediately react defensively. He asked me if I knew anyway to insulate himself from this threat. I pondered his question for a moment and the Lord brought to mind *1 Corinthians 1:30*. I said, "Start meditating on this verse and it will be your insulation."

When we remember (and believe) that Christ is our *total* righteousness before God, we are no longer driven by the compulsion to angrily defend ourselves. The truth is: We are flawless before God, not because we have something "good" of our own to defend, but solely because of Christ's righteousness *in us*. When we see ourselves as God sees us, we finally recognize there is *nothing* good in us to defend. This wisdom sets us free from all deception about our own value, and allows us perhaps for the first time to acknowledge how ugly our flesh truly is. When we have no good in ourselves to defend (because Christ is our total worthiness to God), that understanding bridles our tongue whenever we are criticized.

A JOYOUS THOUGHT FOR TODAY:

*But by **the grace of God I am** what I am ....*

—1 CORINTHIANS 15:10

For Today, join Paul in recognizing that *all* that you are is the grace of God; which leaves *nothing* about yourself to defend. Paul spent much of his early life persecuting and killing Christians, yet the person who did all of that horrible stuff was not him anymore. He was now only the grace of God. Pray that God will bring you to this wonderful truth. YOU are just the grace of God today. These are not just words, but the truth and freedom that lives in you! This truth definitely increases our joy.

DAY 82

*Pure and undefiled religion **in the sight of our God** and Father is this: **to visit orphans and widows** in their distress, and to keep oneself unstained by the world.*
—JAMES 1:27

In the last two verses of chapter one, James is sharing with us three essential elements of *true* religion and how we can expect it to manifests itself in our daily living. Verse twenty-six gave us the first element (Day 77). Now, in verse twenty-seven, we learn the next two. The second manifestation of *true* religion is that Christ gives us a desire to help the needy, or as James puts it: *"to visit orphans and widows."*

Two important observations must be made about this verse before we go further. *First*, the phrase *"in the sight of our God"* does not mean that God is *smiling* on us when we are visiting orphans and widows and *frowning* on us when we are not. It simply means that this is a manifestation (an example) of *true* Christianity.

Second, James is not suggesting that the total definition of *true* religion is visiting orphans and widows. He's just saying that *true* religion is God changing our lives *from within*, including caring for orphans and widows (and the poor), instead of thinking only of ourselves and our own pleasures. God etches His words into our hearts and changes our desires, conversations, purposes, and actions. According to James, *true* religion is God changing us from thinking only of ourselves to caring about others.

A JOYOUS THOUGHT FOR TODAY:

Bear one another's burdens, *and thereby fulfill the law [the word] of Christ.* —GALATIANS 6:2

For Today, bringing help to others does not always come in the form of food or money, but often in being a person willing to *listen* to their burdens. Be sensitive to God bringing someone into your life today who just needs to talk. Pray that God will direct your thinking and response as you listen. This brings joy to them and to you.

DAY 83

*Pure and undefiled religion in the sight of our God and Father is this: to visit orphans and widows in their distress, and to **keep oneself unstained by the world.***
—JAMES 1:27

The third manifestation of *true* religion, according to James, is *"to keep oneself unstained by the world."* The word *unstained* means uncorrupted by this world's immorality (that which destroys lives, marriages, and families), and uncorrupted by selfishness, anger, and critical or abusive speech (which cause the same destruction in our lives as immorality).

Is this verse telling us that WE are responsible to KEEP OURSELVES unstained by the world? No. James is assuming we are reading his entire letter in context. Only a few verses back, he told us (verse twenty-one) what *puts aside all filthiness and all that remains of wickedness* is *receiving the word implanted in humility.* It is God's word that keeps us unstained from the world. God's word keeps us freed from getting caught in the entanglements of the world. Our *flesh-trap* (Day 46) is ready to spring and ensnare us in anger, abusive speech, and all manner of selfishness, but God's word imprints our hearts and protects our life. For James, this is *true* religion.

A JOYOUS THOUGHT FOR TODAY:

*Your testimonies [God's word] also are **my delight;** they are **my counselors.*** —PSALM 119:24

For Today, take a moment to consider how much importance King David placed on God's words. They were his delight and his counselors! They were important because they kept him from being corrupted by this world. Try David's approach; write a few verses on 3x5 cards and read them throughout your day. Pray that God will etch them deeply within you and protect your heart and mind from the entanglements of this world. *God will do this.* Praise Him!

Day 84

Those who love Your law [God's word] **have great peace,** *and* **nothing causes them to stumble.**

—Psalm 119:165

From time to time, it is good to expand our look at God's word beyond James to see the same principles taught throughout scripture. This verse comes from *Psalm 119*, the longest chapter in the entire Bible—a chapter dedicated in all respects to God's word. James is not the only one who encourages us to spend time reading God's word if we want our lives filled with joy and direction from God.

From every side, enticements and threats press in to ensnare us and bring us down to despair and defeat. James tells us that *true* religion manifests itself as a growing love for God's word. What is the result of turning regularly to God's word in the midst of our daily living? *Great peace!* God's word produces a security and well-being in our heart that cannot be shaken. In James' vernacular, we would be those who *consider it all joy* in the midst of various trials.

Psalm 119:165 assures us that for those who love God's word: *nothing will cause them to stumble.*

A JOYOUS THOUGHT FOR TODAY:

This book of the law [God's word] shall not depart from your mouth, but **you shall meditate on it day and night** *[or think about verses throughout your day], so that you may be careful to do according to all that is written in it; for* **then you will make your way prosperous,** *and* **then you will have success.** —Joshua 1:8

For Today, notice the order in which *prosperity* and *success* are found. *First*, meditate on verses throughout your day, *THEN* your words to your spouse, kids, neighbors, friends, and co-workers—in whatever circumstance—will be refreshing. They will also make your day successful. Praise God for His powerful, life-changing word!

My Joyous Thoughts

WHO DO I ADMIRE?

JAMES 2:1-13

My brethren, do not hold your faith in our glorious Lord Jesus Christ with an attitude of personal favoritism. [2]For if a man comes into your assembly with a gold ring and dressed in fine clothes, and there also comes in a poor man in dirty clothes, [3]and you pay special attention to the one who is wearing the fine clothes, and say, "You sit here in a good place," and you say to the poor man, "You stand over there, or sit down by my footstool," [4]have you not made distinctions among yourselves, and become judges with evil motives? [5]Listen, my beloved brethren: did not God choose the poor of this world to be rich in faith and heirs of the kingdom which He promised to those who love Him? [6]But you have dishonored the poor man. Is it not the rich who oppress you and personally drag you into court? [7]Do they not blaspheme the fair name by which you have been called? [8]If, however, you are fulfilling the royal law according to the Scripture, "YOU SHALL LOVE YOUR NEIGHBOR AS YOURSELF," you are doing well. [9]But if you show partiality, you are committing sin and are convicted by the law as transgressors. [10]For whoever keeps the whole law and yet stumbles in one point, he has become guilty of all. [11]For He who said, "DO NOT COMMIT ADULTERY," also said, "DO NOT COMMIT MURDER." Now if you do not commit adultery, but do commit murder, you have become a transgressor of the law. [12]So speak and so act as those who are to be judged by the law of liberty. [13]For judgment will be merciless to one who has shown no mercy; mercy triumphs over judgment.

DAY 85

*My brethren, do not hold your faith in our glorious Lord Jesus Christ with an **attitude of personal favoritism.***

—JAMES 2:1

You may wonder what joy can be found in a verse like this. You are going to see there is joy in *all* of God's word when it is correctly understood. Remember, the fruit of the Spirit is love, *joy*, peace, patience, and things like these *(Galatians 5:22)*. James told us in *James 1:21* (Day 71) that receiving God's word with a soft-pliable heart changes our life. Now, he continues this theme in chapter two by speaking to us in very practical terms and examples. As God continues to draw us to His word, His word eliminates our noticing, respecting, and admiring the rich more than we do the poor.

The Living Bible reads: *"Dear brothers, how can you claim that you belong to the Lord Jesus Christ, the Lord of glory [or how can you claim to be a Christian], if you show favoritism to rich people and look down on poor people [or think less of poor people]?"*

Obviously, some of James' readers were impressed with wealthy people (just as many people are today). James tells us that being enamored with wealth and popularity is the *antithesis* of true faith in Christ. Since we can never lose our salvation, James is not suggesting that this fleshly attitude negates our Christianity. He's just telling us that admiring the wealthy over the poor is sourced in our ugly flesh and is the *opposite* of the way Christ thinks.

A JOYOUS THOUGHT FOR TODAY:

*He who **oppresses the poor taunts his Maker**, but he who is gracious to the needy honors Him.*

—PROVERBS 14:31

For Today, pray for God to shine His light on the attitudes you hold toward *all* others. Ask Him to make you sensitive to the loving and nurturing attitude which Christ (who lives in you) holds for *all* the people you meet. Ask the Lord to honor Himself by eliminating from you any feeling that wealthy and popular people are more special than the poor and insignificant. You can be sure, more joy is coming to you and through you to those you meet.

PRAYER

*Dear God, throughout these coming days, please imprint on my heart from Your living word how deeply You love each and every person. No matter how unappealing a person may look or act, keep me mindful that You loved them enough to endure the cross and die for them. Show me that from Your righteous perspective, I am not one bit better in any respect than anyone else. Without Your mercy and grace we all deserve equally to perish eternally. I pray that You will create in my heart a pathway for Your **equal** compassion, love, and respect to flow to all others. Amen.*

DAY 86

*For if a man comes into your assembly **with a gold ring and dressed in fine clothes,** and there also comes in a poor man in dirty clothes, ³and you **pay special attention to the one who is wearing the fine clothes,** and say, "You sit here in a good place," and you say to the poor man, "You stand over there, or sit down by my footstool."*

—JAMES 2:2-3

In the days when James wrote his letter, the wearing of a *gold ring* was a sign of wealth. This would be equivalent today to the size of house we own, or the make of car we drive, or the title we hold at work. The poor man's *dirty clothes* is better translated "threadbare clothes," which refers to old, worn-out clothes.

James is presenting a contrast between someone who *appears* to be wealthy and someone who *appears* to be poor. Christ who lives *within us* is not attracted to people based on their outward appearance. He regards and loves all people equally.

As God etches His word deeper in our hearts, we too will make no distinction between rich and poor, famous, infamous, or completely unknown. We will not admire the rich, or respect them more than a person who is poor and without earthly possessions. God pours His love out on all people, and as His word is written on our hearts, we will too!

A JOYOUS THOUGHT FOR TODAY:

*Better is the **poor who walks in his integrity** than he who is crooked though he be rich.* —PROVERBS 28:6

For Today, as you come into contact with others, ask God to give you His eyes to look past the outward appearance of wealth or poverty to see each person as Christ sees them. This will free you to love them with God's love, which always gives *joy* to both the lover and receiver (and honors God).

IMAGINE THIS!

Imagine coming to church one Sunday and there are two notices in the church bulletin. The *first* notice announces that Tom Brady (famous NFL quarterback), Bill Gates (the wealthiest person in the world), or Meryl Streep (academy award-winning actress) will be speaking at the church on Monday night. The *second* notice announces a Tuesday night gathering to hear the testimony of what an elderly lady from your church has experienced over decades of intercessory prayer. Which one will you go see?

Isn't it wonderful that James was inspired to expose our ugly flesh in such practical ways? If it were me, for most of my life I would have been the first to go see Tom Brady (or some other famous person) before seeing the prayer warrior from my church. Who knows, maybe I could get his autograph to hang in my office or den (I would have no thought for the prayer warrior's autograph).

Now, try all you want in your own effort to rid yourself of feeling a special awe of rich and famous people. You will never be successful. Only God's word has the power to change this preferential attitude in us so we *feel* the same toward rich and poor, significant and insignificant, alike.

> *Opening his mouth, Peter said: "I most certainly understand*
> *now that **God is not one to show partiality.**"* —ACTS 10:34

Give thanks to God that He is not one who shows partiality. Otherwise, He would not have included us Gentiles in His wonderful plan of salvation through His Son Jesus. As we remember that God saw and chose to include insignificant us in His eternal family, this causes us to feel no partiality in those we meet every day. Praise God for this glorious *power in His word* to accomplish what it says in our life!

DAY 87

*Have you not made distinctions among yourselves, **and become judges with evil motives?** ⁵Listen, my beloved brethren: did not God choose the poor of this world to be rich in faith and heirs of the kingdom which He promised to those who love Him? ⁶But you have dishonored the poor man. Is it not the rich who oppress you and personally drag you into court? ⁷Do they not blaspheme the fair name by which you have been called?"*
—JAMES 2:4-7

The word *motives* in the NASB is translated as *thoughts* in the NIV Bible. It refers to our flesh's prideful attraction to people of worldly importance and success over those who are poor and insignificant.

I remember having a conversation with my Dad, who had been a church pastor for most of his adult life, concerning why it is that the church boards we had served on together throughout the years had all preferred wealthy board members (over people gifted in prayer or showing mercy). At the end of this conversation, my Dad hung his head and said, "It's because of the ugliness in our flesh, Daryl. Even as church leaders we would never admit this, but we have more 'faith' in getting the money we need (to support the church and run all our programs) *if* we have wealthy members on the board who can pick up the slack when the giving falls short. We have more faith in that than we have in God supplying our needs ... *we are so miserably human.*"

Yes, we are miserably human. But as God's word flows through us in a fresh way each day, His life is greater than our miserable flesh and worldly preferences. Praise Him!

A JOYOUS THOUGHT FOR TODAY:

You are from God, *little children, and have overcome them; because* **greater is He who is in you** *than he who is in the world.* —1 JOHN 4:4

For Today, thank God that He does not expect you to change any preferential attitude on your own. Pray that the God who is *"greater"* and *"who is in you"* will conform your attitudes and motives to what *James 2:1-7* says. As God instills in you His equal joy and love for others, praise Him. More joy is coming.

DAY 88

*If, however, you are fulfilling the **royal law according to the Scripture,** "YOU SHALL LOVE YOUR NEIGHBOR AS YOURSELF," you are doing well. ⁹But **if you show partiality, you are committing sin** and are convicted by the law as transgressors. ¹⁰For whoever keeps the whole law and yet stumbles in one point, he has become **guilty of all.** ¹¹For He who said, "DO NOT COMMIT ADULTERY," also said, "DO NOT COMMIT MURDER." Now if you do not commit adultery, but do commit murder, you have become a transgressor of the law.*

—JAMES 2:8-11

The *royal law* referred to is *God's supreme law* which according to *Matthew 22:36-40* is to love *God* and *others* unconditionally; without respect for their status, wealth, achievements, or failures. All of the Law and the prophets rest upon this irreducible foundation.

To become *guilty of all* the law, means if we break just one aspect of God's law, we are as ungodly before God as if we broke *all* of the law! This makes it impossible to satisfy the law on our own. Yet, as Christians, we continue to deceive ourselves by coming up with our own pecking order for the "seriousness" of sins. Respecting the rich would be very low on our list. But James tells us that when we admire the wealthy and successful people more than the poor, we are just as ungodly as a murderer. (I honestly never realized this was such a great evil!)

A JOYOUS THOUGHT FOR TODAY:

"Teacher, which is the great commandment in the Law?"
³⁷And He said to him, "'YOU SHALL LOVE THE LORD YOUR GOD WITH ALL YOUR HEART, AND WITH ALL YOUR SOUL, AND WITH ALL YOUR MIND.' ³⁸This is the great and foremost commandment. ³⁹The second is like it, 'YOU SHALL LOVE YOUR NEIGHBOR AS YOURSELF.' ⁴⁰On these two commandments depend the whole Law and the Prophets." —MATTHEW 22:36-40

For Today, rejoice in the fact that Christ in you *is drawing you to love God, is causing* you to *love and care for others equally*, and has *fulfilled all of God's royal law* FOR YOU!

DAY 89

*So speak and so act as those who are to be judged by the **law of liberty.***
—JAMES 2:12

Ow is it possible to *not* feel any preference or greater respect for some people over others? In my experience, the more God draws us into His word to learn of His great mercy and compassion for us, the more compassion we find ourselves having for the poor (and the less special admiration we have for the rich).

The phrase *"law of liberty"* refers to the glorious truth that Christ has fulfilled all of God's law for us, thereby *liberating* us from any judgment for failing any aspect of God's law! What, then, does it mean to be *judged by* the law of liberty? This is James' way of driving home the truth of what Christ has accomplished on our behalf. If He has fulfilled the law on our behalf and set us free from any and all judgment from God, then being judged by that freedom is to *not be judged at all,* which verse thirteen (Day 90) goes on to explain. If God is so rich in mercy toward us, how can we be less than that to others?

A JOYOUS THOUGHT FOR TODAY:

*But God, being **rich in mercy,** because of His great love with which **He loved us,** ⁵even when we were dead in our transgressions, **made us alive** together with Christ **(by grace** you have been saved).* —EPHESIANS 2:4-5

For Today, consider these verses. Does God threaten to *punish* you? No! Well then, does He *reward* you for good behavior? No! How about requiring you to *cooperate* with Him to live a better Christian life? Again, the answer is no. These verses reveal one thing: God is *rich in mercy.* He *made you alive* with Christ, even when you were DEAD in your transgressions. What can a dead person do for themselves? Nothing! Throughout the day, pray that God would imprint your heart with these glorious words. The result will be that you will be less enamored with the accoutrements of the rich and have more compassion for the poor. As God causes you to see everyone else as just an object of His mercy, He reminds you this is how He sees you. Great joy!

DAY 90

*For judgment will be merciless to one who has shown no mercy; **mercy triumphs over judgment.***
—JAMES 2:13

H ere is a verse that is often misinterpreted and can be quite controversial. But remember the context. *James 1:2* tells us that James was writing to the "*twelve tribes who are dispersed abroad.*" These were Jewish believers steeped in the Old Testament Mosaic law. James is concluding this section of his letter (regarding the sin of partiality) by observing that some among his readers were judging others just as though they were still under the old covenant law.

Under the old covenant, *God responds to our actions.* If we obey the law, He will bless us. If we don't obey, He will remove His blessings or even curse us. In the context of James' letter, James is contrasting the covenants of law and grace in the lives of these Jewish believers. Under the law, God won't forgive us if we don't first show mercy to others. But under grace, *God acts on our behalf.* He has forgiven us even though, at times, we don't forgive others. "*Mercy triumphs over judgment.*" This new covenant is not dependent on our actions, but only on the actions of Christ. Christ has paid the price and forgiven us, once and for all, for *all* past, present, and future sins *(1 John 2:12).*

A JOYOUS THOUGHT FOR TODAY:

*My sheep hear My voice, and I know them, and they follow Me; [28] and **I give eternal life to them,** and they will never perish; and **no one will snatch them out of My hand.*** —JOHN 10:27-28

For Today, rejoice in the fact that once you were dead in your own transgressions, but God made you alive with Christ. He did so, all because of His love, mercy, and grace for you. Under the old covenant you were subject to judgment, but no longer! Praise the Lord that He has given you a new covenant, based solely on what Christ accomplished for you, to bring you into His saving grace. You can never lose this salvation because no one can ever snatch you out of His hand. "*Mercy triumphs over judgment.*" This is the greatest of joys!

CONNECTING THE THEOLOGICAL DOTS

James 2:13 illustrates why it is so important to properly distinguish between scripture written under the old covenant and scripture written under the new covenant. This can be confusing because many think the old covenant is restricted only to the Old Testament. This is not true. The old covenant is still in effect through the four gospels in the New Testament, until its culmination upon the cross. Christ's crucifixion, burial, and resurrection ushered in the new covenant between God and man. Here are two examples from scripture to illustrate what I mean:

Matthew 6:14-15 are verses which record an event that took place under the *old covenant* (Law). Jesus, speaking to the Jews, said, *"For if you forgive others for their transgressions, your heavenly Father will also forgive you. ¹⁵But if you do not forgive others, then your Father will not forgive your transgressions."* This is classic phraseology reflecting directly from the old covenant. This is what the first phrase in *James 2:13* (*"For judgment will be merciless to one who has shown no mercy"*) is referring to.

But compare that to a verse written under the *new covenant* (Grace) on the same subject. *Ephesians 4:32* tells us, *"Be kind to one another, tender-hearted, forgiving each other, Just as God in Christ also **has** [past tense] forgiven you."* This is consistent with the second phrase in *James 2:13* (*"mercy triumphs over judgment"*). Paul is not encouraging believers to forgive others so they can be forgiven by God (threatening them that if they do not forgive they won't be forgiven and end up in hell). Under the new covenant of grace, Paul is encouraging them, based on the fact that they have *already been forgiven* by God's mercy and grace toward them, they in turn, are free to be kind and tender-hearted to others. Under the new covenant, we forgive *because* we have already been forgiven; we do not forgive in order to be forgiven.

Scripture tells us that God did not give the law to the Jewish people so they could keep it. He gave it to them to prove that in their own self-effort they could never keep it. Only God's mercy, not their own performance, could save them from their sins and ultimate eternal destruction. In this capacity, the law served as a tutor *(Galatians 3:24)* to lead them to look forward to Christ, so they might be justified by faith.

PRAYER

Dear God, I can't praise You enough for the truth of Your goodness and mercy toward me. You know that the brighter You shine this truth in my heart, the greater my own heart cries out to simply be a vessel of goodness and mercy to others. Amen.

My Joyous Thoughts

FEELING SAVED

What use is it, my brethren, if someone says he has faith but he has no works? Can that faith save him? [15]If a brother or sister is without clothing and in need of daily food, [16]and one of you says to them, "Go in peace, be warmed and be filled," and yet you do not give them what is necessary for their body, what use is that? [17]Even so faith, if it has no works, is dead, being by itself. [18]But someone may well say, "You have faith and I have works; show me your faith without the works, and I will show you my faith by my works." [19]You believe that God is one. You do well; the demons also believe, and shudder. [20]But are you willing to recognize, you foolish fellow, that faith without works is useless? [21]Was not Abraham our father justified by works when he offered up Isaac his son on the altar? [22]You see that faith was working with his works, and as a result of the works, faith was perfected; [23]and the Scripture was fulfilled which says, "AND ABRAHAM BELIEVED GOD, AND IT WAS RECKONED TO HIM AS RIGHTEOUSNESS," and he was called the friend of God. [24]You see that a man is justified by works and not by faith alone. [25]In the same way, was not Rahab the harlot also justified by works when she received the messengers and sent them out by another way? [26]For just as the body without the spirit is dead, so also faith without works is dead.

James 2:14-26 contain some verses used to bolster one side of a controversy that has existed for thousands of years: whether a person is saved by "doing good works," or by "faith alone," or by some combination of the two.

For those who believe that a person must do works to be saved, they go right away to *James 2:21, "Was not Abraham our father **justified by works** when he offered up Isaac his son on the altar?"* and *James 2:24-26, "You see that a man is **justified by works and not by faith alone**. ²⁵In the same way, was not Rahab the harlot also **justified by works** when she received the messengers and sent them out by another way? ²⁶For just as the body without the spirit is dead, so also **faith without works is dead.**"*

For those who believe that a person's salvation comes from faith alone, they quickly counter with *Ephesians 2:8-9, "For by grace you have been saved **through faith**; and that not of yourselves, **it is the gift of God; not as a result of works**, so that **no one may boast.**"*

Do these sections of scripture contradict each other? Absolutely not! God's word never contradicts itself! Then how do we reconcile what Paul says in Ephesians and what James says in James? The answer is in understanding the different false teachings each was confronting and the different audiences they were writing to.

Paul in Ephesians was confronting the false teaching gaining ground among the *Gentiles* (from their Greek philosophy and pagan heritage) that a person could be good enough on their own merit to gain salvation. To defeat this false teaching, Paul stressed that salvation is by grace *through faith alone* and not of works.

James, on the other hand, was speaking primarily to *Jewish believers* scattered abroad (*see* Day 4) who were *professing* to be Christians but displayed no manifestation of any Christ-like qualities in their lives. To battle this false teaching, James highlighted that true faith changes a person's life. Those who truly have Christ Jesus living in them will be affected by His life. Christ will progressively change their life.

The reality is that both Paul and James are speaking divine truths that do not conflict each other. We will see in the coming days that salvation is not dependent on works, but works is something that naturally flows out of true faith. God, through His Son dwelling in us, progressively changes a person's life consistent with His word!

Day 91

*What use is it, my brethren, if someone says he has faith but he has **no works**?*
Can that faith save him?

—James 2:14

In this section of his letter, James first describes what *"un*-saving" faith is. Or what we would call a *false* faith or a *false* profession of being a Christian. James isn't trying to make *us* worry about whether *we* are saved or not! He is not trying to make us try harder to act like a Christian so we can prove to ourselves (and to others) that we are one! He is simply distinguishing between those who are (from those who likely aren't) saved. This distinction will become clearer in the coming days.

It is also important to understand the meaning of the word *faith* as used by James. *Faith*, in this context, means a *firm belief in Christ*. This is apparent from *James 2:1* which refers to *faith in our glorious Lord Jesus Christ*. The *NIV* uses the word *believers* instead of *faith*. It reads, *"My brothers, as believers in our glorious Lord Jesus Christ."*

If I were to paraphrase what James is saying, it would go something like this: *"How can a person, who claims to be a Christian with Christ living in them 24/7, continue to be totally self-absorbed, uncompassionate toward the needy, and live just as immorally as those in the world (without remorse or troubled spirit); how can these people really be Christians?"* The answer James gives in the next two verses (Day 92) makes it clear that he believes it's likely they are not Christians in spite of their claims. One thing James believed above all else: Jesus Christ, living in us, works changes in our lives to make us more like Him.

A Joyous Thought for Today:

*For **we are His workmanship, created in Christ Jesus***
***for good works,** which **God prepared beforehand** so that*
we would walk in them. —Ephesians 2:10

For Today, as you pray for another, seek God's guidance, read your Bible, think about God, call to encourage a friend, tip a server, or simply praise God, know that *all* of these things are the *good works* God has prepared beforehand for you to walk in this day. Thank God that *He* is producing these *works* in you, which confirms that you have saving faith. *This is Great Joy!*

DAY 92

*If a brother or sister is **without clothing** and in need of daily food, ¹⁶and one of you says to them, "Go in peace, be warmed and be filled," and yet you do not give them what is necessary for their body, what use is that? ¹⁷Even so faith, if it has no works, is dead, being by itself. ²⁴You see that a man is **justified by works and not by faith alone.***
—JAMES 2:15-17, 24

The phrase *without clothing* refers to a person who is in very serious need. James uses this particularly harsh example to make an important point: if a profess-ing "Christian" can see a person in such deep need and have no compassion toward helping them, how can God's word really be implanted in them (or how can Christ be living in them)? He concludes that if there is *no evidence* of Christ's life in this person (who claims to be a Christian), then this person's professed faith is dead (or false).

I confess that this used to give me fits of worry and anxiety. I would wake up in the middle of the night worrying about how much evidence of Christ in my life is necessary to affirm that I am truly saved. Now, I praise God for the understanding that He *never* leaves His children wondering or worrying about their eternal security. He *always* makes us *feel saved* regardless of our circumstances (for "feeling saved," *see* Days 96-97).

A JOYOUS THOUGHT FOR TODAY:

*This was in accordance with the eternal purpose which He carried out in Christ Jesus our Lord, ¹²in whom we have boldness and **confident access through faith in Him.** —EPHESIANS 3:11-12*

For Today, be confident in your salvation. God has given you compassion for the needy, which is evidence of your salvation. Lord willing, as you read future days, you will identify with many more evidences of Christ in you. This is truly *great joy*!

DAY 93

*You believe that God is one. You do well; the **demons also believe**, and shudder.*
—JAMES 2:19

Before we look deeper into what *saving faith* is in verse eighteen, we first must jump down a verse to see what *non-saving faith* looks like; by addressing a strongly held belief by some of those Jews who James was addressing in his letter. Throughout their entire history, from the very founding of their nation, the Children of Israel were completely surrounded by other nations who worshipped *multiple* gods. *Only* the nation of Israel believed in *ONE* God. Over the centuries preceding Christ's first advent, this belief not only made the nation of Israel unique among nations, but protected them from harm.

Many of the Jews that James was writing to took great pride in their belief in *One God*. This belief, in their thinking, made them special and yielded a great deal of "religious" credit toward saving them. James gave them the harsh reminder that even the demons believed in the *One God* and that didn't save them!

James is telling us all that just any faith won't do, even when its object is nothing less than the *One God* of all creation. It is *"faith in our glorious Lord Jesus Christ"* (*James 2:1*, Day 91) that truly saves and from which good works flow.

A JOYOUS THOUGHT FOR TODAY:

*Many more believed **because of His word;** [42]and they were saying to the woman, "It is no longer because of what you said that we believe, for we have heard for ourselves and know that **this One is indeed the Savior of the world."** —JOHN 4:41-42*

For Today, be thankful to God! He has revealed to you that Jesus Christ is your full salvation, without the need for any additional works. This frees you to understand that while it is *faith alone* (in Christ) that saves you, your faith is *not alone*. The divine things you do: like praying to God, reading your Bible, your heart's praise to God, are simply the "works" of His Spirit manifest in your life. And all these "works" continue to confirm your salvation.

DAY 94

*But someone may well say, "You have faith and I have works; show me your faith without the works, and I will show you **my faith by my works**."*
—JAMES 2:18

The first thing we should note about *saving faith* is that James makes clear in this verse that *works*—or what we think of as Christ-like attitudes and actions—are the *result*, not the cause, of *true* faith. They are not "add-ons" to faith, but manifestations of the faith we already have. This is obvious from his statement, *"I will show you my faith BY my works."* From this we can see that James is not talking about *faith* AND *works* being needed for salvation. Only that our saving faith logically expresses itself in ways that can be observed in terms of Christ-like attitudes and actions. Those attitudes and actions are *evidence* in our lives of what we *say* we believe.

James then gives two examples of this principle. *First*, he recalls Abraham's willingness to sacrifice Isaac as evidence of his faith *(James 2:21-23)*. *Second*, he tells us how Rahab evidenced her faith through her compassion for the spies and her loyalty to God *(James 2:25)*. In these examples, it wasn't that they needed both faith and works to save them, but rather, each displayed a faith that *produced* evidence of what they believed.

A JOYOUS THOUGHT FOR TODAY:

*Peace be to the brethren, and love **with faith, from God** the Father and the Lord Jesus Christ.* —EPHESIANS 6:23

For Today, pray that God will shine His light in your heart to understand that whatever you believe about God comes *from* God. Many people can read the scriptures, but there is no power in it for them. There is no light for them to see by. But you, as a chosen child of God, can be assured that the Holy Spirit uses God's words in your life to shape your life, attitudes, actions, and beliefs. Remember, God's word is *equal* to God's presence in your life (Day 30; and *"Imagine This!"* on page 57) So, today, enjoy the freedom and confidence of knowing that you do not even muster your own faith (or belief in Christ). God gives you that belief. Great joy for another day!

Day 95

*And on the basis of **faith in His name**, it is the name of Jesus which has strengthened this man whom you see and know; and **the faith which comes through Him** [or through Christ] **has given him this perfect health** in the presence of you all.*
—Acts 3:16

In Acts we see a similar principle to what James has been sharing with us. In Acts, Peter is explaining to the religious leaders at the Jerusalem Temple how this lame man came to be healed. To paraphrase what Peter said, *"The faith that God gave to this lame man contained the power to heal him."* So, *true faith* contains God's power to conform our lives according to what His scripture says. Many of us may think that it is up to us to apply scripture to our lives, but we are no better than that lame man in *Acts 3*. We don't have any power to heal ourselves. It is only God's power, through His word, that has the power to conform our lives to His word. Praise God for this freedom. He is the Potter and we are the clay. He is molding and shaping us into exactly what pleases Him! For example, the more God grows our faith in His love for us—the more He conforms our lives to that same love—which causes us to *love others* with that same love. This is why *works* are always associated with *faith*.

Paul tells us that *"no one seeks for God" (Romans 3:11)*. This means that no one comes to God's word (through individual reading of the Bible, or attending a Bible study, or going to church) unless the Holy Spirit draws them to it. Whenever we turn to Him in any fashion, it is *all Him* causing us to do so. In the same fashion, it is *all Him* who takes that word and uses it to mold and shape our lives. This is what changes our lives progressively. And it is what others see reflected in our lives as godly works.

A Joyous Thought for Today:

*For by grace you have been saved **through faith;** and that not of yourselves, it [or saving faith] is the **gift of God.*** —Ephesians 2:8

For Today, meditate on what Paul is really saying in *Ephesians 2:8*. Christ is *in you* as a gift from God. Your faith is His faith in you! *Every* godly thing in you is a manifestation of Christ in you. It's *ALL* God, and *NONE* of you. *Praise Him!*

DAY 96

Test yourselves to see if you are in the faith [or test if you are truly saved]; examine yourselves! Or do you not recognize this about yourselves, that Jesus Christ is in you—unless indeed you fail the test?

—2 CORINTHIANS 13:5, NASB

Check up on yourselves. Are you really Christians? Do you pass the test? [Here is the test:] Do you feel Christ's presence and power more and more within you? Or are you just pretending to be Christians when actually you aren't at all?

—2 CORINTHIANS 13:5, TLB

Some Christians read the verses in *James 2* and worry over the fact that they are still struggling with some bad habit, or whatever, might mean that their faith is dead. Time to test ourselves, as Paul puts it, to see whether we are truly saved. And what is that test? Is it calculating how many good works we do compared to how many bad habits we have? Is it taking our whole life and grading it on a curve (a "C" grade is passing). Paul tells us that none of these ideas are the test. Read the test in *The Living Bible* to understand it with clarity. *"Do you feel Christ's presence and power more and more within you?"*

In order to know that we are really saved we need to *first* know that *saving faith* is not confirmed by evaluating whether we have enough good works to save us, but simply by *sensing Jesus Christ* (the author of faith) working in our life. Tomorrow (Day 97), we will explore what it means to "sense" or "feel" Christ's presence and power within us.

A JOYOUS THOUGHT FOR TODAY:

For it is God who is at work in you, both to will and to work for His good pleasure. —PHILIPPIANS 2:13

For Today, acknowledge this simple truth: that you are not a Christian because of your good works, but because of the good work that God has done (and is doing) in you through His Son Jesus who dwells in you. Praise Him for this glorious good news!

Day 97

He who is of God [or every believer] **hears the words of God;** *for this reason you do not hear them, because you are not of God.*

—John 8:47

The word *hears* means God's words have meaning. They are not just dead words on a page that our spirit has no response to. But what does it "feel" like to sense Christ's words working in us? Or what is the feeling of being saved? Here are some examples:

- If you come to the word of God which says, *"Be still, and know that I am God"* and you *feel* it unburden your heart and comfort you—*That is the feeling of being saved;*

- If you are anxious about something, and you are drawn to cry out to God in prayer—*That is the feeling of being saved;*

- If you are reading God's word, or go to a Bible study or to church, or read a book like this one, and you have a growing desire for God to increase in you, and for Him to decrease your flesh—*That is the feeling of being saved!*

This is what John means by God's children *hearing His voice*. His words have meaning to us. They comfort us. They cause us to cry out to God in prayer. They give us the desire to know more and more of Christ. *That is the feeling of being saved.* God didn't choose to save us for eternity, then leave us to worry about our salvation today. *Every* day He confirms our salvation through His Spirit's working in our lives.

A Joyous Thought for Today:

And ***you were dead*** *in your trespasses and sins.*

—Ephesians 2:1

For Today, pray that God would open your eyes to see the myriad ways He assures you each day that you are His child. If you were still dead in your trespasses and sins, you would not think of God at all, let alone hunger and thirst for Him more and more. You would have no desire to pray, or read His word, or fellowship with other believers. All of this confirms that He has given you saving faith.

PRAYER

Dear God, I can't find the words to thank You
for revealing this glorious truth to me.
I am but dust, and purely out of Your love
for me, You daily prompt me to pray, and
read Your word, and to fellowship with other
believers. And through these promptings,
***I know** the feeling of Your work within me.*
I know the feeling of being saved by
Your grace alone. Amen.

A SPECIAL WORD TO THE READER...

In the next series of devotionals, all relating to chapter three of *James* (Days 98-107), we will discover the enormous importance James places on *how we talk to others*. He gives nearly an entire chapter (one out of only five in his letter) to this topic.

I used to think that most, if not all, of our talk is benign. You could blow-off steam, say anything in the process, and people would just brush it off and forget about it. Boy, was I wrong! We will see in James, that *not one word* that passes our lips is benign. *Every* word either tears-down or builds-up. *WOW!*

James makes a point in this section of his letter that is worth acknowledging upfront: We have *all* made mistakes in how we speak to others. We have *all* spoken destructive words that hurt others. James is not judging us for this, nor is he raising this issue to condemn us (or make us feel guilty). His purpose is to encourage us in Christ. This is the purpose of *all* scripture. The purpose of God's word is *never* to make us feel guilty, but *always* to grow more of Christ's likeness in us.

My Joyous Thoughts

MY MOUTH BRINGS ME TO MY KNEES!

JAMES 3:1-12

Let not many of you become teachers, my brethren, knowing that as such we will incur a stricter judgment. [2]For we all stumble in many ways. If anyone does not stumble in what he says, he is a perfect man, able to bridle the whole body as well. [3]Now if we put the bits into the horses' mouths so that they will obey us, we direct their entire body as well. [4]Look at the ships also, though they are so great and are driven by strong winds, are still directed by a very small rudder wherever the inclination of the pilot desires. [5]So also the tongue is a small part of the body, and yet it boasts of great things. See how great a forest is set aflame by such a small fire! [6]And the tongue is a fire, the very world of iniquity; the tongue is set among our members as that which defiles the entire body, and sets on fire the course of our life, and is set on fire by hell. [7]For every species of beasts and birds, of reptiles and creatures of the sea, is tamed and has been tamed by the human race. [8]But no one can tame the tongue; it is a restless evil and full of deadly poison. [9]With it we bless our Lord and Father, and with it we curse men, who have been made in the likeness of God; [10]from the same mouth come both blessing and cursing. My brethren, these things ought not to be this way. [11]Does a fountain send out from the same opening both fresh and bitter water? [12]Can a fig tree, my brethren, produce olives, or a vine produce figs? Nor can salt water produce fresh.

DAY 98

*Let not many of you become teachers, my brethren, knowing that as such **we will incur a stricter judgment.***

—JAMES 3:1

James begins by pointing out that our tongue exposes any hypocrisy in our life. We often are quick to speak words of correction to our kids (or spouse). We rationalize these comments as trying to "teach" them something. But is what we are "teaching" them true in our own life? If it isn't, we are exposed as hypocrites in their eyes.

Some commentators interpret *"incur a stricter judgment"* as judgment coming from God. Other commentators see this judgment as coming from people. I believe this latter interpretation is the scriptural one. *Romans 8:1* supports this understanding: *"Therefore there is **now no condemnation** [or no judgment] for those who are in Christ Jesus." Matthew 7:1-2* uses the same Greek word for "judge/judgment" as is found in *James 3:1: "Do not **judge** so that **you** will not be **judged**. ²For in the way you **judge, you** will be **judged**; and by your standard of measure, it will be measured to you."* The context of these verses is people judging people. *Matthew 7:1-2* in *The Living Bible* makes this meaning clear: *"Don't criticize, and then you won't be criticized. ²**For** others will treat you as you treat them."*

Apparently, in the earliest days of the church, some new Christians (possibly out of genuine enthusiasm) wanted to immediately teach others what they, themselves, were learning. And James told them that not many of them should do this because *their lives* did not yet reflect what they were teaching, and this would result in them being judged by their listeners as hypocrites. We know from God's word that the *fruit* of the Spirit *grows* in our life as we grow in knowing the Lord. And this growth takes time!

A JOYOUS THOUGHT FOR TODAY:

*The **Lord is good** to all, and His mercies are over all His works. ¹⁰... and **Your godly ones shall bless You.***

—PSALM 145:9-10

For Today, if you say the *Lord is good*, but complain about some aspect of your life, what will your listeners conclude? Ask God to check your words, and make sure all you say reflects the truth of scripture. This will give *you* (and your listeners) joy.

DAY 99

*For **we all stumble in many ways**. If anyone **does not stumble** in what he says, he is a perfect man, able to bridle the whole body as well. ³Now if we put the **bits into the horses' mouths** so that they will obey us, we direct their entire body as well. ⁴Look at the ships also, though they are so great and are driven by strong winds, are still directed by a **very small rudder** wherever the inclination of the pilot desires. ⁵**So also the tongue** is a small part of the body, and yet it boasts of great things. See how great a forest is set aflame by such a **small fire!***

—JAMES 3:2-5

How comforting are the words *all* and *many* in verse two. James acknowledges from the outset our common humanness. He states that ALL of us, in MANY ways, stumble by speaking ungodly words. *None* of us are perfect when it comes to our tongue. He doesn't say "*some* of us stumble more than others." He says we *all* stumble. We are *all* in need of God's mercy and grace.

James uses three metaphors to emphasize his point about the power in our tongue to control and direct relationships. A *small bit* in a horse's mouth directs the whole animal; a *small rudder* directs a great ship in heavy winds; and a *small fire* sets loose a forest fire resulting in massive damage and destruction. *So also is our tongue.* It is powerful to either kill or give life, to destroy or to heal. If we desire for God to control our entire life, our testimony in the world, and how people respond to us, we will pray for Him to *control our tongue.* If we want our own lives to be happy (and not miserable) we will ask God to bring our tongue under His control *for every word we speak.*

A JOYOUS THOUGHT FOR TODAY:

Death and life *are in the **power of the tongue.***

—PROVERBS 18:21A

For Today, pray that God will rule as sovereign Lord over your tongue. Ask Him to impress on your heart how *none* of the words you speak are benign, but each has great power to bring life or death into your life, and into the lives of your family and everyone you come in contact with during the day. Speaking only words of life to others is a priceless joy *(Ephesians 4:29).*

Day 100

*So also the tongue is a small part of the body, and yet **it boasts of great things**. See* ***how great a forest*** *is set aflame by such a small fire!* ⁶*And **the tongue is a fire**, the **very world of iniquity**; the tongue is set among our members as that which defiles the entire body, and **sets on fire the course of our life**, and is **set on fire by hell**.*
—James 3:5-6

The word *boast* is most commonly used in scripture in a derogatory sense. So, the phrase *"boasts of great things"* is generally understood to mean our tongue says things that result in great, negative consequences. The phrase *"how great a forest"* refers to the *number of people* we hurt when our tongue spews forth an ungodly word. Within that *number*, we should not overlook ourselves—the one who sparked the fire in the first place (*see* Day 99). Have you ever driven through a region that has suffered a recent forest fire? The spot where the fire started is often times more charred and damaged then the rest of the forest. Even years later, the smell of the conflagration lingers. The broken remains of what were once vibrant trees stand in dead vigil over a blackened landscape. James creates this image to sensitize us to how great the damage is from a *single* ungodly word ("spark") spoken in haste.

James goes on to say that our tongue is *"the very world of iniquity."* The tongue is the realm (the world) in which *all evil* (such as lying, pride, murder, child abuse, slander, gossip, etc.) can be found. This is the channel through which all evil flows and it (the tongue), in truth, *"is set on fire by hell."*

A Joyous Thought for Today:

*Set a **guard, O Lord**, over my mouth; **keep watch over** the door of my lips.* —Psalm 141:3

For Today, this is a great verse to write on a 3x5 card to keep with you during the day. Ask God to shine His divine light on each word you speak; and to imprint this verse on your heart as He sensitizes you to how powerful your tongue is for either good or evil in your life and in the lives of others. Notice that God, not you, is the *only* guard capable of watching over your mouth. And He will, as we just pray for Him to do so.

DAY 101

For every species of beasts and birds, of reptiles and creatures of the sea, is tamed and has been tamed by the human race. ⁸But no one can tame the tongue; it is a restless evil and full of deadly poison.

—JAMES 3:7-8

Isn't it amazing to think of the truth contained in James' words? In India, the locals train elephants to lift large trees and haul them to collection points. Alexander the Great used these same animals for warfare. Humans have trained dogs, cats, goats, horses, monkeys, talking Myna birds, even mice. Lion trainers perform with all manner of predatory cats. Dolphins perform at SeaWorld. There are people who make a living as snake (and even earthworm) charmers in this world. Yet, mankind has *never* been able to tame the tongue.

James tells us that the tongue *"is a restless evil and full of deadly poison."* He has given us another word-picture to consider when he refers to the tongue as *"full of deadly poison."* This describes our natural, fallen, human tongue (with all the fleshly words it holds), ready to strike out with deadly venom (like a serpent) into any victim we come in contact with. That is the kind of tongue we have apart from Christ. It will speak poison from our flesh, our selfishness, our ego, our worries and fears, or from whatever we want for ourselves. Yet what a great mercy of God we have with Christ living in us, and the ministry of the Holy Spirit progressively transforming and renewing our mind—and thus, our tongue. God is faithful to increasingly control our conversation day by day as He draws us to yearn more and more after Him.

A JOYOUS THOUGHT FOR TODAY:

He who guards his mouth and his tongue, guards his soul from troubles. —PROVERBS 21:23

For Today, continue to pray that the Lord will guard your mouth. This continual prayer will keep you out of innumerable heartaches, hurt feelings, broken relationships, and painful memories. Again, this is not something you can amp up in yourself. God is faithful! He will guard your mouth as you continually turn to Him. This is truly "good news!"

DAY 102

With it we bless our LORD and Father, and with it we curse men, who have been made in the likeness of God; [10] from the same mouth come both blessing and cursing. My brethren, these things ought not to be this way.

—JAMES 3:9-10

In these verses, James points out a fundamental inconsistency in our lives apart from Christ. One minute we pray and sing praise songs to the Lord (like on Sunday). But later (on Monday) we say "un-Christ-like" things to (or about) the people God made! James asks how both of these things can come out of the same mouth? When we are critical of the people God made, we are actually being critical of God! We are criticizing the people who are made, not only *by* God, but in the *likeness of* God.

I've mentioned *1 Peter 3:10* before (Day 77), but it is worth repeating here. *"For, THE ONE WHO DESIRES LIFE, TO LOVE AND SEE GOOD DAYS [meaning happy days/ joyous days], MUST KEEP HIS TONGUE FROM EVIL AND HIS LIPS FROM SPEAKING DE- CEIT."* Notice that Peter did not say the person must keep some *other person's tongue* from saying evil things; he said a person must keep *his own tongue* from evil. How important it is, when discussing what James is saying about the evil in our tongue, to realize that this evil not only poisons others but *us* as well. This may sound depressing, but it's not. It is actually very *good news*. James tells us that *no one* has the power to "zip it" by themselves. This isn't about *you* being stronger, exercising more "will power," or more self-discipline to bite your tongue. It's about simply recognizing that Christ lives in you, and just being sensitized to Him throughout your day. He, in turn, will rule your tongue.

A JOYOUS THOUGHT FOR TODAY:

*The one who guards his mouth **preserves his life;**
the one who opens wide his lips **comes to ruin.***

—PROVERBS 13:3

For Today, before you open your lips to speak to others, silently contemplate what you are about to say before God. Ask Him to guard your lips from speaking evil. Ask Him to search your words to find any evil motive or harmful thing in them. He *will* protect you and the listener, and give you *both* greater joy.

DAY 103

*Does a **fountain** send out from the same opening both fresh and bitter water?*
*¹²Can a **fig tree**, my brethren, produce olives, or a **vine** produce figs? Nor can*
***salt water** produce fresh.*

—JAMES 3:11-12

James concludes this section of his letter by directing us to the *source* of our spoken comments and attitudes. He asks what can be *produced* from the fountain, tree, vine, and salt water. To say it differently, *where do all of the words we say come from?*

Matthew 12:34 records a condemnation Jesus pronounced on the Pharisees who were opposing Him. He said, *"You brood of vipers, how can you, being evil, speak what is good [or say godly things]? For the **mouth speaks out of that which fills the heart**."* This is a divine principle: *Our mouth speaks out of what our heart is feeling*. We can't see our heart, but once we know this principle, we know that what we say is a manifestation (or reflection) of what we are feeling in our heart.

So, our heart is the *source* of all the words we say. This means, in practical terms, that when our heart is *feeling* rejected, impatient, disrespected, angry, stressed (to name but a few things the heart may feel), *we will say* unkind things to others as those feelings flow out of our mouth from our heart. As God progressively makes us aware of this, our heart increasingly yearns to pray constantly the same prayer King David prayed in *Psalm 139:23-24*.

A JOYOUS THOUGHT FOR TODAY:

*Search me, O God, and know **my heart**; try me and*
*know **my anxious thoughts**; ²⁴and see if there be any*
*hurtful way [or hurtful feelings] **in me** [toward others],*
*and **lead me** in the everlasting way.* —PSALM 139:23-24

For Today, recognize that God knows you through and through. Pray to Him to search your heart in ways that you have no power to search yourself. Ask Him to search out any anxious thoughts you may have hidden there. Trust Him, as your heavenly Potter, to mold the clay of your heart into His image as it pleases Him and in His timing. Then praise Him because this is *exactly* what He is doing.

*Dear God, I pray that You would deeply imprint King David's prayer from Psalm 139:23-24 into **my** heart. Search **me**, O God, and know **my** heart. Try **me** and know **my** every anxious thought. Reveal any hurtful way in **me**, any attitude or unforgiving spirit within **me**, that would hurt another person. I acknowledge from Your word that I have no power to control **my** speaking or to cleanse **my** own heart. You know **me** far deeper than I know myself. Please mold **my** heart. As Your word in Isaiah 64:8 says, "we are the clay, and You our Potter." Lord, please shape **my** clay in a way that pleases You. I pray that You will guard **my** mouth and keep **me** from ever hurting anyone again from any word that I say. I pray that only words that bring life to the hearer will cross **my** lips from this day forward. Amen.*

A SPECIAL WORD TO THE READER...

Over the last few days (Days 98-103) we traveled with James as he addressed how *negative words* shipwreck marriages, alienate kids, and make our own lives miserable. He spoke with clarity about the evil (poison) in the tongue and how only one critical or demeaning word can set a whole forest ablaze.

Over the next few days (Days 104-107) I want to depart from our James study to consider *godly words*: which are words (and word tones) that produce peace, joy, comfort, and positive change in the very people we most want to encourage and lift up; our spouse, kids, family, and friends.

Of course, this topic could fill an entire book with scripture. For purposes of these next few days, I want to share just three foundational principles upon which all godly communications rest. I have selected these three principles because they have had the greatest impact on *my life*.

DAY 104

*If I speak with the tongues of men and of angels, **but do not have love,** I have become a noisy gong or a clanging cymbal.*

—1 CORINTHIANS 13:1

Principle One: Heart Tones of Love

We all know *1 Corinthians 13* as the "love" chapter, but how much do we really understand how incredible Paul's message is in this section of scripture? Paul tells us that although we might speak with the most eloquent of words to our spouse, kids, family, and friends, and those words may have been carefully picked to be intentionally positive; *if they don't flow from a source of love* (which gives our words the *tone* of love), these words will be received by the listener as nothing more than a source of empty noise and irritation. The words themselves may be wonderful, but the *tone* will tell the listener that our words are not true.

Many parents have heard one or more of their children say (when the parent is trying to correct them), "Why are you mad at me?" or "How come you don't like me?" That response flows from the child's *interpreting the tone* of what is being said. We might be trying to take care with our words, but the child picks up on our heart because *"the mouth speaks out of that which fills the heart" (Matthew 12:34).*

A JOYOUS THOUGHT FOR TODAY:

*The **teaching of the wise** [from God's word] **is a fountain of life**, to turn aside from the snares of death [or to turn aside from the snares of discouragement, poor self-image, worry, fear, etc.].* —PROVERBS 13:14

For Today, pray for God to replace any stress, anger, selfishness, fear, or worry that may be lurking in your heart with His love. This is the first prerequisite for constructive communication. Then, while you are listening to others, continue to quietly pray for God to create a *fountain of life* in your heart from which will flow *His words* of encouragement to those you are speaking to. This is the path to great joy for you and for others you come in contact with.

A PRACTICAL APPLICATION OF LOVE

Scripture is a wonderful thing. It truly is a love letter from God to each of us. When scripture says that God is at work in us *(Philippians 2:13)*, this is what it is talking about. Christ comes into our life and begins a good work in us; that is to say, He begins to grow and transform our lives into His image. He bears the fruit of His Spirit within us *(Galatians 5:22)* in terms of *His love*, joy, peace, patience, kindness, goodness, faithfulness, gentleness, and long-suffering. Scripture tells us that the first fruit of God in us is *love*.

Then, in *1 Corinthians 13:4-8,* He further defines this *love*. Again, the first description of the love God is producing in us (as a fruit of the Spirit) is **patience**. I always thought if I lacked patience, I just needed to pray for more patience. But God's word says that love is patience. Love doesn't try to be patient—*it IS patience*.

Consider for example, someone saying to you: "I'm really trying to be patient with you!" Does that make you feel they are being patient? Or does it make you feel the opposite, that they are rapidly becoming impatient and upset with you? That kind of impatience communicates the message that they really don't love you at that moment because love is patience. It doesn't struggle to be, or *try* to be, it *is*!

When we foster anger toward our spouse for not meeting some perceived need, or lash out at the kids for something, we distance ourselves from the very people we say we love the most. We may feel justified in acting the way we do, but we are undermining the mutual love and respect inherent in the supportive communication critical to family life.

> *But now faith, hope, love, abide these three;*
> *but the greatest of these is love.*
>
> —1 CORINTHIANS 13:13

Day 105

Let NO unwholesome word proceed from your mouth, **but only such a word as is** **good for edification** *according to the need of the moment,* **so that it will give grace to** **those who hear.**
—Ephesians 4:29

Principle Two: Words that Lift up

The second principle is to speak words that lift up, rather than demean, criticize, and put down. It would be great to put this verse on a 3x5 card and read it everyday, especially if the word *"NO"* was printed in bold and all CAPS! This means "let not one" word, *not even one*; proceed from our mouth that does not lift up. The word *edification* means to lift up and encourage spiritually. And the phrase *"it will give grace to those who hear"* means to promote the spiritual qualities of love, joy, peace, patience, etc., in those we are talking to. It may not be instant, but the listener will feel encouraged by what is said.

Having read this far in this devotional book, you know that it is impossible to accomplish these encouraging words on your own. When I am listening to someone, I am silently praying for God to give me direction (whether to say anything or not), and if so, what to say. Often, when God directs me to share something, it is usually a scripture verse that He has recently touched my own life with. When God's words, or words that are sourced in biblical truth, are shared with another person, the result is encouragement. However God accomplishes this, the hearer will feel uplifted. Their burden will feel lighter.

A Joyous Thought for Today:

There is one who speaks rashly like the thrusts of a *sword,* **but the tongue of the wise brings healing** *[lifts* *up and encourages].* —Proverbs 12:18

For Today, ask God to impress on your heart an even greater importance for regularly reading His word, so you will have His living word *flowing through your veins,* ready to encourage and uplift those He brings in touch with your life.

THE DYNAMICS OF SHARING
UPLIFTING WORDS

In my experience, here is how the process works: God is continually drawing us to fill our minds with His words. As we meditate on them, they become our life. They don't become an objective to achieve, or an ideal for us to strive for, or a complex tapestry of theological doctrines to argue over (with other Christians). We are drawn to God's words which touch us as the *living God*. We have nothing to boast about in this process. It is all God, drawing us and caring for us. His word becomes increasingly who we are, as He enlightens us to the *true knowledge of His Son (2 Peter 1:2-3)*. It transforms us day by day into a new person in Christ. As *we* think about what verses say, instead of focusing on our circumstances and failures, the Lord produces peace in us in the midst of whatever we are going through. *"And the peace of God, which surpasses all comprehension, will guard your hearts and your minds in Christ Jesus" (Philippians 4:7)*.

God's living word, however, doesn't stop here. While we are personally experiencing the above, God brings us in contact with others, and we listen to the troubles afflicting them. God's love in us flows out to them because we have gone through similar trials. It is in these times, as we are prayerfully listening to His Spirit in us, that God brings a verse to mind to share with this person. You may not remember the chapter and verse, but you do remember the gist of what the verse says because God has touched your life with it. It could be about **guilt** *over something (Psalm 103:12-14, Romans 5:1, Colossians 2:13, and Hebrews 10:10-18)*; or the **illness** *of a loved one (2 Corinthians 1:3-4, Psalm 23, Psalm 94:19, and 1 Peter 5:7)*; or **selfishness** *(Psalm 34:10, Matthew 5:6, and Philippians 2:3)*; or feelings of failing to live up to God's expectations *(2 Corinthians 3:5, Romans 10:4, and Galatians 5:1)*; or *struggles with* **loneliness** *(Psalm 68:6, 2 Corinthians 1:3, and Psalm 32:10)*.

For every circumstance in our life, God has breathed verses (His living word) into us to bring us through to His joy and peace. His word is living and operative, caring for us His children in every situation in life. Sometimes a verse comes to us by others sharing with us; and sometimes God directs His word to others through what He impresses upon our hearts.

Day 106

*Finally, brethren, whatever is true, whatever is honorable, whatever is right, whatever is pure, whatever is lovely, whatever is of good repute, if there is any excellence and if anything worthy of praise, **dwell [or think] on these things.***
—Philippians 4:8

Principle Three: Praise-Worthy Thoughts

In Days 103 and 104 we saw how *"the mouth speaks out of that which fills the heart" (Matthew 12:34)*. Philippians 4:8 declares this same principle. Notice that Paul did not exhort us in this particular verse to say praise-worthy things, but to *dwell* on praise-worthy things. The *NIV* translates this phrase as *"**Think** about things excellent and worthy of praise."* This verse is addressing how we occupy our time for most of the day when we are not engaged in speaking to others. Our mind is still full of thoughts and considerations. Paul encourages us to take non-speaking times and dwell on praise-worthy things.

Why should we do this? Well, let's say we spend the entire day ruminating over thoughts about our spouse being lazy, inconsiderate, and unappreciative, what will we likely speak to them at the end of the day? You got it—we are almost certain to say the same negative words that filled our heart during the day. By contrast, dwelling on how God is faithfully performing His good work in them *(Philippians 2:13)* and how He will continue to do so until completion *(Philippians 1:6)*—fills our heart with praise-words.

A Joyous Thought for Today:

*Watch over your heart [the source of your thoughts] with all diligence, for **from it flow the springs of life.***
—Proverbs 4:23

For Today, recognize that your heart fills up and overflows with either evil *words that poison* others, or words that are *a spring of life* to others. *The Everyday Bible* reads: *"Be careful what you think because **your thoughts run your life.**"* Pray that God will make you increasingly sensitive to your thoughts (which reflect the desires of your heart). For out of them flow the *springs of life!*

DAY 107

*The **heart of the righteous ponders** [thinks about] how to answer [or how to speak], but the mouth of the wicked pours out evil things.*

—PROVERBS 15:28

How do we say words that *lift up* and *have tones of love* throughout our day? We know now that our thoughts run our life, but how do we check our thoughts? *Proverbs 15:28* says *"The heart of the righteous **ponders** how to answer."* The *"heart of the righteous"* refers to every child of God. The word *ponders* means to consider our words (and our thoughts) before the Lord *before* we speak them.

Let's say you are going through your day and suddenly you are hit with a stressful thought concerning your spouse, kids, a friend, or circumstance at work. *First*—begin to recognize that this *stressful* thought is a "red flag," warning you to ponder it before the Lord. *Then*, ask the Lord to search your heart, and show you anything poisonous in you (which in a few seconds or minutes, if left unchecked, will be poisonous to someone else). Pondering in this way gives the Holy Spirit an opportunity to reveal anger, worry, guilt, pride, sense of rejection, resentment, fear, jealousy, or lack of trusting the Lord *behind* our words. I can't tell you how many times the Lord has completely changed what I was about to say by revealing that the *source* of my thoughts was my ugly flesh!

A JOYOUS THOUGHT FOR TODAY:

*We are taking **every thought captive** to the obedience of Christ.* —2 CORINTHIANS 10:5B

For Today, when you enter any conversation, particularly a problematic one, ask yourself; *what am I feeling? What am I thinking right now?* By checking every thought with Christ, making sure it is something He would think—you will not have to worry whether your words are godly words. As God builds this pondering habit in you, it frees you to speak uplifting words out of love. This brings great joy to you and to those who are listening to you.

My Joyous Thoughts

EARTHLY WISDOM

JAMES 3:13-16

Who among you is wise and understanding? Let him show by his good behavior his deeds in the gentleness of wisdom. [14]But if you have bitter jealousy and selfish ambition in your heart, do not be arrogant and so lie against the truth. [15]This wisdom is not that which comes down from above, but is earthly, natural, demonic. [16]For where jealousy and selfish ambition exist, there is disorder and every evil thing.

DAY 108

*Who among you is **wise and understanding**? Let him show by his good behavior his deeds in the gentleness of wisdom.* ¹⁴*But if you have bitter **jealousy** and **selfish ambition in your heart,** do not be arrogant and so lie against the truth.*
—JAMES 3:13-14

In verse seventeen (Days 111-132) James describes a *heavenly wisdom* by telling us of eight qualities that Christ is gently working into our lives. First, however, he wants us to understand the opposite form of *wisdom (earthly wisdom)*—which comes from within our own *human* hearts without God. James asks us to test what we believe about ourselves to see whether we are living a delusion or not. Do we consider ourselves to be wise and full of understanding? "Yes, I do," some will respond. Okay, if you do, test that belief by asking whether your life manifests any *jealousy* or *selfish ambition*. If it does, then believing you are wise and understanding is not true.

Over the next few days (Days 108-110), we will explore the incredible destructiveness of our own human wisdom compared to the uplifting power of God's wisdom, which is Christ in our lives. Consider these next days as a wonderful opportunity for God to show us that He is the How-Great-Thou-Art Potter and we are just clay. If God did not want us to understand the ugliness of our own fleshly *wisdom* He would not have given us these scripture verses to expose it. This does not mean He expects us to fix the problem on our own. Only God can do that; which He does, as we consider these verses. Scripture tells us again and again that He is shaping our clay into the eight qualities that James describes in verse seventeen.

A JOYOUS THOUGHT FOR TODAY:

Behold, You desire truth in the innermost being,
*and in the hidden part **You will make me know***
***wisdom** [God's wisdom!].* —PSALM 51:6

For Today, dwell on just six words from this verse: *"You will make me know wisdom."* This is a glorious promise, assuring us that in the coming days, as scripture reveals the ugly, destructive wisdom of our flesh, God is in the process of replacing our wisdom with His. Praise God!

DAY 109

*This wisdom is not that which comes down from above, **but is earthly, natural, demonic**.*
—JAMES 3:15

James continues his description of the *wisdom* that flows from jealousy and *selfish ambition* rather than from God. He uses three distinctive terms to identify the *source* and *focus* of this form of knowledge.

First, this wisdom is *earthly*. The closest synonym to this adjective is *worldly*. This wisdom is fully absorbed in earthly pleasures and matters related to this world. It doesn't pray, read God's word, or trust in God for any leading; but draws all of the information it needs from earthly sources. It prefers to accumulate (and then trust in) knowledge gleaned from the Internet, advice from a trendy book, magazine, or fortune cookie, or a headline from a tabloid magazine while standing in line at the grocery store. All of this is the stuff from which this kind of wisdom is derived.

Second, this wisdom is *natural.* This adjective highlights that such wisdom operates solely in the realm of the physical, with *human* reason rather than spiritual revelation. This is often referred to as our flesh.

Third, this wisdom is *demonic.* This is a sobering adjective! It means "of the devil" or under the influence of Satan's demons. Have you ever thought that your own wisdom (logic, reasoning), apart from God, is actually under satanic influence? There is nothing neutral or benign about our earthly, fleshly, wisdom. It can be as destructive as the forces of hell when influenced by demonic powers.

A JOYOUS THOUGHT FOR TODAY:

Trust in the LORD with all your heart and do not
lean on your own understanding. ⁶In all your ways
acknowledge Him, and He will make your paths straight.
—PROVERBS 3:5-6

For Today, realize that as your heart simply turns from earthly, natural, demonic wisdom (your own logic and reasoning) to God's wisdom, God guides your path away from all evil, and in all circumstances increases your joy, peace, and fulfillment.

DAY 110

For where jealousy and selfish ambition exist, there is disorder and every evil thing.
—JAMES 3:16

I have never forgotten this verse since the first day I read it. I put it up there with *John 3:16* for life-changing content. In the context of verses thirteen through fifteen, James is warning us that our earthly, natural, demonic *wisdom* is primarily driven by two evil and destructive forces: *jealousy* and *selfishness*. He says: *disorder and all evil in our life results from this!*

Jealousy primarily refers to jealousy between Christians. We may be jealous of another Christian's spiritual gifts: a gifted speaker, Bible teacher, singer, or person who is financially positioned to give aid to others. We may be jealous of others who appear to be doing better than us; they seem to have a great job, better marriage, angelic kids, etc. We can conclude that they do not struggle as much as we do, and that makes us jealous. We may even be jealous of another church's growth, youth program, or recognition in the community. As God shapes our clay, however, we grow to realize there is nothing to be jealous about.

Selfish ambition simply refers to all forms of selfishness. Pride, lust of the flesh, and lust of the eyes are all spawned from selfishness. We want *what* we want, *when* we want it. We want our spouse to change, and our kids to obey. We want fewer problems in our life (and greater appreciation and respect). We want all of this *for ourself* (regardless of how we justify it). In truth, selfishness strikes at the heart of our sinfulness against God—it is the essence of *idolatry*—we want to be the god who rules our life (without having to rely on Almighty God for anything). One thing is certain: our selfishness *never* brings us the satisfaction we seek. On the contrary, it only brings disorder, disunity, arguing, hurt feelings, resentment, anger, broken relationships, and loss of respect.

A JOYOUS THOUGHT FOR TODAY:

I said to the LORD, "You are my LORD; I have no good besides You." —PSALM 16:2

For Today, pray with the psalmist, "You are my Lord; I have no good wisdom in myself. I desperately need the wisdom that comes from You." *This is where all joy resides!*

SELFISHNESS TEST

Thank God that James does not leave us with only our earthly, natural, demonic wisdom that flows from a heart filled with jealousy and selfish ambition. James puts these verses in context with the next verse that speaks of eight qualities of a heart flowing with heavenly wisdom. Before we move on, however, ask God to search your heart *(Psalm 139:23-24)* to deeply expose any evil of "selfishness" in your life:

- One brother told me that the hardest thing for him to deal with in his life was his wife's negativism. Consider whether your own selfishness makes your spouse's comments "difficult" (because you want a more comfortable marriage for yourself);

- I heard a non-Christian retail store manager comment about a prominent Christian in the community: "I just wish he wasn't always trying to get something from me for nothing—FOR HIMSELF!" Consider how much we sacrifice our integrity when others see us solely being out for our (selfish) selves;

- Consider how we sacrifice time with our family and kids when we are selfishly driven to advance ourselves in our career, hobby, or whatever;

- Through my counseling of couples, I know men who always needle their wives about their weight because they want her thinner—all for their benefit! Consider how these sarcastic (selfish) remarks deeply hurt the ones we say we love;

- One person told me as a child they would go to bed every night in fear that their parents were going to divorce because of hearing them argue all the time. They would run into their bedroom every morning to see if both of them were still there. Consider how arguing, and the evil that results in our kids' lives, is sourced in our selfishness;

- Consider how our selfishness puts unreasonable demands on our kids to perform in sports (or whatever)—to make us proud (or make us look good).

- Add your own experiences here:_____

_____

_____

_____

MY JOYOUS THOUGHTS

WISDOM
FROM ABOVE

JAMES 3:17-18

But the wisdom from above is first pure, then peaceable, gentle, reasonable, full of mercy and good fruits, unwavering, without hypocrisy. [18]And the seed whose fruit is righteousness is sown in peace by those who make peace.

DAY III

*But the **wisdom from above is first pure**, then peaceable, gentle, reasonable, full of mercy and good fruits, unwavering, without hypocrisy.*
—JAMES 3:17

In this verse, James turns to describe the wisdom that comes from above (from God). In contrast to our earthly, natural, and demonic wisdom (Days 108-110), the *first* defining quality about God's wisdom is that it is *pure*. The word *pure* is used in contrast to the *impurities* of *jealousy* and *selfishness* from our earthly wisdom that produces *disorder* and *every evil* thing in our lives.

But how is it possible to experience purity (no resentment, impatience, or selfishness) in our heart throughout our day? How is this possible when we face difficult bosses, inconsiderate neighbors, rude drivers, and our flesh's continual temptations? It is only possible by *looking to God alone to overcome our selfishness!* Note that James 3:17 says that this purity *comes from above*. It is not something we can generate or achieve in our own effort. King David recognized this reality in *Psalm 51:10, "Create in me a clean heart, O God [he recognized that only God could do this], and renew a steadfast spirit within me."*

Many years ago I had an employee that always gave me fits. Quite honestly, I deeply resented him. I knew my feelings were wrong, but I couldn't help myself. Then one day, the Lord caused me to begin to earnestly pray this verse (and I continued to pray it daily): *Create in me, Lord, a clean heart.* To my amazement, in the coming weeks I began to feel *love* taking the place of my *resentment*. I felt *joy* replacing the *stress* associated with working alongside this person. Did this person change in anyway? No, he remained as gnarly as ever, but God worked a joyous miracle in my heart.

A JOYOUS THOUGHT FOR TODAY:

*But as for me, **the nearness of God is my good.***
—PSALM 73:28A

For Today, simply ask God to create a clean heart in you; and realize that the closer you stay in touch with Him (through prayer and reading His word), the more evil He purges from your heart and, thus, the more freedom and joy you will feel in your spirit. The nearness of God is truly *your* good!

DAY 112

*But the **wisdom from above** is first pure, **then peaceable**, gentle, reasonable, full of mercy and good fruits, unwavering, without hypocrisy.*

—JAMES 3:17

The *second* defining quality of God's wisdom is that it is *peaceable*. Remember, *James 1:17* assured us that: **"Every good thing given** *and every perfect gift is from above, coming down from the Father of lights, with whom there is no variation or shifting shadow."* God's wisdom from above (His word and His Spirit), is always peaceable. Note what James did not say. He did not say that God's wisdom is sometimes peaceable and *sometimes* fearful. Or sometimes it is peaceable and sometimes it makes us feel guilty. James simply states that all that is of God (His word and leading in our life) is *always peaceable!*

For many Christians, this is not their experience. They go to church, hear a sermon, and leave feeling more weighted down and guilty than when they arrived. James is giving us an acid test: The more we understand God's word correctly, and pray (have a conversation with Him), the more *peace* we have. The entire Bible is one big, unified, love letter from God. It *is all peaceful.* I don't want you to take my word for it. Let's take the next few days (Days 113-118) to explore other verses that tell us *all* of God's word, all of His direction in our life, is peaceable. In my experience, *if* any part of God's word makes us feel bad, or weighted down, or guilty, *then* we are not reading it right, or hearing it right, or being taught right.

A JOYOUS THOUGHT FOR TODAY:

*For whatever was written in earlier times was written for our instruction, so that through perseverance and the **encouragement of the Scriptures** we might have hope.*

—ROMANS 15:4

For Today, hold up your Bible before you and ask God, "Why did You go to the trouble of inspiring the writing of all this?" His answer is contained in this verse from Romans: *for encouragement!* Not to do a guilt trip on you. Not to weigh you down. Not to make you fearful; and not to make you try harder yourself. But to lift you up, encourage you, and give you hope each and every day as your manna (spiritual food) from heaven. How joyous!

DAY 113

*Her ways [meaning, all of wisdom's ways, or all of God's ways] are pleasant ways
and **all her paths are peace.***

—PROVERBS 3:17, NASB

Wisdom** will make your life pleasant. **It will bring you peace.

—PROVERBS 3:17, TEB

The author of Proverbs was Solomon, the wisest man who ever lived. He sought after God's wisdom with such fervor that he often thought of wisdom, not as some esoteric concept, but as a "she"—a real, live person. Through his writing of Proverbs, we get to peek through a window into the very heart of Solomon and his living testimony of hungering after God's wisdom. It was his personal experience that all of God's wisdom produced two important attributes within him: wisdom is always pleasant and *peaceful.*

Romans 14:17 tells us the same thing: *"For the kingdom of God is **not eating and drinking**, but righteousness and peace and joy in the Holy Spirit."* The *"kingdom of God"* refers to our new life in *Christ.* God *"rescued us from the domain of darkness and transferred us to the kingdom of His beloved Son" (Colossians 1:13).* The kingdom of God is not a long list of religious "dos and don'ts" (earthly things like eating and drinking) that require us to exhaust ourselves trying to live up to them. It is a *person,* God's Son Jesus, who is called the *Word of God (John 1:1-5; Revelations 19:13)* who comes to bring us into the realm of God's *peace* and *joy* today.

A JOYOUS THOUGHT FOR TODAY:

*Those who love Your law [God's word] **have great
peace,** and **nothing causes them to stumble.***

—PSALM 119:165

For Today, hold up your Bible before you again and ask God, "What can bring me to a place where I *never* stumble, no matter what circumstance afflicts me?" The answer is in your hands. By reading God's word, praying to God, and listening to His spoken word (through the Holy Spirit in your heart), He will deliver you from *stumbling,* meaning: He will make His word more powerful in your life than any circumstance, so nothing can rob you of God's peace in your heart, or divert you away from Him. *That's real peace!*

DAY 114

*Grace and **peace be multiplied to you** in the **knowledge of God and of Jesus our Lord;** ³seeing that His divine power has granted to us **everything pertaining to life** and godliness, **through the true knowledge of Him** who called us by His own glory and excellence.*
—2 PETER 1:2-3

Hold your Bible up before you one more time and ask: "What is this?" These verses tell us the answer: it is the *"knowledge of God and of Jesus our Lord."* It is through this *"true knowledge of Him"* that He grants us *"everything pertaining to life"*—grace, **peace**, godliness—EVERYTHING we need in every circumstance. So, as we are drawn deeper into this Bible:

- We grow in *peace*—regarding our relationship with God;

- We grow in *peace*—regarding a child who wants nothing to do with God;

- We grow in *peace*—regarding the conflicts and problems in our family;

- We grow in *peace*—regarding our ungodly work environment/job demands;

- We grow in *peace*—regarding our own daily failures and spiritual growth!

Who is God? *What* is the extent of His love, mercy, and grace for us? *When* can we expect Him to respond to our needs? *Where* has He made Himself available to us? *How* sovereign is He over our lives? These questions are answered as we grow in the true knowledge of Him (through His word). The more understanding we have, the more we realize that even our spiritual growth is not up to us; but entirely up to His working in us *(Philippians 2:13)*, in His timing *(Philippians 1:6)*, and for His glory *(Philippians 1:11)*. We are truly free just to love Him and be at *peace* in *"everything pertaining to life"!*

A JOYOUS THOUGHT FOR TODAY:

*But the **fruit of the Spirit** is love, joy, **peace** [in all things], patience, kindness, goodness, faithfulness.*
—GALATIANS 5:22

For Today, thank God for His fruit (not yours) in your life. Ask Him to increase your *love for His word*, so that you may grow in *more peace* regarding all the otherwise troubling matters in this life. There is no greater source of joy.

A long-time Christian friend of mine showed up one morning at my office and urgently needed to talk. This meeting turned out to be a venting session of rage, discouragement, and all manner of other emotions. After about 10-15 minutes, he stopped long enough to tell me the obvious, "Daryl, I needed to vent; is there any advice you have for me?"

I had been quietly listening through all of it. I said, "Yes, I have one thing to tell you, not 7 things or 10 steps, but just one thing. When you finish venting, if you want to hear it, I'll tell you."

My friend nodded and immediately proceeded to vent for another 10 minutes. In his view, his life was awful. He and his wife were both miserable. His kids didn't want anything to do with the Lord, or with either of them. He didn't have any friends (although he was sitting in the office of one). His new job was not going well. He felt a great deal of guilt and anxiety over failing God in all of this; and actually wondered if he was even saved. He wanted to go to a liquor store, buy a six-pack and some cigarettes, and skip town.

Finally, he ran out of steam and asked, "What is wrong with me?"

I said, "I still have only one thing to share with you." I picked up the Bible that was open on my desk and held it out to him. "This is the Bread of Life! This nourishes your spiritual life just as three meals a day nourish your physical life. When the children of Israel were wandering through the wilderness, just as we are doing in our sojourn through the broken world we live in, God sent them daily manna to eat so they would not starve. They couldn't store it up beyond the day or it would rot and be inedible. They gathered it fresh *each day* from God's bountiful hand. That is what God has provided us in this Bible. Eat a little bit of God's word *each day* and you will experience God's growing peace in all of your circumstances."

He asked again, "But how can I have peace when my wife is so troubled and my kids don't even come around?"

"Fair question," I said. "I'll give you four verses to demonstrate this for you. When you have these four verses *fresh* in your life—that means they are *flowing freshly* in your veins, not something you remember reading years ago—you will experience God's peace that passes all understanding:

Be anxious for nothing, but in everything by prayer and supplication with thanksgiving let your requests be made known to God. ⁷And the peace of God, which surpasses all comprehension, will guard your hearts and your minds in Christ Jesus.

—Philippians 4:6-7

[This verse tells you that there is NOTHING in all of creation for which you need to be anxious about. Is there anything you can think of that is excluded from this nothing?]

*Casting **all** your anxiety on Him, because **He cares for you.***

—1 Peter 5:7

[This verse tells you to cast all (not some, or part, but all) your anxiety on God. What part of *all* do you not understand? God IS caring for you!]

*The LORD will accomplish **what** [or all that] **concerns me.***

—Psalm 138:8a

[This verse tells you the Lord Himself will do what needs to be done to accomplish all that concerns you. He does this in His way and timing; and it will all be for your good, according to *Romans 8:28.*]

*Be still, and know **that I am God** [or I am being God.]*

—Psalm 46:10a, KJV

[This verse tells you to stop fretting and experience God being God in your life.
If He needs your help, He'll let you know.
He is being sovereign over all the things that trouble you.]

My friend lowered his head and admitted that he had not read his Bible or prayed for weeks. I asked him how he would feel if he had not eaten any physical food for that long. He said, *"I'd be dead!"*

"Enough said."

Whenever God reminds us, from His word made *fresh* to us, that He is *continually* caring for us *and for* all that concerns us; and there is *nothing* for us to worry about because He is being sovereign over our lives and is accomplishing all His good purpose for us in His timing; we will feel our hearts lifted up in priceless praise for His comfort *and peace!*

DAY 115

*Therefore, having been justified by faith, **we have peace with God through our Lord Jesus Christ.***

—ROMANS 5:1

The word *therefore* means "because of" or "as a result of." Paul has just concluded his argument that we all have been justified by faith. Notice that the next phrase *having been* is in the past tense. It is not referring to what we are doing in the present to please God, but what Christ has already done (past tense) on the cross for us. The word *justified* means "to be declared righteous." The closest way to think of this is to imagine never having done anything wrong in your entire life. Lots of us would like to start life over and make different choices, but this is even better. The word *justified* means that all of our past mistakes have been erased, as if none of them ever occurred. This has happened because of the next two words: *by faith.* All of our past, present, and future failures have been erased—just by our faith (or belief) in Christ's death and resurrection on our behalf. And even this faith was given to us by God *(Ephesians 2:8).*

This brings us to a wonderful place in the present: *"we have peace with God."* Let that sink in for a moment. As radical as Paul's statement is, it is the pure gospel—we have *peace* with God! This means we are not failing Him; or disappointing Him in any way; nor are we guilty of anything in His eyes! He has no angst or claim against us that He wants to hold us accountable for. He declared us righteous and perfect in His eyes because of the faith He gave us to believe in His Son. We have peace with God *"through our Lord Jesus Christ."* What a wonderful, wonderful basis for our joy!

A JOYOUS THOUGHT FOR TODAY:

*He who was delivered over because of **our transgressions,**
and was raised because of **our justification.***

—ROMANS 4:25

For Today, rejoice in this glorious fact—God is completely at peace with you as a believer in His Son Jesus. Not only that, rejoice in the fact that He gave you the very belief which now justifies you fully in His eyes. He also quickened your heart to respond to Him in love. He further established your entire relationship with Him based on His love *for* you and His peace *with* you. Rejoice in all of this, for this is unspeakable joy!

DAY 116

*But by **His doing** [God's doing] **you are in Christ Jesus**, who became **to us wisdom from God**, and righteousness and sanctification, and redemption, ³¹so that, just as it is written, 'LET HIM WHO BOASTS, **BOAST IN THE LORD.'***

—1 CORINTHIANS 1:30-31

O ur fleshly tendency is to believe that we *ought* to feel guilty about our bad behavior. But don't confuse the working of the Holy Spirit (to draw us toward Christ and away from evil things) with this false obligation to feel guilty. If we are "feeling guilty," then two things have happened in that moment. *First*, we have temporarily lost the *freshness of God's word* regarding His accomplished work through His Son. It is this *wisdom from above* that James assures us will always result in *peace* and *joy*. *Second*, we have replaced God's *living wisdom* (resulting in *liberty*) with our own *earthly wisdom* (resulting in *bondage*) which is telling us that *WE* have some part to play in pleasing God. But Paul tells us in *1 Corinthians 1:30*, "But by *His* doing you are in Christ Jesus." God's peace with us does not come from our efforts to quit some bad habit. It comes *solely* through *God's action* of putting *us into* Christ Jesus. We have nothing to boast about—just the Lord!

I always find it ironic when someone raises the concern, as others have throughout church history in accusing Paul, Martin Luther, and others, that somehow the preaching of the gospel of grace will make the believer lazy and give them a license to sin. Does anyone really believe that any true believer who has Christ's new nature in them (which has a predisposition to godliness) will be comfortable sinning? Not possible! Any true believer will become increasingly miserable doing the very same things they once enjoyed as a non-believer.

A JOYOUS THOUGHT FOR TODAY:

Peace be to you all who are in Christ. —1 PETER 5:14B

For Today, praise God that He is at *complete peace* with you, and you can't do anything to make Him *MORE* pleased with you! He is the sovereign potter in your life, not to condemn, but to lovingly mold you (all in His timing) into the person He desires you to be. It is *all* Him—*none* of you! How could this joy get any better?

A PERSONAL TESTIMONY
The Pen and the Kleenex

Some years ago, I had just finished speaking at a marriage conference. I was back in my car and slowly working my way to the exit of the parking lot. A young woman in her mid-thirties came running up to my car. I slowed to a stop and rolled down my window, asking her if I could help.

She got right to the point. "Mr. Kraft," she said, "I've had several abortions; I'm in my third marriage; I've experienced times of heavy drugs and alcohol; I don't know either my mother or my father. You talked about love in your message, but honestly, I don't know what love is, or anyone who loves me." Turning up her wrists, she showed me the scars from her multiple attempts to commit suicide. With tears now streaming down her face, she choked out a final plea, "Can you help me?"

I didn't know this woman. I wasn't prepared for such an intense confrontation. But at that very moment, God brought to me a thought, and I quickly scanned my car to produce an illustration for her. I found exactly what I needed: a pen and a Kleenex.

I said, "Let's let this black pen represent you. It's fortunate that it is black because I know that is how you feel about yourself. All of your pain comes from looking at all of this black. You can't stand it and you've tried to kill yourself in an attempt to escape it. But here is what this Bible [I had one in the seat next to me] tells you that God has done for you. It says that God put *you in Christ* and clothed *you* in His righteousness. Let me illustrate:"

I took the black pen and wrapped it completely in the white Kleenex to where all the black was gone. I was quiet for a moment and just held the white Kleenex up in front of her. Then I said, "This is who you are in God's eyes. He never looks under the Kleenex. This is your new identity today, tomorrow, and forever. God accomplished this for you. When you just believe this, all of your pain will go away."

I'll never forget what she said. With a quivering voice, she asked, "Can I have that?" referring to the pen and Kleenex. I gave it to her. Then holding it tight to her chest, she said, *"Please pray, that I can believe this."*

DAY 117

*The **steadfast of mind** You will keep in **perfect peace**, because he trusts in You.*
—ISAIAH 26:3, NASB

*He will keep in perfect peace all those who trust in Him, **whose thoughts turn often to the Lord!***
—ISAIAH 26:3, TLB

This verse reveals something very practical about *peace*. It reveals the way to *know* without question *when* God is speaking to us, and *how* to understand what He is saying! Notice how uncomplicated Isaiah's message is. He didn't say, *"He will keep in perfect peace"* all those who live a perfect life! Or who haven't made any major mistakes! No, his message was simple: *"He will keep in perfect peace all those who trust in Him"* and *turn often* to Him throughout the day.

Many of us don't think about God's *peace* when it comes to discerning what to do in everyday circumstances. What do we do when we suddenly become unemployed? What do we say to our spouse or child when a certain problem arises? What do we do when our finances are tight and we are not sure how we will meet future obligations? Isaiah tells us that the answer to all of these challenges is *God's peace*; not just any kind of peace, but God's *perfect peace*. How do we live in a state of God's perfect peace? By *trusting* Him and *turning our* thoughts to Him often throughout the day. In practical terms, this means thinking often about what verses say, and trusting everything to the Lord instead of trying to work out our circumstances using our own earthly wisdom.

A JOYOUS THOUGHT FOR TODAY:

*For the mind set on the flesh ["flesh" referring to our human life] is death [meaning: misery], but the **mind set on the Spirit** [which includes God's word] is **life and peace.** —ROMANS 8:6*

For Today, surround yourself with verses and ask God to turn your thoughts to Him (through these verses) often throughout the day. He will speak to you in a new and fresh way—everyday.

DAY 118

*For the LORD gives wisdom; from His mouth come knowledge and understanding. [7]He stores up sound wisdom for the upright [meaning: all believers]; He is a shield to those who walk in integrity, [8]guarding the paths of justice, and He preserves the way of His godly ones. [9]Then you will discern righteousness and justice and equity and **every good course.***

—PROVERBS 2:6-9, NASB

*For the Lord grants wisdom! His every word [or every verse] is a treasure of knowledge and understanding. [7]He grants good sense to the godly—his saints. He is their shield, [8]protecting them and guarding their pathway. [9]**He shows how to distinguish right from wrong, how to find the right decision every time.***

—PROVERBS 2:6-9, TLB

These verses continue to announce this wonderful truth: that God *will confirm His leading in our lives, every day, through peace.* Isaiah joins this joyous chorus by declaring, *"And the **work of righteousness** will be peace [referring to all of God's work in our life], and the service of righteousness, quietness and confidence forever"* (Isaiah 32:17). God gives wisdom to every believer and James tells us that God's wisdom from above is peaceable. This is how we can *"distinguish right from wrong"* and *"how to find the right decision every time."*

The question to ask, as you seek God's leading, is not complicated. We either *have peace* or *we don't have peace.* If your circumstance is filled with ambivalence or complex options from which to choose, you are likely trying to handle the situation using *earthly wisdom* rather than turning to *God's wisdom.* Ask yourself: Do I have peace about this? If not, then *wait.* If God is silent, then He is telling you that He doesn't need your help at the moment. *Be still, and know that I am God [handling everything](Psalms 46:10a KJV).*

A JOYOUS THOUGHT FOR TODAY:

*For **God is** not a God of confusion but of **peace.***

—1 CORINTHIANS 14:33A

*For **Today,*** set aside anything that is confusing or convoluted. Trust God to guide you, both by His direction and in His timing, *through His peace.*

Day 119

*But the **wisdom from above** is first pure, then peaceable, **gentle,** reasonable, full of mercy and good fruits, unwavering, without hypocrisy.*
—James 3:17

The *third* defining quality of God's wisdom is that it is *gentle.* We still use the word today with essentially the same meaning as James used in his letter. Its meaning is analogous to a mother's gentle caring and compassion for a fussy child; or to describe a horse that has been trained to be careful with its rider; or the caution a parent gives to an older child who wants to hold his new baby sister: "Be very gentle with her." We mean by that to be careful not to hurt her.

We see this same meaning from Paul in *1 Thessalonians 2:5-7, "For we never came with flattering speech, as you know, nor with a pretext for greed—God is witness—⁶nor did we seek glory from men, either from you or from others, even though as apostles of Christ we might have asserted our authority. ⁷But we proved to be **gentle among you,** as a nursing mother tenderly cares for her own children."* So, the prevailing meaning of *gentle* is living with, and caring for, others in a way that doesn't hurt them physically or emotionally. It is a word that should be included in all marriage vows. The preacher should ask, "In sickness and in health, and in all of your spouse's insensitivity and unkindness, do you promise to be *gentle* with them?"

A Joyous Thought for Today:

*Like a shepherd He will tend His flock, in His arm
He will gather the lambs and carry them in His bosom;
He will gently lead the nursing ewes.* —Isaiah 40:11

For Today, as a Christian, you may know with certainty that you are part of God's flock. You are safe in His arms and He is carrying you close to His heart. He will never abandon you, nor will He ever beat (punish) you. Your God is always a loving God who *gently* leads you in the way He has planned for you. As a child who has been so gently treated, pray that God would imprint this gentle spirit on your heart so you will treat others with the same gentleness. *"Let your gentle spirit be known to all men. The Lord is near" (Philippians 4:5).* Praise God, yet again, that *He is doing this!*

DAY 120

*Take My yoke upon you and learn from Me, for **I am gentle** and humble in heart, and **YOU WILL FIND REST** FOR YOUR SOULS.*
—MATTHEW 11:29

In my experience, you can't read *James 3:17* and simply "decide" to be gentle. A "gentle spirit" is the work of the Holy Spirit within us that develops progressively over the entire span of our lives. There is, however, a beginning to this process. God first leads us into a personal awareness of how *completely* and *consistently* gentle He is with us. Read again what Christ shared with us in *Matthew 11:29*. He promised that as we enter the Christian journey with Him, He will always be *gentle* with us as He teaches us along the way. He is not some narcissistic, arrogant ruler bent on punishment and inducing fear in His people. Christ is *gentle,* with a humble heart. He *is* our *gentle* Good Shepherd.

Many Christians, at some point during their Christian journey, picture God in terms that are not so gentle. Have you ever heard someone say, "You better be careful what you pray for" (implying that God's "answer" may be hard to take), or "I wouldn't want to be standing where you are right now" (implying that God might strike you down with lightning if you step out of line too many times). Whenever such lies enter our thinking, it is time to return to *Matthew 11:29* and *1 Thessalonians 2:5-7* for God's truth. Scripture tells us that God always deals with us like a nursing mother cares for her baby–*GENTLY!*

A JOYOUS THOUGHT FOR TODAY:

Now I, Paul, myself urge you by the meekness and ***gentleness of Christ.*** —2 CORINTHIANS 10:1A

For Today, imagine yourself in the arms of the God of all creation! He is able to speak into being exactly what you need, precisely when you need it. Imagine Him caring for you, not only for this day but for every day in your future and forever, as carefully and lovingly as a nursing mother cares for her child. That will bring you *huge joy* for today!

DAY 121

*But God, being **rich in mercy**, because of His great love with which He loved us, ⁵even when we were dead in our transgressions, made us alive together with Christ (by grace you have been saved), ⁶and raised us up with Him, and seated us with Him in the heavenly places **in Christ Jesus,** ⁷so that in the ages to come He might show the surpassing riches of His grace **in kindness toward us in Christ Jesus.***

—EPHESIANS 2:4-7

Paul tells us that God always deals kindly (or He is always *gentle*) with *all of us* who are *in* Christ Jesus. He never punishes us because there is *nothing* to punish us for. Christ took *all* of our punishment upon Himself on the cross. God will not punish both Christ and us for our sins. That would be unfair and unjust, something God cannot be.

This discussion about God's *gentleness* sometimes raises the question about Jesus' wrath in the temple when He overturned the moneychangers. He certainly wasn't very gentle with them! This section of scripture demonstrates that while God is long-suffering in many ways, He can and does often deal with sin directly, and sometimes, urgently. The real question for us Christians is what does that have to do with us? The answer is *nothing!* It is enlightening to see God's sinless anger expressed against unbelief because this gives us a sweeter appreciation of the love and grace He shows *us.* These verses (in context) are not speaking about Christians. God does *not see us in sin* anymore! He has hidden *us in Christ!* Read *Ephesians 2:4-7* and recall the illustration (of the black pen and white Kleenex) I gave you on page 196.

A JOYOUS THOUGHT FOR TODAY:

*Surely goodness and **lovingkindness** [including gentleness] **will follow me** all the days of my life, and I will dwell in the house of the LORD forever.* —PSALM 23:6

For Today, God wants you to see how much He is first gentle with you; even when you fail and feel like you don't deserve God's mercy and grace. He is still *gently* drawing you toward Himself on the path of the righteous. Surely, God's goodness and lovingkindness is following you today! AS the Holy Spirit etches this glorious truth into your life, He makes you more (and more) *gentle* with others. *Praise the Lord!*

DAY 122

The Lord's bond-servant must not be quarrelsome, but be kind to all, able to teach, patient when wronged, ²⁵***with gentleness*** *correcting those who are in opposition, **if perhaps God may grant them repentance** leading to the knowledge of the truth.*
—2 TIMOTHY 2:24-25

In Days 120-121, we saw an important wisdom about *gentleness:* that God has *first* been gentle with us. When God touches our heart with this truth, our own fleshly lack of gentleness toward others begins to drain away. How can we treat others harshly when our Lord treats us with relentless gentleness? This reality is a humbling experience.

Another wisdom about *gentleness* is revealed in *2 Timothy 2:24-25.* When Paul uses the phrase *with gentleness,* he is not meaning that we are to be wishy-washy in standing for the truth of the gospel. We can be *gentle* precisely because we are assured from scripture that it is *not* our responsibility to argue and convince others of anything. The phrase, *if perhaps God* means that *only* God can change a person's heart; *only* He has the power to do so. Paul tells us in verse twenty-five that it is God who may *"grant them repentance,"* not our fancy vocabulary or skilled logic.

When we don't trust others to the Lord, our earthly *wisdom* kicks in and we begin to stress over how we can change them ourselves. We may be convinced that our motives are pure, but they really manifest a spirit of *ungentleness* and harshness. This produces the fruit of disorder and every evil thing: like rebellion and resentment within the hearer. By contrast, *God's gentleness* truly changes others!

A JOYOUS THOUGHT FOR TODAY:

*So, as those who have been **chosen of God,** holy and beloved, **put on a heart of** compassion, kindness, humility, **gentleness** and patience.* —COLOSSIANS 3:12

For Today, ask God to give you a spirit of *gentleness.* Trust others totally to His care. This will free you from relying on your own stressful (and argumentative) earthly wisdom and give you increasing peace and joy. Over time, God will manifest His life-changing *gentleness* through you to others *(1 Peter 3:1, 4).*

Day 123

*A **gentle answer** turns away wrath, but a harsh word stirs up anger.*
—Proverbs 15:1, NASB

*A **gentle answer** turns away wrath, but harsh words causes quarrels.*
—Proverbs 15:1, TLB

This verse gives us a practical contrast between our *earthly wisdom* and God's *wisdom*. God's wisdom always offers a soft and gentle answer when confronted with anger. This goes a long way in calming the other person as well. Perhaps one of our children is angry about something and comes to us in a disrespectful manner. A gentle answer will often cool their attitude before the exchange grows into a full-blown quarrel which could turn into something permanently destructive to the relationship.

The two verses referenced yesterday are good examples of this: *1 Peter 3:1, 4, "In the same way, you wives, be submissive to your own husbands so that even if any of them are **disobedient to the word**, they **may be won** without a word by the behavior of their wives ... ⁴but let it be the hidden person of the heart, with the **imperishable quality of a gentle and quiet spirit**, which is precious in the sight of God."* This verse is using the relationship between a wife and her husband as an example, but the same principle is applicable in reverse. When we are in a relationship with anyone who is being *"disobedient to the word"*—meaning they are being gnarly, unkind, ungentle, selfish, prideful, or demanding, to name just a few fleshly things— *"they may be won"* (or changed) without a word by our *gentle* and quiet behavior.

A Joyous Thought for Today:

*But flee from these [worldly] things, you man
[and woman] of God, and **pursue** righteousness,
godliness, faith, love, perseverance and **gentleness**.*
—1 Timothy 6:11

For Today, pray that God would grant you His wisdom, as a spirit of quiet *gentleness* in all your dealings throughout the day. It is this *wisdom of God*, flowing peaceably and gently through you, that changes people's lives and draws them to Him. In this way, you serve God as a bond-servant and are blessed by Him with great joy!

DAY 124

Just as a father has compassion on his children, so the LORD has compassion on those who fear Him. ¹⁴For He Himself knows our frame; He is mindful that we [all of us] are but dust [equal to dust].

—PSALM 103:13-14

Yet another wisdom about *gentleness* is recognizing that we are *all* made of the same *dust*. This humbling realization is a wonderful safeguard for maintaining a spirit of gentleness toward others. The moment we begin to think that we are better than dust, our spirit of gentleness evaporates. In my experience, one of the fastest ways to lose our gentle spirit is to look at the faults in other's lives more than we do in our own life.

All of our observation of others—like our spouse, children, relatives, and co-workers—leads us down a dangerous path; first to an *ungentle* spirit that is harsh and critical toward the person we are observing. This soon leads us away, in our thinking, from a *grace-based relationship* with God and others (where we recognize that God has done, is doing, and will do it all for us and others); to a *works-based relationship* (where we have some part to play in earning credit toward our salvation or sanctification). This, in turn, leads to either *pride* or *despair*. If we compare ourselves to others and think we are better, this yields the fruit of *pride* in our heart, a critical spirit, and the idolatry of self-worship. By contrast, if we view ourselves as inferior to others, this can lead to *despair* because we believe we can never please God. Christ died to save us from both extremes.

When the Lord causes us to remember that we are made of *exactly* the same dust as everyone else—and we *all* struggle with our flesh—that turns us back to being gentle with others. We stop observing others judgmentally, and return to *our joy* in the Lord.

A JOYOUS THOUGHT FOR TODAY:

Why do you look at the speck that is in your brother's eye, **but do not notice the log that is in your own eye?**

—MATTHEW 7:3

For Today, thank God that He is completely sovereign in your life. Only He can make the blind to see. Only He can grant you *a spirit of gentleness* in your heart toward others. Here is great news: He is, *right now through His word,* making you—increasingly *gentle!*

DAY 125

*But the **wisdom from above** is first pure, then peaceable, gentle, **reasonable,** full of mercy and good fruits, unwavering, without hypocrisy.*
—JAMES 3:17, NASB

*But the **wisdom that is from above** is first pure, then peaceable, gentle, **willing to yield,** full of mercy and good fruits, without partiality and without hypocrisy.*
—JAMES 3:17, NKJV

The *fourth* defining quality of God's wisdom is that it is *reasonable.* The word *reasonable* is translated a number of ways to reflect the fullness of its meaning. In addition to the above two translations, the *Amplified Bible* translates the word as *"willing to yield to reason."* The *New International Bible* uses the word *submissive.*

Regardless of the translation, this defining quality reflects a willingness to listen to others (and yield to what is reasonable according to God's word), rather than continue to remain entrenched in unyielding demands to get *our* way. The essence of what is *reasonable* from God's word is found in *Psalm 34:14b, "Seek peace and pursue it."* Instead of arguing to make a point or gain something for ourselves, God's word tells us to *seek peace;* that is, *be reasonable.*

In the previous three verses, when describing earthly wisdom, James has been discussing the *evil* of our *selfish ambition.* Now, in verse seventeen, he is talking about the *opposite* attribute—to *yield* to the reasonable wishes and desires of others, rather than insist on our own selfish ways.

A JOYOUS THOUGHT FOR TODAY:

*Do nothing from selfishness or empty conceit, but with humility of mind **regard one another as more important than yourselves.*** —PHILIPPIANS 2:3

For Today, listen carefully to others. Silently ask God to direct your side of the conversation with His wisdom, both in listening and in being willing to yield to what the other person is saying. As God gives you understanding of their point of view, follow His leading to be agreeable. This will give you greater joy.

DAY 126

*But the **wisdom from above is** first pure, then peaceable, gentle, reasonable, **full
of mercy and good fruits,** unwavering, without hypocrisy.*
—JAMES 3:17

The *fifth* defining quality of God's wisdom is *mercy*. James tells us that God's wisdom is *"full of mercy and good fruits."* The phrase *good fruits* is descriptive of the *acts* of mercy which flow from God's wisdom. *Mercy* means showing *undeserved kindness* toward those who are in need. At our salvation, when we deserved nothing but hell for our sins, God showed us mercy instead. This was God's undeserved kindness to us.

This, of course, is not the way of the world. Everything in the world is performance-based. People are treated according to what others believe they deserve. For example, work hard for your employer and you may earn a promotion or a raise; make a mistake or "goof-off" and you'll likely be shown the door. By contrast, mercy responds to people's needs, regardless of what they deserve. Mercy does not negate performance-based considerations, but operates independent of it.

Sometimes we learn of someone who has a financial crisis, like a sudden major car repair or unexpected funeral expense. It is easy to judge them with the thought: *IF* they would have budgeted *better,* saved a little *more,* bought *fewer* new clothes, or eaten out *less,* they would now have the funds for their emergency. On that basis, we make some excuse for not helping them. We judged them based on their performance rather than God's mercy. Mercy doesn't consider how they got there, only that they are in need.

A JOYOUS THOUGHT FOR TODAY:

*But **God, being rich in mercy,** because of His great love
with which He loved us, ⁵even when we were dead in our
transgressions, made us alive together with Christ (by
grace you have been saved).* —EPHESIANS 2:4-5

For Today, thank God that He has *always* been, currently is, and *always* will be *rich in mercy* toward you. He never will treat you according to what you deserve! He will forever be merciful to you. Ask Him to etch this defining quality of His wisdom into your heart. Then thank Him because He is doing the very thing you ask *(1 John 5:15)*!

DAY 127

*But the **wisdom from above** is first pure, then peaceable, gentle, reasonable, full of mercy and good fruits, unwavering, without hypocrisy.*
—JAMES 3:17

God's mercy is *full* of *good fruits.* But sometimes, we worry that we can show mercy too much. Let's say one of our kids or relatives gets into trouble of their own making. This isn't some serendipitous problem that could hit anybody. They created the problem themselves through poor life choices. Would it not be interfering with the life-lesson they need to learn through dealing with the hardship themselves? Aren't we enabling poor behavior in the future if we keep bailing them out each time they call?

There is a three-fold answer to this concern:

First, If we are walking sensitive to God's Spirit in us *(Galatians 5:16)*, He will make us know *(Psalm 25:12-14)* when we should grace the person *directly* with mercy, and when that mercy should come indirectly in the form of letting them work it out on their own.

Second, we can't ever be merciful to a fault because God's ability to teach the other person what they need to learn is not dependent on our mercy (or lack of it). This is particularly applicable to parents. I know some Christians who have lived for years with the guilt of feeling that their failures have scarred their children for life. But God has good news for all of us! He knew all along that we would "fail" our kids many times and He is providing a *greater grace* to them according to *James 4:6* (Day 141).

Third, we can't be too merciful to others because God is *full of mercy* toward us! He always treats us—every hour of every day—with a kindness we don't deserve!

A JOYOUS THOUGHT FOR TODAY:

*I know that You can do all things, and that **no purpose of Yours can be thwarted.*** —JOB 42:2

For Today, thank God for this glorious promise: *"no purpose of Yours can be thwarted"*! This allows you to ask God to *fill you* with His mercy toward all others without concern for whether you are wrongly enabling them! This is a priceless joy.

DAY 128

*But the **wisdom from above** is first pure, then peaceable, gentle, reasonable, **full of mercy and good fruits**, unwavering, without hypocrisy.*
—JAMES 3:17

We can associate God's mercy only with our new life in heaven. But this is not entirely scriptural. God's word tells us that His mercy began way back before the foundation of the world when He decided to choose *underserving US* to be children in His family! Then His mercy continued when He revealed His Son in us and put us *IN* Christ, so He could dwell with us and relate to us every day in *this life*. This relationship is always gentle (Days 119-124), never judgmental. God never whacks us, even though we fail daily. He just continues to advance the good work He began in us *(Philippians 1:6)*. God doesn't get mad at us (or think less of us when we don't fully trust Him). He just continues to gently shape our clay for His purpose and glory, and our peace and joy!

Living God's mercy can be a troubling thought: when our kids don't respect us; or our spouse hurts us deeply; or our in-laws still don't accept us; and our employer treats us unfairly. *Luke 6:32-36* asks us: What good is it if we only love those who love us? Christ commands that we love our enemies (or those who disrespect us), *"for He Himself is kind [meaning merciful] to ungrateful and evil men."* So, *"be merciful, just as your Father is merciful [to you!]."* Nothing compels my desire to be merciful to my offenders more than realizing that for as long as I still feel cool and resentful toward them, I'm still lacking the quality that saved me—*MERCY!*

A JOYOUS THOUGHT FOR TODAY:

*O give thanks unto the LORD; for He is good: for **his mercy** [toward you] endureth forever [or every day, day after day, forever].* —PSALM 136:1, KJV

For Today, meditate on the immense scope of God's mercy toward you. Before He made the earth and set forth the heavens, He had mercy on you. Knowing every sin you would ever commit, *He chose you* to be His child. Pray that God will grant you this quality of His wisdom: *Mercy.*

DAY 129

As He was getting into the boat, the man who had been demon-possessed was imploring Him that he might accompany Him. ¹⁹And He did not let him, but He said to him, "Go home to your people and **report to them what great things the Lord has done for you, and how He had mercy on you."**

—MARK 5:18-19

Christians have asked me over the years: "How do I share Christ with my unsaved relative or supervisor?" I refer them to *Mark 5:18-19* to see an example from Jesus' life. Jesus healed a man from demon possession, and the man was so full of joy that he wanted to follow the Lord wherever He went. Jesus sent him home, however, to report what God had done for him and *"how He had mercy"* on him.

Too often, we are ashamed of our past failures and think that God could never use us. We want to hide our past so we aren't an embarrassment to God, but just the opposite is what Jesus told the man to do. He didn't tell him to go home and report what a wonderful person he had been, but rather, *how God had mercy on him.*

I remember a young woman sobbing deeply in a meeting I attended. When I asked if I could help, she told me how sad she was over her past life. She was a new Christian and wanted to serve the Lord (and saw so many hurting people at the place she worked), yet she felt unworthy to talk to any of them. I asked her: "What do your friends need to hear most: how they can become worthy of God? Or how God mercifully forgave you, and has given you a whole, new life in Him, none of which you deserved, and the same is freely offered to them?" These verses brought tears of joy to her eyes. Praise God for His mercy!

A JOYOUS THOUGHT FOR TODAY:

*The LORD is good to all, and **His mercies** are over all His works.* —PSALM 145:9

For Today, trust God's word to set aside any worry that your past living is too shameful for God to use you in showing mercy to others. No one's actions are worthy of God. *Not one! (Romans 3:12).* It is God's *mercy* to those who are *undeserving* that is the *good news*, and source of great joy.

DAY 130

*But the **wisdom from above** is first pure, then peaceable, gentle, reasonable, full of mercy and good fruits, **unwavering,** without hypocrisy.*
—JAMES 3:17

The *sixth* defining attribute of God's wisdom is the quality of being *unwavering.* The word *unwavering* in this verse means to be *without doubt, without any uncertainty,* or *without any ambivalence, wondering,* or *questioning.* James gives us the good news that God's wisdom (His truth) never wavers. In terms of our daily living, this means that as God establishes His truth in us He stabilizes our life and makes us unwavering. He gently conforms our beliefs, feelings, and actions into an unwavering reflection of what scriptures say.

In considering this truth, I am drawn back again to *Psalm 34:10, "The young lions do lack and suffer hunger; but they who seek the* LORD **shall not be in want of any good thing."** God is absolutely unwavering; and He gives this attribute to us as part of His wisdom from above. This *unwavering* quality *infuses us* with confidence that we will never (daily) lack any truly good thing, even in the most adverse of circumstances. Our attitudes and feelings don't skyrocket up one day and plunge into the depths the next. More each day, God causes Himself to be who we trust in difficult times. As He increases this *unwavering* quality in us, *we feel* stable and secure. Regardless of the difficulties of each day, we are stable in Him, without wondering, confusion, or questioning: *unwavering.*

A JOYOUS THOUGHT FOR TODAY:

*And **He will be the stability of your times,** a wealth of salvation, wisdom and knowledge; the fear [reverence, worship] of the* LORD *is his treasure.* —ISAIAH 33:6

For Today, rest in God as your *stability.* He will provide you with a wealth of salvation, wisdom, and knowledge to meet what He knows you need today. Thank Him that He is the *unwavering* One in you; who keeps you secure and safe on the path of the righteous—today, tomorrow, and forever. Rest in this profound joy!

DAY 131

*Even in darkness light dawns for the upright. ⁷**He will have no fear of bad news; his heart is steadfast**, trusting in the LORD. ⁸**His heart is secure,** he will have no fear.*
—PSALM 112:4A, 7, 8A, NIV

Not long ago, I visited an old friend in a local rehabilitation hospital. He recently experienced a stroke, which paralyzed the left side of his body, and he was working on physical therapy to regain his strength. What he told me I'll never forget. He said, "You know, when this stroke hit me, and the left side of my body went numb, I had no fear of dying or even being handicapped. I just knew—what God had established in me from His word—that I was in the arms of the *Great Shepherd* and perfectly cared for by Him."

This peaceful awareness is reflected in *Psalm 119:165, "Those who love Your law [God's word] have great peace, and **nothing causes them to stumble** [or nothing causes them to be afraid or waver]."* Zephaniah 3:17 (NIV) adds this joyous chord: *"The LORD your God is with you, he is mighty to save. He will take great delight in you, he will quiet you with his love."* For over half of my adult life, I wavered tremendously over whether I was really saved. Part of me tried hard to accept what *John 3:16* said, yet I still found myself worrying whether I would actually wake up in heaven when I died. Another part of me really didn't want too much God because I feared He would take all the fun out of my life.

It wasn't until my later years in life that God brought me to a place where I earnestly desired to experience more of Christ's life in me. Is there anything I did to make this happen? No. As far as I know, I wanted the opposite. Yet God one day placed a hunger for His word in my heart as He did for the psalmist in *Psalm 119:165*. Ever since, I have never wavered regarding my salvation. God has established that confidence in me!

A JOYOUS THOUGHT FOR TODAY:

*And the work of righteousness **will be peace,** and the service of righteousness, quietness **and confidence** [or unwavering] forever.* —ISAIAH 32:17

For Today, praise God for His work of righteousness in your heart. He is working peace and confidence into your life. He is making you stable and unwavering.

DAY 132

*But the **wisdom from above** is first pure, then peaceable, gentle, reasonable,
full of mercy and good fruits, unwavering, **without hypocrisy.***
—JAMES 3:17

The *seventh* defining attribute of God's wisdom is the quality of being *without hypocrisy.* The essence of *hypocrisy* is to believe and claim something about yourself that isn't true. The interesting thing about hypocrisy is that others around the hypocrite can usually see right through the hypocrisy. Only the hypocrite is blind to its ugliness. I once did business with another company whose owner constantly witnessed to my employees and sent gospel tracks with every invoice. At the same time, my accounting people told me how this same man was always trying to manipulate the books in order to either cheat the IRS or his partners. *Without hypocrisy* means to say (and act) according to what is true—where others can see what is said and done—is true.

What makes us aware of this ugly hypocrisy in our life and eliminates it? Or, to ask this question in another way: If we claim to be "Christians," what causes our life to look like (and sound like) the seven defining qualities of God's wisdom given to us in *James 3:17?* One thing is certain; we don't have the power to rid ourselves of hypocrisy—it is too deceptive. Paul tells us in *1 Thessalonians 1:5* that it is the *word of God* that causes this change in us: *"For our gospel [or God's word] did not come to you **in word only,** but also **in power and in the Holy Spirit** and with full conviction; just as you know **what kind of men we proved to be** among you for your sake."* Paul didn't deliver *lip service,* but a word in power and in the Holy Spirit, with his own life reflecting (or proving) that truth.

A JOYOUS THOUGHT FOR TODAY:

*For this reason we also constantly thank God that when
you received the **word of God** which you heard from
us, you accepted it not as the word of men, but for what
it really is, **the word of God, which also performs its
work in you who believe.*** —1 THESSALONIANS 2:13

For Today, as you consider this verse before the Lord, it will revolutionize your thinking. It will cause you to realize that it is God's word performing in you what verses say, not you trying to apply verses to your life. This is an awesome joy.

Day 133

*Let the **word of Christ** [or verses] **richly dwell within you.***

—Colossians 3:16a

The phrase *"richly dwell within you"* means for God's word to be what we *continually* think about; and what we *desire most* to shape and direct our daily life. A longtime friend told me recently that he still struggled with a lot of guilt. I asked him why—when many verses assure us there is no guilt! Verses like *Romans 8:1: "Therefore there is now **no condemnation** for those who are in Christ Jesus"; and Hebrews 10:22 (NIV): "Let us draw near to God with a sincere heart in **full assurance** of faith, having **our hearts sprinkled to cleanse us from a guilty conscience** and having our bodies washed with pure water."* This verse tells us that God has removed all of our guilt from us forever! My friend paused for a moment, then said, "I guess it's because I'm still listening to lies."

When we meditate on God's words instead of Satan's lies, God not only tells us that we are not guilty of anything, but He makes us feel that way and live that way before others. This brings me back to *Psalm 119:165* (Day 131): *"Those who love Your law [God's word] have great peace, and **nothing causes them to stumble** [or nothing causes them to feel guilty or hypocritical]."* God's word removes our stumbling over hypocrisy in our life in the same way it does for every other ugly thing. God's word makes our words consistent with our actions. When we tell someone (like our spouse or kids) to trust the Lord, they will be able to see in *our* life a model of that trust!

A Joyous Thought for Today:

*But his **delight is in the law of the Lord** [God's word],*
*and in His law he **meditates day and night** [continually].*
³He will be like a tree firmly planted [or unwavering]
by streams of water, which yields its fruit in its season
and its leaf does not wither [or there is no hypocrisy in
his life]; and in whatever he does, he prospers.

—Psalm 1:2, 3

For Today, pick a verse from God's word and delight in it. While you go through your day, meditate on its meaning and ask God to guide and nourish you. The Holy Spirit will turn that verse into streams of living water that bear God's fruit in your life!

DAY 134

*And the **seed whose fruit is righteousness** is **sown in peace** by those who **make peace.***
—JAMES 3:18

This verse finishes James' comparison of our *"earthly, natural, demonic"* wisdom (verse fifteen) with God's wisdom (verse seventeen) which comes from above. In verses fourteen to sixteen, James has told us that earthly wisdom is pursued by those who have bitter jealousy and selfish ambition in their hearts; who sow these seeds of jealousy and selfish ambition in whatever they do; resulting in the fruits of disorder and every evil thing. By contrast, God's wisdom is pursued by those who make (seek) peace in their hearts; who sow this seed of peace in whatever they do; resulting in the fruit of righteousness filling their daily living.

The Living Bible says, *"And those who are peacemakers [because of God's peace in their life] will plant seeds of peace and reap a harvest of goodness."* James is telling us three things:

- **First,** *when our life is peaceful,* we act in godly ways. We don't act from anger, fear, stress, bitter jealousy, or selfish ambition in our relationship with others;

- **Second,** *when our life is peaceful,* it ministers hope and encouragement to others (*see* Days 79, 104-105); and

- **Third,** *when our life is peaceful,* others are attracted to know our God of peace because God's peace is foreign to the world (they don't see it anywhere)!

Psalm 34:14 confirms what James is telling us: *"Depart from evil and do good; seek peace and pursue it."* To *pursue peace* means rather than argue—*pursue peace;* rather than judge or criticize—*pursue peace;* rather than demand what we want—*pursue peace!* Trust the Lord *with everything,* which leaves you with a heart at peace.

A JOYOUS THOUGHT FOR TODAY:

*A **peaceful heart** leads to a healthy body.*
—PROVERBS 14:30A, NLT

For Today, pursue peace by trusting the Lord for everything that concerns you *(Psalm 138:8).* This peace will not only affect your health, but will extend hope and encouragement to your family and friends. Praise the Lord!

Day 135

*Finally, brethren, rejoice, **be made complete,** be comforted, be like-minded, **live in peace;** and the God of love and peace will be with you.*
—2 Corinthians 13:11

This verse echoes what James has shared with us in *James 3:17-18* about God's wisdom. Living by the wisdom of God brings to our living a pure heart, a peaceable life, a gentle spirit, a reasonable disposition, and a character that is merciful and full of good fruits, unwavering, and without hypocrisy. Now we know the specific nature of the wisdom that James was referring to at the beginning of his letter: *"But if any of you **lacks wisdom,** let him ask of God, who gives to all generously and without reproach, and it will be given to him" (James 1:5).* This explains the call from James to *consider it all joy* in the midst of trials *(James 1:2)*; knowing that these trials produce endurance and endurance produces a perfect result: *"that you may be perfect and complete, lacking in nothing" (James 1:3-4).* To say it another way, *these trials produce God's wisdom in us!*

Paul also writes to the church in Corinth to *"rejoice"* and *"be made complete"* and *"live in peace."* We know from James that it is *God's wisdom* that brings peace into our lives and makes us complete. God's wisdom gives us reason to rejoice! Perhaps this is why in *Ephesians 4:3,* Paul says, *"Being diligent to preserve the unity of the Spirit in the **bond of peace."*** God has given all of His children (every Christian) the *same Spirit,* who lives in *all* of us. That means He is equally at work in all of our lives and will complete His work in each of us *(Philippians 1:6).* There is *nothing* for us to be stressed about in each other. *LIVE IN PEACE!*

A Joyous Thought for Today:

***Let the peace of Christ rule** [or prevail] in your hearts,*
to which indeed you were called in one body;
and be thankful. —Colossians 3:15

For Today, thank God for His wisdom, which He offers you generously and without reproach. He is faithfully growing His wisdom in *you* to make *you* complete and bring you fully into His peace. This is a great cause to rejoice and praise the Lord. This is truly great joy!

PRAYER:

*Dear God, I pray only for Your wisdom to
prevail and rule in my life. Search my heart,
O God, and make it pure. Grow in me a life
that is peaceable, gentle, reasonable, merciful,
unwavering, and without hypocrisy. Touch
my lips that I might speak only encouraging
words to others and maintain the unity of the
Spirit in the uniting bond of peace. Make me
a person of peace who sows only seeds of peace
into the lives of others. Your word promises
me that You are not done with me yet, and
You will not give up until You have perfected
me into exactly what you desire me to be for
Your glory. I praise You for this great promise.
Amen.*

GOD ALWAYS LIFTS US UP!

JAMES 4:1-6

What is the source of quarrels and conflicts among you? Is not the source your pleasures that wage war in your members? ²You lust and do not have; so you commit murder. You are envious and cannot obtain; so you fight and quarrel. You do not have because you do not ask. ³You ask and do not receive, because you ask with wrong motives, so that you may spend it on your pleasures. ⁴You adulteresses, do you not know that friendship with the world is hostility toward God? Therefore whoever wishes to be a friend of the world makes himself an enemy of God. ⁵Or do you think that the Scripture speaks to no purpose: "He jealously desires the Spirit which He has made to dwell in us"? ⁶But He gives a greater grace. Therefore it says, "GOD IS OPPOSED TO THE PROUD, BUT GIVES GRACE TO THE HUMBLE."

DAY 136

What is the source of quarrels and conflicts among you? Is not the source your pleasures that wage war in your members?

—JAMES 4:1

This passage of scripture is typical of many in the Bible which initially sound harsh and negative. You remember from *Romans 15:4* (Day 112), that all scripture was written to encourage us and give us hope. With that in mind, a careful study of the next series of verses in James will leave us praising the Lord. Beginning in chapter four, James moves back to the topic of *how* we make ourselves unhappy (Days 136-140), as a prelude to showing us *how* **God always lifts us up** and makes our lives purposeful, fulfilled, and joyous as we progressively depend on Him for everything (Days 141-142).

The word *quarrels* refers to tense and heated verbal exchanges. This happens when Person One tries desperately to get his point across to Person Two; while Person Two is equally passionate about getting their point across to Person One. The word *conflicts* refers to what all "heated exchanges" produce: A polarization of relationships (the feeling of a wall going up between us and the person we are quarreling with).

James asks a direct question: *"What is the **source** of quarrels and conflicts among you?"* Or, where does all arguing and feeling at odds with others come from? James says the source is US! We will look at this more in the coming days (Days 137-140). For now, know that James' goal is *never* to discourage us, but to speak truth that leads us into lasting joy.

A JOYOUS THOUGHT FOR TODAY:

Keeping away from strife [arguing] is an honor for a
*man, **but any fool will quarrel.*** —PROVERBS 20:3

For Today, ask God to sensitize you to the source of any quarrels and conflicts in your life. He will *both* shine His light in your heart to expose any personal agendas, needs *you* have to be right or control, fear, impatience, selfishness, etc.; and simultaneously use that light as a killing agent against all those fleshly motivations. He will set you free from all troubling feelings within you for His glory and your increasing joy!

Day 137

What is the source of quarrels and conflicts among you? ***Is not the source your pleasures that wage war in your members?***

—James 4:1

Do you remember the "flesh trap" from Days 46-48? James has returned again to this subject to underscore its importance as an insidious source of unhappiness in our lives, and to point us to Christ as the source of all happiness. *The Living Bible* translates this verse: *"What is causing the quarrels and fights among you? Isn't it because there is a whole army of evil desires* ***within you?"***

Not long ago, a friend called me from out of state. During our conversation, he confessed, "My wife and I fight all the time." I asked, "Why?" He was silent for a moment before answering, then said, "I guess it's because I feel so angry at her because she's gained so much weight since we got married." James is asking: Is the *real source* of this husband and wife fighting, her weight gain, or something else?

The phrase *your pleasures* is a topic James covered on Day 45. Our *selfish flesh* wants *more* pleasure, *more* material things, a *more* positive and shapelier spouse, *easier* finances, *perfect* kids, *less* problems and inconveniences, and of course, *more* respect from others and more time for—*OURSELVES!* James is telling us that what our flesh wants is the source of all our discontent and unhappiness. The truth is: ***We make ourselves unhappy, no one else does!***

A Joyous Thought for Today:

*You will make known to me the **path of life;** in **Your presence is fullness of joy;** in Your right hand there are **pleasures forever.*** —Psalm 16:11

For Today, God promises to make known to *you* His path of life which includes His pleasures and fullness of joy. He says these pleasures and joy are in His presence, meaning, you experience them regardless of your circumstances, *through His word and prayer.* What great hope and encouragement is found in just focusing on the Lord. He always gives us more joy!

DAY 138

*You lust and do not have; **so you commit murder.** You are envious and cannot obtain; so you fight and quarrel. ⁴**You adulteresses,** do you not know that friendship with the world is hostility toward God?*

—JAMES 4:2A, 4A

J ames is not accusing all of us of *murder* here. He is pointing out one of the extreme consequences of our selfishness, to demonstrate the deceptive power in what *our flesh wants*. He speaks a harsh truth: our fleshly desires will deceive some people to the point that they will contemplate (or actually commit) murder in hopes of satisfying what *they* want. They may want vengeance over some perceived wrong, or money from a life insurance policy, or attaining "freedom" from a problem they want to be rid of.

If you thought James could get no harsher, jump to verse four where he calls those who lust after their fleshly desires *adulteresses*. He means by this blunt word that selfishness is equivalent to having an "affair" with Satan. In *Philippians 4:19* we read: *"And my God will supply **all your needs** according to His riches in glory in Christ Jesus."* God wants us to trust Him (and *no one* else) to meet our every need. When we believe we still need our spouse to change in some way, or we want a different job, more income, or a larger retirement nest egg, we are saying that God *alone* is not enough to satisfy us. We need something more from the world (or from Satan) to be happy. James calls this spiritual adultery. We will see more of what this means tomorrow (Day 139).

A JOYOUS THOUGHT FOR TODAY:

*But I say, walk by the Spirit, and **you will not carry out the desire of the flesh.** ¹⁷For the flesh sets its desire against the Spirit, and the Spirit against the flesh; for these are in opposition to one another.*

—GALATIANS 5:16-17A

For Today, recognize that you can never defeat your flesh by trying harder yourself, but only by resting in the fact that greater is He who is within you than he who is in your flesh *(1 John 4:4)*. As you remain sensitive to God's Spirit in you and to His word, He defeats your flesh and gives you more of His peace and joy!

Day 139

You adulteresses, do you not know that friendship with the world is hostility toward God? Therefore whoever wishes to be a friend of the world makes himself an enemy of God.
—James 4:4

James uses the word *world* in this verse in reference to Satan's entire system of evil; including the counterfeit (and temporary) peace and happiness Satan offers to lure us away from looking *only* to God and relying *only* on Him. When I say *counterfeit* I mean the belief a person has that more money, more time for pleasure, or something else changing in some way, will make them happy.

Some Christians are confused by this verse, thinking that it teaches we can lose our salvation if we are too attracted to the world. This is not what the verse is saying. No Christian is a *"friend of the world."* *"No one who is born of God practices sin, because His [God's] seed abides in him" (1 John 3:9).* To *practice* sin means to dwell in sin *continually* and to *continually* love its pleasures. But God's seed, the Holy Spirit, abides in us and is faithfully doing battle with our flesh *(Galatians 5:16-17).* While our flesh continues to be attracted to the world's pleasures, we *hate* that it is! When James talks about being an *enemy of God,* he is not talking about every Christian's ongoing struggle with the flesh; but a primary and continual desire of the heart that befriends the world with open arms. This describes a person who is, as yet, unsaved.

A JOYOUS THOUGHT FOR TODAY:

*The one who **practices sin is of the devil;** for the devil has sinned from the beginning. The Son of God appeared for this purpose, to destroy the works of the devil. ⁹**No one who is born of God practices sin,** because **His seed abides in him;** and he cannot [continually] sin, because he is born of God.* —1 JOHN 3:8-9

For Today, thank God that He has given you new birth, and has planted His seed within your heart to abide on a continual basis and oppose the antics and desires of your flesh. Thank Him that He didn't leave you to the daily painful destruction of your flesh, but He is growing His greater new life in you daily. This is *great peace and joy!*

DAY 140

*You do not have because **you do not ask**. ³You ask and do not receive, because **you ask with wrong motives**, so that you may spend it on **your pleasures**.*
—JAMES 4:2B-3

James tells us two destructive habits of those who are filled with quarreling and conflict. *First,* in the latter half of verse two, he tells us that we are not satisfied because we don't pray and seek God's answers and directions to our needs and frustrations. *Second,* when we do pray (in verse three), we often end up praying only for our own selfish benefit! We act like God is some kind of personal servant, who waits silently and patiently for our beck-and-call, to fetch us pizza and cold drinks (or whatever) whenever we give Him the order to do so; merely to satisfy some perceived need we have at any given moment.

Let's take a minute for a reality check. Take a minute to consider what you prayed for this last week. In the midst of your daily hassles and frustrations, what was the motivation for your prayers? Were you trying to negotiate with God or get Him to give you something (more money, better job/boss, a change in your spouse/kids, or to solve one of your problems); or was it a simple prayer for Him to manifest more of Himself (His love, wisdom, trust, patience, peace, joy, kindness, forgiveness, long-suffering, self-control) in your life? This single prayer: asking God to manifest more of Himself in you, replaces all *your* frustration with *His* peace.

A JOYOUS THOUGHT FOR TODAY:

Declaring the end from the beginning, and from
ancient times things which have not been done, saying,
*'My purpose will be established, and **I will accomplish***
all My good pleasure.' —ISAIAH 46:10

For Today, consider your prior week of prayer to God and the questions posed above. Regardless of your answers, there is no reason to be discouraged. God *is at work in you (Philippians 2:13),* and He promises that *He will* accomplish *ALL* of His good pleasure *in your life.* It is His good pleasure to *draw you* closer to Himself and grant you greater peace and joy each day. It is priceless joy to know that He is doing this.

Day 141

*Or do you think that the Scripture speaks to no purpose: "He **jealously desires the Spirit** which He has made to dwell in us"? ⁶But **He gives a greater grace.** Therefore it says, "GOD IS OPPOSED TO THE PROUD, BUT GIVES GRACE TO THE HUMBLE."*
—JAMES 4:5-6

Verse five can be a bit difficult to understand. I believe the best interpretation of what James is telling us is this: *God "jealously" wants His Spirit (which now dwells in us) to be our complete fulfillment;* or to say it a different way, to permeate fully and completely every aspect of our life. This is what God's work in us day by day is all about *(Philippians 2:13)*—being *"transformed into the same image [as His Son] from glory to glory, just as from the Lord, the Spirit" (2 Corinthians 3:18).*

James then goes on in verse six to tell us how we experience that fulfillment. To me, this verse is one of the most powerful verses in all of scripture: *"God is opposed to the proud, but gives grace to the humble."* We hear Christians quote the first phrase of verse six to each other when they say, "God will give you the grace." But the latter half of this verse reveals a solitary condition for receiving that grace. That one condition is a *humble* heart versus a *proud* heart. A proud heart believes that it can arrange (and rearrange) all the ducks on life's pond to bring about contentment and happiness. God is opposed to that.

The humble heart believes *only God* can satisfy and make us happy. A humble heart believes *THE LORD* is the source of all peace, joy, fulfillment, spiritual growth, and the strength and ability to deal with whatever difficulty in life.—The humble heart trusts in the Lord for *EVERYTHING (Isaiah 33:6)!*

A JOYOUS THOUGHT FOR TODAY:

*He teaches the **humble** His way.* —PSALM 25:9B

For Today, pray that God will grant you a humble heart to receive His grace in the midst of your current circumstances. Ask Him to give you a deeper understanding of His love and care for you *(2 Peter 1:2-4)* to the point where you give up any prideful struggling, and recognize that He alone can satisfy; and teach you His ways of peace and joy! As you pray this prayer, you will feel Him *lift you up;* which is the meaning of James 4:6, *"He gives grace to the humble."*

DAY 142

*Therefore **humble yourselves** under the mighty hand of God [or, trust God with everything], that **He may exalt you** at the proper time, ⁷casting all your anxiety on Him, because **He cares for you.***
—1 PETER 5:6-7

W hen we trust the Lord for everything, God *exalts* us (in His way and in His timing). The word *"exalt"* means to be lifted up to a jubilant, glorious sense of well-being *by God*. To be exalted means to have no unfulfilled desires, or any sense of real need. It means to be totally satisfied! James will further explore being exalted by God in future days (Days 147-150); for now, recognize that exaltation is the result of God's work to humble us, and make us totally dependent on Him—the *How-Great-Thou-Art Almighty God!*

When I came to understand that God *alone* will meet my every need; and *lift me up* no matter what circumstance I find myself in, to a jubilant sense of well-being—as I just depend on Him—I was compelled to look at everyone else in a new light. I recognized that any unhappiness I am feeling is never because of something someone else did or didn't do, but always because of some remaining awful, ugly, fleshly desire in me. This realization, in turn, caused me to never want the people I say I love the most (my wife and family) to feel inadequate in any way because of a less-than-humble me! This has been a profound life-changing truth for me!

A JOYOUS THOUGHT FOR TODAY:

*I will **rejoice greatly** in the LORD, **my soul will exult in my God;** for He has clothed me with garments of salvation, He has wrapped me with the robe of righteousness.* —ISAIAH 61:10A

For Today, rejoice greatly and exult in your God, for He has done (and is doing) *everything* for you! He promises to always lift you up. He has clothed *you* in salvation and adorned *you* in righteousness. He is continuing, day by day throughout your life, to bring *you* fully and completely to trust Him for everything. *He is doing it all!* You are left to just praise and worship Him. What could be greater joy!

PRAYER

Dear Lord, Your uplifting word leaves me speechless as to how I can adequately thank You for all You have done and are continuing to do in my life. I confess that my human tongue is inadequate to give You the praise, honor, and worship You deserve. Grant me a humble heart, dear God, to exult You and declare Your wondrous acts in my life which give comfort and total fulfillment to my heart. As I continue through the remainder of my days in this fallen world, I desire only to praise You! Amen.

MY JOYOUS THOUGHTS

THE FREEDOM
OF
"SUBMISSION"

JAMES 4:7-8A

Submit therefore to God. Resist the devil and he will flee from you. [8]Draw near to God and He will draw near to you.

DAY 143

Submit therefore to God. Resist the devil and he will flee from you.

—JAMES 4:7

In the preceding verses (one through six) James talked about the cause of all our arguments and conflicts in life. We learned that it was *our* selfish desires, which we pursue instead of God, because we believe that a bit more respect, money, or time for ourselves (or less problems) will make us happy. James tells us in verse seven, however, that the *one thing* which truly makes us happy is just submitting to God. God always makes our happiness—*SIMPLE*—because we are His dearly-loved children.

Of course, our flesh hears the word *submit* and instantly bristles; interpreting it to mean "to surrender our happiness." We may have to do it because God says so, but we don't have to like it. James, however, intends for us to understand an entirely different meaning. To *submit* to God is an invitation to just *trust in Him,* and *rest in what His word says,* which produces true happiness, peace, and joy in our lives.

We see this principle throughout scripture. *Psalms 144:15b (KJV)* says, "*Happy is that people, ... whose God is the LORD,*" meaning the people who submit to (or trust in) the Lord. *Proverbs 16:20 (KJV)* declares, "*He that handleth a matter wisely shall find good: and whoso trusteth in the LORD, happy is he.*" We find an example of what it means to trust in the Lord in *Psalm 25:12,* "*Who is the man who fears [reveres, worships] the LORD? He **will** [not He may or He might, but He will] instruct him in the way he should choose.*" Submitting to God simply means trusting and resting in the fact that God, out of His enormous love for us, is directing (and will continue to direct) our life—*DAILY!*

A JOYOUS THOUGHT FOR TODAY:

*But they who seek the LORD **shall not be in want**
of any good thing.* —PSALM 34:10B

For Today, join King David in submitting to God by *just resting* in His glorious promises to you. You no longer need to stress over not having enough retirement. You don't have to be concerned about people taking advantage of you, or saying negative things about you. You don't even have to worry about your children or friends *(Philippians 4:6).* God is actively drawing you to seek Him more and more—to the point where you feel no lack, no need, nor want of any good thing. *Praise the Lord!*

A PERSONAL TESTIMONY

DEFENDING MY REPUTATION

A number of years ago, when I first moved my business to Coeur d'Alene, Idaho, we had to let a Christian employee go. This was not a surprise to him. We had worked with him for an extended period of time with much counseling and effort to find accommodation for his needs—all without success.

The entire separation package the company gave him was generous under the circumstances, yet as soon as he left, we began to hear through the grapevine a series of horrible, hateful, and angry things about the company and me personally. I was perplexed and puzzled how so many negative attacks could come from what I thought was an amiable parting.

My first thoughts were full of stress. I was very new to the community and felt I needed to defend my reputation. I wanted to investigate this man further, track down every person he had spoken to, and set them all straight!

Then the Lord brought His word from *1 Peter 5:7* to my mind and spoke it as though he had written it personally to me: "Daryl, when I said, 'cast all your cares upon Me because I am caring for you,' I was including your reputation!"

That timely word stopped me in my tracks. In the middle of all my stressing and anxiety about a situation (that I felt was completely undeserved and unfair), God brought His word to me. As I simply submitted to that truth, and left my reputation to the Lord's care—I can't tell you how much weight and worry I felt lifted from my shoulders. It was not long, through other timely verses, that I actually grew to empathize and feel compassion for this man. Through the course of this situation, I realized that God had used all of this negative experience to grow a firmer faith in me—to trust Him with EVERYTHING!

DAY 144

Submit therefore to God. **Resist the devil and he will flee from you.**
—JAMES 4:7

This verse sounds like James is calling on us to both *submit* to God and *resist* the devil in our own effort. But we already saw in Day 143 what it means to "submit" to God: to *trust* in Him and *rest* in the promises He gives us in His word.

But now James tells us to *resist the devil* and he will flee from us. How do we do that? Let's begin by understanding what James is referring to when he mentions the devil. All of us have experienced *worry* that we cannot shake, *anger* that eats away at us like cancer, *guilt* that troubles us deeply, or *discouragement* that oppresses us. James tells us to resist the devil (or resist the worry, anger, guilt, or discouragement) and he will flee from you (including all the manifestations of his evil). But how do we resist him?

A wondrous thing about scripture is it explains itself. In *1 Peter 5:9* God's word says, *"But resist him [the same word for resist in James 4:7],* **firm in your faith,** *knowing that the same experiences of suffering are being accomplished by your brethren who are in the world."* In this verse, Peter tells us that it is a firm faith that "resists" the devil! Or to say it another way, *a firm faith* keeps us from feeling discouraged, worried, angry, guilty, impatient, selfish, to name a few of the devil's evil devices that distract us from God. But that raises a further question: *Where* does a *firm faith* come from?

Look at *Romans 10:17* for the answer: *"So faith [or a firm faith] comes from hearing, and hearing by the word of Christ."* From this verse we see that it is *God's word* that produces *a firm faith* in us, and resists the devil!

A JOYOUS THOUGHT FOR TODAY:

But the **Lord is faithful,** *and* **He will strengthen and protect you** *from the evil one.* —2 THESSALONIANS 3:3

For Today, gain from James this glorious, freedom-producing understanding: resist the devil (his discouragement, selfishness, worry, fear, anger, guilt, etc.) *by reading and meditating on God's word (Psalm 119:165).* The Lord is faithful to strengthen and protect you from *all* of Satan's attacks, because He loves you more than you know.

Day 145

*Let us draw near to God with a sincere heart in **full assurance of faith** [or firm faith, or firm belief], having our hearts sprinkled [in Christ's blood] to **cleanse us from a guilty conscience** and having our bodies washed with pure water.*
—Hebrews 10:22, NIV

This verse in Hebrews gives us a great example of what James has been talking about. The author of Hebrews tells us to come before the presence of God, not in a shy or embarrassed way, but in total peace; with full assurance of faith, having our hearts sprinkled with Christ's blood to cleanse us from what? From a guilty conscience!

Not long ago, I talked to a dear Christian brother over lunch. He was about my age and ministers to a lot of people. During our conversation, he shared that he still struggled with deeply-held guilt, particularly over so many of his failures from before he came to know the Lord. I have no doubt this brother has quoted this same scripture to others, but during this lunch period, he had lost sight of it. I had just been studying this verse, so I asked him to take out his phone and call up *Hebrews 10:22.*

I tell you, just watching him read this one verse, and to see the relief on his face, was priceless. I watched as that word penetrated deep within him *(Hebrews 4:12)* and showed him that he has been clothed with the righteousness of Christ (and he has no more sin before God), so there is no more guilt (past, present, or future) for him to worry about again. I watched that *WORD OF GOD* instantly counter Satan's lies with the only power that can—God's Power! God causes His word to become *firm faith* (what we truly believe). This faith resists every attempt by the devil to make us feel guilty.

A Joyous Thought for Today:

*As for you, **you meant evil against me, but God meant it for good** in order to bring about this present result, to preserve many people alive.* —Genesis 50:20

For Today, rest in the *firm faith* that God converts all the wrongs that others intend for you into something for your good. This faith mightily resists the devil when he tries to make you angry or resentful as others do you wrong. This *firm faith* is true peace and joy!

Day 146

Draw near to God and He will draw near to you.

—James 4:8a

The phrase *"draw near to God"* does not mean that we are far away from God and need to get closer to Him. It simply means *"trust God."* Let's look to God's word to confirm this understanding. In *Psalm 73:28a (KJV)* the psalmist declares, *"But it is good for me to draw near to God."* This phrase, *"draw near to God"* is the same phrase used in *James 4:8*. Then in the second half of this verse, the psalmist explains what it means to *draw near to God: "I have put my trust in the Lord God, that I may declare all thy works."* From this verse, we see that trusting God is what "drawing near to God" means. As God draws us to trust Him (which includes trusting in what verses say), or believing every verse of scripture with a *firm faith* because God wrote it, we will declare how wonderful it is to experience God caring for us! Our faith will grow firmer—and our acts of human self-effort will grow weaker. We will increasingly experience the truth contained in *Romans 8:28:* God is working *all* things together *for our good!*

This is precisely what James is sharing with us in *James 4:8,* when he declares, *"and He [the Lord] will draw near to you."* This means we will *feel* His wonderful care so much that we will be unable to contain our praise.

A Joyous Thought for Today:

The Lord your God is with you, He is mighty to save. He will take great delight in you, He will quiet you with His love [or we will feel Him doing this], He will rejoice over you with singing. —Zephaniah 3:17, NIV

For Today, pray for God to bring you to fully trust this verse in your heart. It says that God is mighty to save. You know that He hung His own Son on the cross in order to redeem you by name and include you in the Lamb's book of life. And He required *nothing* from you! Yes, you believed in Him, but God gave you the faith to believe. How marvelous is that? This verse is contemplating all of this. He will take great delight in you—every day. Part of that delight is that He will *quiet you* with His love, meaning you will *feel* His love more and more in you—and surrounding you *(Psalm 32:10). Great joy!*

A PERSONAL TESTIMONY
QUIETING MY LIFE WITH HIS LOVE

Many Christians get uncomfortable or cautious when anyone begins to talk about "feelings." Overall, this is a wise caution if feelings are being promoted as a preliminary or primary object and goal of faith. That is the opposite of what I am sharing with you from James. My own testimony concerning "feelings" relates to the consequence (or result) of all of God's work within me over decades of my life. There is no other way to describe it but to share with you how much I feel the Lord continuing to "quiet my life" with His love." He continues to:

- Quiet my fear of dying;

- Quiet my guilt over my many past failures;

- Quiet my guilt over feeling that I am still not doing enough for Him;

- Quiet my feeling that I am still not a "good enough" Christian;

- Quiet the disunity I felt for years with other believers who had different understandings of scripture than mine, and wanting to argue with them all the time;

- Quiet my angry responses to being criticized;

- Quiet my stress amidst the ups and downs of everyday circumstances;

- Quiet my need to be right;

- Quiet the feeling that "I need to fix" whatever;

- Quiet my worry about my children.

My testimony is this: I could *never* have made progress on even a single one of these issues in my own effort. But by trusting, or just by submitting to what scripture verses say, I have experienced a progressive quieting of my life in all of these areas and many more. It genuinely brings you to a place where you can no longer contain the overflow of your praise and worship to God for all *HE* has done. Praise the Lord!

MY JOYOUS THOUGHTS

GOD EXALTS US

Cleanse your hands, you sinners; and purify your hearts, you double-minded. ⁹Be miserable and mourn and weep; let your laughter be turned into mourning and your joy to gloom. ¹⁰Humble yourselves in the presence of the Lord, and He will exalt you.

Day 147

*Cleanse your hands, you sinners; and **purify** your hearts, you double-minded.*
—James 4:8b

Yet again, James' tough speech can sound harsh, like an angry command from God. But that is not what James is saying. To understand James at this point in his letter, we may look to other scripture to gain meaning and insight, which always produces joy.

In *2 Corinthians 7:1,* Paul says, *"Therefore, having these promises, beloved, let us **cleanse ourselves** from all defilement of flesh and spirit, perfecting holiness in the fear of God."* The word *cleanse* is the same word used in *James 4:8.* The word does not mean to strive to make ourselves more righteous than Christ has *already* made us! It simply means to separate ourselves—in terms of our daily living—from all that is evil (like, our flesh's selfishness, immoral thoughts, arguing, anger, and all such things).

James has already counseled us as to what separates us from all our flesh's ugly and painful thoughts, feelings and actions. He said in *James 1:21,* *"Therefore, putting aside all filthiness and all that remains of wickedness, **in humility receive the word implanted,** which is able to save your souls."* To receive the word implanted does not mean to try harder in our own effort to apply God's word, but rather in *humility* to *receive it* (with a heart of soft wax, Days 70-71); to be a receptacle of God's word which He has implanted into us. His word is able to conform our entire life into what it says, like the potter molds his clay.

This reminds us that the Christian life *never* grows out of focusing on ourselves for *anything,* but always directs back to focusing on God for *everything.* Praise Him!

A Joyous Thought for Today:

*For this reason we also constantly thank God that when you received the word of God which you heard from us, you accepted it not as the word of men, but for what it really is, **the word of God, which also performs its work in you who believe.*** —1 Thessalonians 2:13

For Today, thank God that His word alone contains the power to accomplish **all** that God desires in your life. Thank Him that He is continuing to battle your flesh *(Galatians 5:17)* and "purify your heart" *(Philippians 1:6).* This is enormous joy!

CONNECTING THE THEOLOGICAL DOTS

Always remember that God's word, from *Genesis 1:1* to *Revelation 22:21* is a divinely revealed *personal love letter* from God *to you* (*see* page 115). This means, in practical terms, that when you think a particular scripture sounds harsh, like *James 4:8-9* may initially sound to you; it is most likely due to the fact that you do not yet fully understand what the verse means, and *how* what it says is accomplished.

Some of this misunderstanding comes from the fact that many well-intentioned Christians believe that once we "get saved," we need to "get going" with the work of discipleship and do as much for God as we can in appreciation for our salvation. This is a presupposition that they bring to their understanding and interpretation of every scripture they read.

Similarly, if we adopt an impression of God from the Old Testament as a stern taskmaster who expects us always to be righteous and perfect in all of our actions, then verses like *James 4:8-9* will be interpreted as demanding *even more* commitment and effort from us. From this perspective, scripture appears to be always demanding that we try harder and harder because it is our responsibility to do so as good disciples.

By contrast, Paul points us in a different direction. He said the goal of his ministry was for *Christ to be formed in you (Galatians 4:19)*. He revealed in *Philippians 3:10* the passion that drove his own life, *"That I might know Him and the power of His resurrection"* [meaning, that I might experience more of Him myself]. This is the fundamental lesson of *Luke 10:38-42*: Mary's overriding desire to be in the Lord's presence. If you see God as your loving father, caring for you as gently as a *nursing mother cares for her own children (1 Thessalonians 2:7)* then these same words in *James 4:8-9* have an entirely different meaning—they are **all** a call to just humbly rest in God's loving care.

That is why *2 Peter 1:3* emphasizes the importance of growing in understanding the *true knowledge* of God. As we have seen in Day 147, and will see in Days 148-150, **all of God's word sheds light on all of God's word!** Many verses need the light of other scripture to be understood correctly. That is why *2 Timothy 2:15 (TLB)* tells us to study scripture, to accurately *"Know what his Word says and means."*

DAY 148

*Cleanse your hands, you sinners; and **purify** your hearts, you **double-minded.***
—JAMES 4:8B

To go deeper into this verse, we must return to *2 Corinthians 7:1, "Therefore, having these promises, **beloved,** let us **cleanse ourselves** from all defilement of flesh and spirit, perfecting holiness in the fear of God."* The word *beloved* means *to you who God loves* (not to you who God is upset with). And the phrase *"having these promises"* refers to the promises that God had previously given (to those He loves) in the last few verses of the preceding chapter. In *2 Corinthians 6:16* we read, *"Or what agreement has the temple of God with idols? For **we are the temple of the living God;** just as God said, 'I **will dwell in them** and walk among them; and I **will be their God,** and they shall be **My people.'"** It does not say we will be the temple of the living God IF we cleanse ourselves, and are righteous enough. No, we *ARE* the temple of the living God. It is not what we *need to* achieve, but what God *has done.* God has already cleansed us with the blood of Jesus and now dwells in us.

With this understanding, we return to *James 4:8.* The phrases *"cleanse your hands," "purify your hearts,"* and *"you double-minded"* are all referring to earlier exhortations of James, particularly the double-minded man in *James 1:8* (Day 27). James exhorts us to humble ourselves and single-mindedly *TRUST GOD*—who lives in us and is caring for us—instead of trusting our fleshly desires (which are the cause of all of our conflicts and unhappiness) that James discussed earlier in chapter four (Days 136-140). It is by trusting God alone that our hands (what we do) are cleansed, and our hearts (what we think and feel) are purified—not by *our effort,* but by *our trust in Him and His work in us.*

A JOYOUS THOUGHT FOR TODAY:

*But if we walk in the Light as He Himself is in the Light [referring to all Christians], we have fellowship with one another, and **the blood of Jesus His Son cleanses us from all sin.*** —1 JOHN 1:7

For Today, to experience even greater joy, simply trust in what scripture tells you. You *have been* cleansed by the blood of Jesus. Christ now resides in you (*you* are the temple of the living God). He is continuing to cleanse your attitudes and actions for His glory and your greater peace and joy *(1 Corinthians 3:17).*

I have listened to many Christians describe their thinking while going through their day. All of their comments boil down to two main classifications (or focus-points):

They are weighted down with *Self-focus:*

- Thinking continually about *their* past failures;

- Dwelling on the way others mistreat—*them;*

- Obsessing over what *they* need to do to solve *their* problems;

- Worrying over how to protect *themselves;*

- Stressing over how to "fix" *their* kids, *their* spouse, or *their* co-workers.

They are lifted-up with *God-focus:*

- "The more I just talk to the Lord, the less stress I have."

- "The more time I spend reading/meditating on His word ...."

What is *YOUR* focus throughout your day?

- _____

- _____

- _____

- _____

DAY 149

*Be miserable and **mourn** and **weep;** let your laughter be turned into mourning and your joy to gloom.*

—JAMES 4:9

To correctly understand this verse, it is first important to note what James is *not* saying. He did not say, "Be miserable, mourn, weep, *and feel guilty.*" Nor does he say, "Be miserable, mourn, weep, *and ask God to forgive you.*" If God wanted us to ask forgiveness every time we failed, this is the perfect verse to tell us that. After all, James is talking about what we should do whenever we fall back into our flesh.

Let's look again to scripture. *Hebrews 10:22 (NIV)* reads, *"Let us draw near to God with a sincere heart in full assurance of faith, having our hearts sprinkled to **cleanse us from a guilty conscience** and having our bodies washed with pure water."* In *1 John 2:12* we read, *"I am writing to you, little children, **because your sins have been** [past tense; all our past, present, and future sins have been] **forgiven you** for His name's sake."* In light of these verses, we see why James does not tell us in *James 4:9* to feel guilty or ask to be forgiven.

What is James saying in verse nine? *The Living Bible* reads, *"Let there be **tears** for the wrong things you have done. Let there be **sorrow** and **sincere grief.** Let there be **sadness** instead of laughter, and gloom instead of joy."* James tells us to grieve over our failures, *not* to feel guilty, discouraged, or rejected by them. What is it to have *sincere grief?* Paul shares of his own struggles with wanting to do what is good but finding his flesh wanting to do what is sinful *(Romans 7:21-24).* In his grief, he cries out *"Wretched man that I am!"* He doesn't ask for forgiveness (because he knows he has been forgiven). He does, however, *sincerely grieve* over his flesh. James and Paul are describing a *process of growing humility.*

A JOYOUS THOUGHT FOR TODAY:

*<div align="center">**Thanks be to God** through Jesus Christ our Lord! So then, on the one hand I myself with my mind [or my heart's desire] am serving the law of God, but on the other, with my flesh the law of sin.</div>* —ROMANS 7:25

For Today, be encouraged by Paul's example. He sincerely grieves over his sins, but in the next breath is thanking God for His deliverance through Jesus Christ our Lord! Like Paul, praise God as you live and experience His joy every day, *even amidst your failures!*

DAY 150

*Humble yourselves in the presence of the Lord, and **He will exalt you.***
—JAMES 4:10

H aving brought us through several verses of tough reflection, James brings us to one of the greatest invitations to daily freedom and rest in all of scripture. He tells us to *humble* ourselves. He didn't say, "Be sure to do these seven things to please God." He said simply, *humble yourselves.* To *humble yourselves* means to *depend on the Lord for everything*—to admit *you can't* accomplish a single good, divine quality (true happiness, patience, unconditional love, peace, joy, fulfillment, etc.) *in your life.* Only God can.

Putting this verse in context gives us more insight into the process God uses to humble us. The mourning and weeping that James exhorts us to do when faced with our sins is part of this humbling process. This, in turn, is part of the Lord's overall progressive work in us to bring us low—so He can lift us up and exalt us. As He shines His light, through His word, into the hidden recesses of our heart, He exposes selfishness and all manner of evil in us. This brings us "low" to a *humble* position (Days 35, 40, 141-142), where we recognize that we are totally incapable of defeating our flesh. We give up trying to make ourselves happy, and work things out with our own earthly wisdom (Days 108-110), and cry out to God for His wisdom (from above) (Days 111-132).

When God brings us to this place of humility, there is a purpose to it. James tells us that it is precisely from this position that *God exalts us!* To say it another way, when we are in this *humble* position (depending on Him for everything), God adorns our life with *His* fulfillment, contentment, fullness of purpose, wisdom, peace, and joy!

A JOYOUS THOUGHT FOR TODAY:

*In all your ways **acknowledge Him,** and **He will
make your paths straight.*** —PROVERBS 3:6

For Today, praise God for being able to experience His total peace and joy by simply acknowledging that He is everything and you are nothing *(Romans 11:36)!* He is the *Potter* and you are clay *(Isaiah 64:8)!* He is the *How-Great-Thou-Art Shepherd* leading you, His beloved sheep, always with goodness and lovingkindness *(Psalm 23:1, 6).* *What great peace and pure joy!*

MY JOYOUS THOUGHTS

I'M JUDGING GOD?

JAMES 4:11-17

Do not speak against one another, brethren. He who speaks against a brother or judges his brother, speaks against the law and judges the law; but if you judge the law, you are not a doer of the law but a judge of it. [12]There is only one Lawgiver and Judge, the One who is able to save and to destroy; but who are you who judge your neighbor? [13]Come now, you who say, "Today or tomorrow we will go to such and such a city, and spend a year there and engage in business and make a profit." [14]Yet you do not know what your life will be like tomorrow. You are just a vapor that appears for a little while and then vanishes away. [15]Instead, you ought to say, "If the Lord wills, we will live and also do this or that." [16]But as it is, you boast in your arrogance; all such boasting is evil. [17]Therefore, to one who knows the right thing to do and does not do it, to him it is sin.

DAY 151

Do not speak against one another, brethren. *He who speaks against a brother or judges his brother, speaks against the law and judges the law; but if you judge the law, you are not a doer of the law but a judge of it.*

—JAMES 4:11

This is the third time James has returned to how we talk to (and about) each other. In *James 1:26* (Days 77-80) he spoke of bridling the tongue; in *James 3:6* (Days 100-101) he described the tongue as a fire that defiles the body and sets on fire the whole course of life (and is set on fire by hell). Now James warns us not to judge or criticize others because when we do, we are actually judging God!

The *NIV* translates the first phrase in verse eleven as, *"Brothers, do not slander one another."* To *slander* means to say something false about someone else. Also in *James 5:9* we read, *"Do not complain, brethren, against one another."* James is telling us in these two verses, taken together in context, that we should avoid any form of speaking negatively *to* or *about* one another. For example, we "speak against" our spouse when we say, "how come you didn't do such and such?" Or we judge others when we say, "they're not very good Christians!" or "they don't discipline their kids properly."

Verse eleven continues, *"He who speaks against a brother or judges his brother, speaks against the law [God's word] and judges the law."* Whenever we criticize anyone, we are actually judging God's law (or God's word). By the phrase *judges the law,* James means that we are deciding *which* laws of God are important enough to follow and *which* laws are not. For example, we say "stealing" is really wrong so we don't do that. But when we "criticize others," this reveals our heart's belief that such conduct isn't as important.

A JOYOUS THOUGHT FOR TODAY:

*I have come as Light into the world, so that **everyone who believes in Me will not remain in darkness.***

—JOHN 12:46

For Today, recognize that God's word brings light and understanding into your life to guide the words you speak *to* and *about* others. God's word does this to keep you walking in joy; and to use your words (God's word flowing through you) to accomplish His good purpose in the lives of others—resulting in peace, joy, comfort, and harmony.

DAY 152

*There is **only one** Lawgiver and Judge, the One who is able to save and to destroy; but who are you who judge your neighbor?*

—JAMES 4:12

James uses strong language to get his point across in this verse. He makes it crystal-clear that there is *only One* who created the law and therefore has the right to make judgments of people concerning His law—there is *only One* who has the power to save and destroy. That ONE is *not* us, but GOD! When we criticize others, we are engaging in the height of idol worship. We are attempting to replace God with ourselves and to act out the role of God (as Lawgiver and Judge). By taking on this task—by making assessments of people that only God has the right to make—we are not only judging the law which God established, but also God Himself as the Author of the law.

Whenever I prayerfully consider these verses from James, it is not long before I am on my knees in my heart before the Lord. It is not long before I am asking Him to search my heart for any hurtful, critical, or judgmental thoughts in me *(Psalm 139:23-24)*. These thoughts are the source of noxious evil and pernicious poison—that deeply affect the lives of others around me in profound ways.

How can we ever free ourselves from this critical and judgmental spirit? We can't; but the context of these verses shows us the way. Verse ten, just two verses back, exhorts us to *"**Humble yourselves** in the presence of the Lord, and **He will exalt you**."* We learned a couple of days ago (Day 150) that to *humble yourselves* means simply to desire for the Lord to manifest His life in us. He doesn't give us a "To-Do" list of seven things to please Him, but rather, manifests all the purposes of His gospel in our lives. Meaning, *HE* removes our critical feelings and makes *all* of our conversation refreshing instead!

A JOYOUS THOUGHT FOR TODAY:

Let no unwholesome word proceed from your mouth,
but only such a word as is good for edification
*according to the need of the moment, **so that it will give**
grace to those who hear.* —EPHESIANS 4:29

For Today, praise God that He purifies your speech *about* and *to* others as you just stay *on your knees in your heart toward God.* He turns criticism into grace for those who hear.

DAY 153

Come now, you who say, "Today or tomorrow we will go to such and such a city, and spend a year there and engage in business and make a profit." ¹⁴Yet you do not know what your life will be like tomorrow. **You are just a vapor that appears for a little while and then vanishes away.** *¹⁵Instead, you ought to say,* **"If the Lord wills, we will live and also do this or that."**

—JAMES 4:13-15

During his day, there were some who James knew were planning to travel somewhere and start a business. This speaks just as plainly to us today concerning the thought process and attitudes we harbor toward "tomorrow." He reminds us that we are *"just a vapor that appears for a little while and then vanishes away."* Have you ever had the opportunity to watch fog roll into a valley or on the coastline, only to see it just as quickly burn off and disappear? James is telling us that our entire lives on earth are just that short in God's eyes. It is like a vapor that appears *for a short time*—and then is gone. James tells us bluntly that we should not assume we are going to be alive tomorrow, next week, or next month.

Why is this distinction important? James is really saying that when we *forget* that God controls everything about our life—including the number of days we live—we can fall into the delusion that *WE*, not God, have control of our life. The moment we think it is up to us to plan out our own lives, *is* the moment when His joy and peace dissolve into fear and anxiety. Of course, if we give conscious thought to it, we will remember the truth that our lives are totally under God's control. Keeping this wisdom fresh in our hearts—that God is in *total* control of our lives in every respect—is the path to abiding joy and peace! There is enormous freedom in just humbling ourselves before God.

A JOYOUS THOUGHT FOR TODAY:

Do not boast about tomorrow, *for you do not know what a day may bring forth.* —PROVERBS 27:1

For Today, pray for God to shine His light on your attitude *about tomorrow*. Ask Him to draw your attention back to living in His presence *for today alone*. As you plan for the future, acknowledge His sovereignty in everything and He will bring you *great peace*.

DAY 154

But as it is, you boast in your arrogance; ***all such boasting is evil.*** *[17]Therefore, to one who knows the right thing to do and does not do it, to him it is sin.*
—JAMES 4:16-17

No one can ever accuse James of dancing around the hard issues. We prefer to shrug off our own cavalier attitudes concerning "tomorrow" as nothing more than semantics. We "know" that God is really in control, but we still *need* to plan for that future promotion at work, our next vacation with the family, retirement, or whatever. To be clear, James is not criticizing our need to plan *(Proverbs 21:31)*, but only our attitude that *assumes* we are going to live *ONE* more day (to accomplish whatever)—that attitude is *evil*. It is evil because we are assuming that WE control our life, not God. We make what we hope to do tomorrow more important than just wanting more of the Lord to be manifest in our life *TODAY!* We lose sight of the fact that just walking sensitive to God's Spirit within us *TODAY* is the *most important thing* we can do during our life on earth.

I still vividly remember how God brought this lesson to me years ago. I was a businessman with visionary plans for the future. I wanted to be counted among the wealthy and successful and I had plans to get me there. Suddenly, in the middle of playing racquetball with a friend, I felt a pain in my chest. One thing led to another and by nightfall I was in the hospital undergoing an angioplasty for a blockage to my heart. God used that surgery to bring me to my senses—to understand just how similar my life is to vapor! Whether my heart beats from moment to moment, let alone tomorrow or the next day, is totally and completely in the Lord's hands. That made me realize that what is most important to me in this life is just being conscious of the Lord—*TODAY!*

A JOYOUS THOUGHT FOR TODAY:

So ***do not worry about tomorrow;*** *for tomorrow will care for itself. Each day has enough trouble of its own.*
—MATTHEW 6:34

For Today, ask God to keep you focused on what is most important for you during your life on earth: just being conscious of the Lord's life *within you* in the *present* moment. This also yields within you a powerful sense of daily peace and joy.

Day 155

LORD, make me to know my end and what is the extent of my days; ***let me know how*** ***transient I am.*** *⁵Behold, You have made my days as handbreadths, and my lifetime as nothing in Your sight; surely every man at his best is a* ***mere breath.***
—Psalm 39:4-5, NASB

Lord, help me to realize how brief my time on earth will be. Help me to know that ***I am here for but a moment more.*** *⁵My life is no longer than my hand!*
—Psalm 39:4-5, TLB

Throughout James' letter, he has shared with us wisdom from God that brings us faithfully to a life of joy in every circumstance. This is another one of these wisdom truths. When we consciously think about it, we readily acknowledge that God is sovereign over our lives and is in complete control, including exactly how many breaths we will take during our sojourn here on this earth.

But our flesh works hard to busy us with all manner of distractions. "Our" schedules can grow so busy, in fact, that it becomes increasingly difficult to "squeeze" into our lives something as simple as praying or reading God's word. As Christians, we are not immune to these distractions. We may fill our days with "good" things, like witnessing, working in our church, Bible studies, and any number of other Christian activities, to the point that we grow bone-tired and numb to why we are doing it all in the first place.

Joy returns when God draws us back to recognize that our lives are *not* governed by "our" schedule, but by His! He has *not* put us in charge! He is in charge! From this perspective we can say, *"If God wills, we will live and do this or that."*

A Joyous Thought for Today:

What is man *that You magnify him, and* ***that You are*** ***concerned about him?*** —Job 7:17

For Today, here is a great new joy: just recognize your *"smallness"* before God; that you are totally dependent on Him. He is managing everything *about* you and *for* you. *This is great joy!*

PRAYER

Dear Lord, keep me mindful of how transient my life is on this earth. I am here for but a moment more and then I will be with You for eternity. In this brief "breath" of time, You have a purpose for my sojourn through this world. I pray that You will not allow me to be distracted from Your purpose. Please keep me sensitive to Your presence and Your leading throughout my day. Make me increasingly hungry to know Your schedule for my life and what is most important—just to know You more and more. Amen.

MY JOYOUS THOUGHTS

THE EVIL OF
WANTING MORE

JAMES 5:1-6

Come now, you rich, weep and howl for your miseries which are coming upon you. [2]Your riches have rotted and your garments have become moth-eaten. [3]Your gold and your silver have rusted; and their rust will be a witness against you and will consume your flesh like fire. It is in the last days that you have stored up your treasure! [4]Behold, the pay of the laborers who mowed your fields, and which has been withheld by you, cries out against you; and the outcry of those who did the harvesting has reached the ears of the Lord of Sabaoth. [5]You have lived luxuriously on the earth and led a life of wanton pleasure; you have fattened your hearts in a day of slaughter. [6]You have condemned and put to death the righteous man; he does not resist you.

DAY 156

*Come now, **you rich,** weep and howl for your miseries which are coming upon you.*
—JAMES 5:1

Most Bible commentators believe *James 5:1-6* are referring to *non*-Christians for two reasons. *First,* James does not address his readers as "brothers" (as he does throughout the rest of his letter; *James 2:1, 5; 3:1; and 4:11*). *Second,* he doesn't encourage his readers to change their ways as he does elsewhere in his letter. These two observations lead to the conclusion that the *slaughter* mentioned in verse five is referring to God's coming judgment of *unbelievers.* This is consistent with all of scripture. Unbelievers are included here, in a letter to Christians, because God is warning them of the consequences of their actions. However, regardless of who the message is directed to, there is always a *benefit* to believers from *all* of God's word *(2 Timothy 3:16).*

To see this benefit, we must first understand who the *rich* are that James is referring to. If you own a car, are you rich? What if you own a large home or a business, or have a high paying job—are you rich? The Apostle Paul tells us in *1 Timothy 6:9,* *"But those who **want to get rich** fall into temptation and a snare and many foolish and harmful desires which plunge men into ruin and destruction."* Note that Paul is not condemning having material things (like a second car, a larger home, or an above-average income), but he says it is the *wanting more* (of whatever) that is an evil which robs us of God's joy, peace, and contentment; and hurts others in the process.

Many Old Testament believers had significant wealth (like Abraham, David, Solomon, and others). In *2 Chronicles 32:29,* we read *"for God had given him [Hezekiah] very great wealth."* Scripture makes it clear that the wealth (or possessing wealth) is not wrong, but it is the *wanting more apart from God* that is destructive.

A JOYOUS THOUGHT FOR TODAY:

*If we have **food and covering,** with these*
we shall be content. —1 TIMOTHY 6:8

For Today, if you have the basics of life, ask God to search your heart and remove anything that you *want more of* other than your hunger for more of Christ in your life. As you hunger for more of Him only—watch your joy and peace grow.

DAY 157

*Your **riches have rotted** and your **garments have become moth-eaten.** ³Your **gold and your silver have rusted;** and their rust will be a witness against you and will consume your flesh like fire. It is in the last days that you have stored up your treasure!*
—JAMES 5:2-3

R*iches* in James' day often consisted of oil, wine, and grain (agricultural produce), richly adorned garments (products of commerce, *2 Kings 5:5*), and silver and gold (currency). James is saying that the riches these so-called rich people have stored away as grain *have rotted* and the expensive clothes they have accumulated have been ruined by moths. Likewise, their gold and silver *have rusted* (meaning, it has tarnished), suggesting that it was wealth that had been stockpiled for many years.

James is telling these "rich" people that in their desire to acquire more and more, they end up wasting the very wealth they accumulate in excess (through natural ruination and destruction—rot, moths, and corrosion), when it could have been used to help others who have real needs *right now*.

What does this look like in practical terms? I remember one family giving a lawnmower to a family who could not afford to buy one themselves. This lawnmower could have been stored away until it went to rust, but instead, it was put to good use by a family who really needed it. That is what James is talking about! It isn't the wealth itself, which all flows from God, but the evil that results from a focus of trying to gather more and more wealth and accumulate more things, rather than focusing on just gaining more of Christ and seeing the present-day needs of others met in the process.

A JOYOUS THOUGHT FOR TODAY:

He who trusts in his riches will fall, but the righteous [those who trust in God] will flourish like the green leaf.
—PROVERBS 11:28

For Today, ask the Lord to give you fresh eyes to see excess wealth that you really don't need and where it might be put to good use by others. God will cause people in need to cross your path. Trusting God, the Giver of all wealth, is the only secure path to peace and contentment. Praise Him again and again for this insight.

DAY 158

*Behold, the pay of the laborers who mowed your fields, and which has been withheld by you, **cries out against you;** and the outcry of those who did the harvesting has reached the ears of the Lord of Sabaoth. ⁵You have lived luxuriously on the earth and led a life of wanton pleasure; you have **fattened your hearts** in a **day of slaughter.***
—JAMES 5:4-5

These verses expose another evil that occurs when we fall into the trap of "wanting more." It is so tempting to cheat and take advantage of others in our manipulations to keep more for ourselves. Verse four says, *"... the pay of the laborers ... which has been withheld by you ..."* means that when our passion is focused on getting more for ourselves financially, it blinds us to what is fair and honest in how we deal with others.

Here is an example. For years, I thought if our business needed to improve its cash flow, the best and cheapest way to accomplish this (rather than get a bank loan) was to delay paying our bills to vendors for thirty to ninety days. I honestly thought this strategy was good business. I never gave thought to the harm I was doing to the vendor when I delayed my payment. How were they going to pay *their* employees and bills without *my* timely payment to them? In truth, I was blinded by my own greed!

James continues in verse five to warn those *unsaved* among the church who are taking advantage financially of others that they have *"fattened your hearts in a day of slaughter."* James is telling them that all unsaved people who are chasing more material gain are adding self-indulgent "weight" to their own coming day of slaughter!

A JOYOUS THOUGHT FOR TODAY:

*You have put gladness in my heart, more than when their grain and new wine abound. ⁸In peace I will both lie down and sleep, for **You alone, O LORD**, make me to dwell in safety.* —PSALM 4:7-8

For Today, give thanks to God for His salvation. He has not left you with the self-delusion that more wealth can save you, or make you happier. He has put *His* gladness in your heart, for He *alone* makes you dwell in safety. This is the basis for true peace, joy, and contentment.

A PERSONAL TESTIMONY

A New Compassion for the Poor

I shared with you on Day 158 how in the early days of building my business I would strategically delay paying my vendors for as long as thirty to ninety days in order to improve my own cash flow. I gave no thought to how damaging this would be to the vendors affected by this selfish act.

Likewise, when buying something new, I would scrutinize every inch of whatever product I was buying in hopes of finding some imperfection (no matter how small) so I could use it to leverage the vendor into discounting their price for the product.

I thought this way until the Lord one day implanted *James 5:4* into me. Here is how verse four reads in *The Living Bible: "For listen! Hear the cries of the field workers whom you have cheated of their pay. Their cries have reached the ears of the Lord of Hosts."* The Lord pierced my heart with this verse in a personal way, *"Listen **Daryl,** hear the cries of the vendors that you have cheated of their pay!"* From that moment forward, I never again delayed payment to any vendor for any reason (other than a legitimate dispute pending resolution).

By the way, speaking of verse four, but on an unrelated topic, this verse has also given me a whole new compassion for people who struggle financially. James clearly implies that those in need, or of modest means are often "poor," not because of their own laziness or their own financial mismanagement, but because of people taking advantage of them—who want more for themselves and are willing to hurt and cheat anyone who gets in their way of achieving more wealth. This realization has made me less judgmental of others who are poor and more willing to help them in practical ways.

DAY 159

*You have condemned and **put to death the righteous man;** he does not resist you.*
—JAMES 5:6

A final evil that James highlights in these verses relates to how our obsession with "making more" often results in our influencing others toward ruin. Verse six tells us that those who obsess over making more have *"put to death the righteous man."* This phrase harkens back to what James said in *James 4:2* (Day 138), that our selfish desires are so strong that some people commit murder out of believing that such an action will make them happy. Here in verse six, he is saying that some people actually "kill" for more wealth!

This verse, of course, is easy to dismiss with the thought: *I wouldn't kill anyone for more money!* But how about when our friends and children see us admiring the financial success of others—the new house, car, or boat they just bought, or job promotion they just got—*more* than we admire people's faith and prayer life, or their walking daily sensitive to the Lord's leading? How much destructive influence does this have on others?

As for me, I want my kids, family, and friends to see *me* admiring the God-given *faith* that one friend has as she deals every day with terminal cancer; and the God-given *peace* that another friend has as he continues to recover from a stroke; and the God-given *trust* in the Lord another couple has as they deal every day with weighty family matters.

A JOYOUS THOUGHT FOR TODAY:

*Instruct those who are **rich in this present world** **not to** be conceited or to **fix their hope on the** **uncertainty of riches, but on God,** who richly **supplies** us with **all things to enjoy.*** —1 TIMOTHY 6:17

For Today, praise God for His exhortation in Timothy concerning the insecurity of money. He is faithful to draw your eyes off of that which can *never* satisfy you in order to refocus you *on Him,* the source of *all* true joy and the supplier of *all* the things you need—*AND MORE!*

PRAYER

Dear Lord, how attractive to my flesh is the glitter of gold and the addition to my storehouse of more and more things that add to my earthly wealth. Please keep me focused on You as the only source of security and happiness in my life as I sojourn through this world. Simplify my understanding that no amount of money can save me! No amount of wealth can produce any amount of true happiness and contentment in my life. You are the source of **all** *blessings and* **all** *wealth. While I thank You for all of the provisions You have blessed my family with, I pray earnestly that You will guard my heart from being distracted by these things, or* **anything,** *and continue to draw my heart to seek* **You alone.** *Amen.*

MY JOYOUS THOUGHTS

WHAT MAKES US PATIENT?

JAMES 5:7-11

Therefore be patient, brethren, until the coming of the Lord. The farmer waits for the precious produce of the soil, being patient about it, until it gets the early and late rains. [8]You too be patient; strengthen your hearts, for the coming of the Lord is near. [9]Do not complain, brethren, against one another, so that you yourselves may not be judged; behold, the Judge is standing right at the door. [10]As an example, brethren, of suffering and patience, take the prophets who spoke in the name of the Lord. [11]We count those blessed who endured. You have heard of the endurance of Job and have seen the outcome of the Lord's dealings, that the Lord is full of compassion and is merciful.

Day 160

Therefore be patient, brethren, until the coming of the Lord. The farmer waits for the precious produce of the soil, being patient about it, until it gets the early and late rains. ⁸You too be patient; strengthen your hearts, for the coming of the Lord is near.
—James 5:7-8

Verse seven begins with the word *therefore* and refers back to verses one through six (Days 156-159), where James talked about the financially "poor" Christians among them being taken advantage of by greedy people of wealth and power in the community. James is referring back to these poor Christians and encouraging them to *be patient!*

If you have ever tried your hand at raising a garden, you know what James is talking about. Your job isn't done simply because you turned over some soil and planted a few seeds. Days often run into weeks before the first signs of growth of those seeds can be seen poking through the soil. Then there are weeks upon weeks of tending the garden as these tiny, frail plants continue to grow. *Patience* is the hallmark of the farmer, but his patience pays off in *precious produce* from the soil. This patience is not *retrospective* in focus, but *prospective*—it always *looks ahead* to a future harvest.

Verse eight exhorts *us* to *be patient* like the farmer. With that in mind, what is the *precious produce* we are looking ahead to? James tells us that our precious produce is the *COMING OF THE LORD*; and *HEAVEN,* our eternal home where there is no more sin, suffering and injustice! Like the farmer, who toils day after day in the dust and hot sun, we toil in the midst of suffering and hardships. We should not expect to be treated fairly, or kindly, *now* (by others); no more than the farmer expects his crop to be fully grown as soon as he plants the seed. Our *impatience* comes from wanting *precious produce NOW!*

A Joyous Thought for Today:

Casting all your anxiety on Him,
because He cares for you. —1 Peter 5:7

For Today, rest in the fact that you are a child of God and He is caring for you. Praise Him for revealing this glorious truth to you in order to give you *patience* with the hardships you face today.

DAY 161

You too be patient; strengthen your hearts, for the coming of the Lord is near. ⁹Do not complain, brethren, against one another, so that you yourselves may not be judged; behold, the Judge is standing right at the door.
—JAMES 5:8-9

The Greek word translated as *complain* in the *NASB* is translated as *grumble* in *The Living Bible*. This is due to the fact that the word includes *both* the sense of *inner distress* (to grumble or be discomforted) and the sense of *verbal criticism (to speak critically)*. James is not only telling us to avoid criticizing others verbally, but also to not agonize within ourselves about the situation. If our spouse has spoken a hurtful word, not only should we not criticize them, but we should not inwardly stew and agonize over the way he or she is mistreating us. The same goes for when our church does something we don't like. It is not enough to avoid speaking critically, we also should not be distressed about it in our hearts. Instead, verse eight tells us to *be patient*—to face calmly whatever difficulty we have at the moment. We will see how God does this in our hearts in Day 163.

Until then, let's look more closely at the word *patient* from both verse seven *("be patient ... until the coming of the Lord")* and verse eight *("be patient ... for the coming of the Lord is near")*. The same word is used in both verses and is derived from two Greek root words. One relates to *personal temperament* and the other to *a measure of time*. To understand James clearly, imagine a cooking oven with two control knobs on top. One is labeled "temperature" (which sets the *temperature* at which our food will cook) and the other is labeled "timer" (which sets *how long* our food will cook). James is telling us to set our personal temperature gauge on "PATIENT" and our *timer* on "UNTIL THE LORD RETURNS."

A JOYOUS THOUGHT FOR TODAY:

*With all humility and gentleness, **with patience**,*
showing tolerance for one another in love. —EPHESIANS 4:2

For Today, ask God to make this a bright light in your life; not to expect your difficulties to go away, or for others to treat you kindly or fairly, but only to look ahead to when *the Lord returns*. Knowing this will give you patience and peace.

What a light went on for me when I first realized that my "patience clock" was set on a very short timer. My flesh wanted difficult circumstances to change in a day or two, maybe a week, or a month at the latest. As the Lord has reset the timer on my "patience clock" to "UNTIL THE LORD RETURNS" it has brought enormous peace into my life.

James never expected the difficulties he experienced in this broken and ungodly world to improve until the Lord returns. He said *consider it all joy when you experience various trials,* not because he thought they would be few and far between, but rather because he knew that difficulties would be a daily challenge for every Christian until the Lord's return. As we read in James to "be patient," God's word is *living* and *active* to bring forth in us the reality of patience in our lives. Patience exposes our fleshly impatience and the desire to get what it wants when it wants it (Days 46-48). Patience leads to a freedom that yields daily joy, peace, and contentment beyond our grandest comprehension.

As you live a life set on "PATIENT" you will experience increased opposition. Sadly, this opposition often comes from other well-meaning Christians, who will insist that rather than patiently endure a situation month after month, action *must* be taken to *fix* the problem *immediately.* But God's word says we cannot be patient to a fault. We never need to worry about being patient *too long!* God has promised to *make us know* His leading *(Psalm 25:14)*; He will instruct us in the way we should choose *(Psalm 25:12)*; He will write His directions clearly on our hearts *(2 Corinthians 3:3-5)*; and He will direct our steps as we just trust Him to do so *(Proverb 3:5-6).* Being patient is actually *being active* in sensing God's speaking and leading in our lives.

I remember serving on a mission board of an orphanage located in a third-world country. When certain financial matters related to the orphanage came up, I encouraged those involved to wait *patiently* on the Lord for direction and timing to solve the problem. There were directors on this same board who repeatedly slandered and ridiculed me for this position. But, like James, the Lord in me was *patient,* with a loving sense of peace and love for each of these brothers in the Lord. Eventually, I quietly and peacefully resigned my position on the board and the remaining directors did what they wanted to do.

Day 162

*Do not complain, brethren, against one another, **so that you yourselves may not be judged; behold, the Judge is standing right at the door.***

—James 5:9

The second part of verse nine requires that we not forget the context of what James is discussing at the time. He has been encouraging poor believers to not complain and grumble, but be patient in the face of greedy rich people (unbelievers) in their midst who were taking advantage of them. With that in mind, two phrases are worth noting:

First, the phrase *"so that you yourselves may not be judged"* is often skipped over by Bible commentators to avoid the difficult language. Some believe James is referring to when Christ comes and sets aside the works of "man" from the works of God's Spirit according to *1 Corinthians 3.* I prefer to understand this verse in light of *Matthew 7:1-2* which says, *"Do not judge so that you will not be judged. ²For in the way you judge, you will be judged; and by your standard of measure, it will be measured to you."* I believe that *James 5:9* is simply saying that any time we criticize someone else, we set a standard by which we invite their criticism of us in return.

Second, the phrase *"behold, the Judge is standing right at the door,"* when read in context, is implying what James has been discussing since verse one—that Christ is coming soon to "judge" all *unbelievers.* Since He is coming soon, we believers can *be patient* and let the Lord do what is His right to do. He has not given us the task to judge other people. This awareness actually has the result of bringing us to our knees even more before God, praying for Christ to remove *all* of our complaining and disunity with one another!

A Joyous Thought for Today:

*Being strengthened with **all** power according to his glorious might so that **you may have great endurance and patience.*** —Colossians 1:11, NIV

For Today, God promises to grant you (to give you) *"great"* power (*greater power* than any of your difficulties) so you may experience *great endurance* and *patience* throughout your day. God knows your trials will continue until glory and He is giving you the patience to endure them. *Praise Him!*

DAY 163

*As an example, brethren, of suffering and patience, take the prophets who spoke in the name of the Lord. ¹¹We count those blessed who have endured. You have heard of the endurance of Job and have seen the outcome of the Lord's dealings, that the **Lord is full of compassion and is merciful.***

—JAMES 5:10-11

In verse ten, James is using the patience of the prophets and the endurance of Job to illustrate that this life has never been easy, just, or fair. But, praise God, James doesn't end there. He reminds us all in verse eleven that the Lord has always been full of compassion and mercy toward His people—meaning that God has *always* given His people the strength, direction, patience, and comfort they need, when they need it!

This is where *patience* comes from. In *2 Peter 1:3*, we read *"Seeing that His divine power has granted to us **everything** pertaining to life and **godliness**, through the true knowledge of Him who called us by His own glory and excellence."* The word *godliness* refers to every divine quality of God's life (which includes *patience*)! Peter is telling us that all godly qualities appear in our life effortlessly as we just grow in the true knowledge of God!

How many Christians feel anxious and *impatient* about what *they need* to do for God? How many are *impatient* about some loved one coming to know the Lord? How many are critical of another person who does not appear to be walking with the Lord like we think they should? When we come to understand that God is truly sovereign over *all* of life, and He will accomplish *all* of His good pleasure in our lives, it causes "patience" to grow *in* our lives and flow *out* to others for His praise and glory!

A JOYOUS THOUGHT FOR TODAY:

Declaring the end from the beginning, and from ancient times things which have not been done, saying,
*'**My purpose will be established, and I will accomplish all my good pleasure.**'* —ISAIAH 46:10

For Today, rest in the fact that God is establishing His purpose in you. He (not you) is accomplishing *all* (not some) of His good pleasure for you. What great joy and contentment this brings you throughout the day.

A SPECIAL WORD TO THE READER...

We are now approaching the final verses in this letter from James. You will recall that James began his letter talking about trials, something that all of us experience virtually every day of our lives, and how problematic this earthly life is and will continue to be. He then shares a series of Wisdoms from God that take the pain out of our trials and enable us to see this life through His divine lens. Now in chapter five, James shares his final exhortations, addressing various conduct and attitudes within the church and in individual lives. In this final set of devotionals, he culminates his letter with a specific clarification of *prayer's power* in our lives. As we will see, according to James, praying is the most powerful thing you can do on earth.

In these final devotionals, I want us to focus on what James tells us about prayer without adding any further speculations. To do this, we must dig deeper into James on three levels: *First,* we need to look into the meanings of the Greek words actually used by James in his epistle; *Second,* we need to compare usage of these same Greek words in other portions of scripture in the New Testament; and *third,* we need to consider the immediate context of these words in James.

When we understand scripture properly, it *always produces joyous freedom in Christ!*

There are few things more intimidating to Christians than praying to God. By shedding light on prayer, James intends to *remove* our fears and stress regarding praying to Him. We know from scripture that God will accomplish *all* of His perfect will in our lives whether we pray for it or not *(Isaiah 46:10)*. We know that Christ is *constantly* interceding on our behalf *(Hebrews 7:25)* and the Holy Spirit is *continually* praying for us *(Romans 8:26)*. Surely, the intercessory prayers of Christ and the Holy Spirit are in alignment with God's will and are certainly answered. At the same time, James puts *on our hearts to pray for one another* and tells us (in a way that perhaps we can't fully understand until glory) the powerful effect that this prayer has in another person's life.

It is my prayer, that our Heavenly Father will enlighten these remaining verses to you in a way that will revolutionize your life by building *within you the simple habit of prayer!*

My Joyous Thoughts

THE
POWER OF PRAYER

JAMES 5:13-20

Is anyone among you suffering? Then he must pray. Is anyone cheerful? He is to sing praises. [14]Is anyone among you sick? Then he must call for the elders of the church and they are to pray over him, anointing him with oil in the name of the Lord; [15]and the prayer offered in faith will restore the one who is sick, and the Lord will raise him up, and if he has committed sins, they will be forgiven him. [16]Therefore, confess your sins to one another, and pray for one another so that you may be healed. The effective prayer of a righteous man can accomplish much. [17]Elijah was a man with a nature like ours, and he prayed earnestly that it would not rain, and it did not rain on the earth for three years and six months. [18]Then he prayed again, and the sky poured rain and the earth produced its fruit. [19]My brethren, if any among you strays from the truth and one turns him back, [20]let him know that he who turns a sinner from the error of his way will save his soul from death and will cover a multitude of sins.

DAY 164

*Is anyone among you suffering? Then he must pray. **Is anyone cheerful?** He is to sing praises. ¹⁴Is anyone among you sick? Then he must call for the elders of the church and they are to pray over him, anointing him with oil in the name of the Lord.*

—JAMES 5:13-14

I n the context of these verses, James is describing various *spiritual conditions* being experienced by his Christian readers. Some were *suffering,* some were *cheerful,* and some were *sick.* What do each of these words mean? Let's start with the most misunderstood.

The Greek word for "sick" is *asthenei*—which means "to be weak." Without further understanding "to be weak" could refer to being "weak" physically or spiritually. That's why we need to look next at how the word is used elsewhere in scripture. In the four gospels (Matthew, Mark, Luke, and John), the word "weak" or "sick" is used to refer to physical illness or being physically sick. This is understandable since a major activity in the gospels shows Jesus healing sickness.

However, from Acts on, and all through the epistles, this same word is used primarily in reference to being *"weak in faith"* or *"weak"* in understanding and experiencing the truth and freedom of God's word. For example, *Romans 14:1* reads, *"Now accept the one who is weak in faith, but not for the purpose of passing judgment on his opinions."* The word *weak* in *Romans 14:1* is the exact same word translated *sick* in *James 5:14!* In *Romans 14:1,* it means to be *weak* in understanding God's word. Or *weak* in experiencing the freedom and peace that a deeper understanding of God's word brings to our life!

A JOYOUS THOUGHT FOR TODAY:

*And He has said to me, "My grace is sufficient for you,
for power is perfected in **weakness.**" Most gladly,
therefore, I will rather **boast about my weaknesses,**
so that the power of Christ may dwell in me.*

—2 CORINTHIANS 12:9

For Today, ask God to give you Paul's attitude toward your weakness (whatever you are struggling with today); recognize that in your weaknesses, Christ makes His power strong in you. As His strength overcomes your struggle (or quiets your heart in the midst of your struggle) you become filled with a new joy and praise to Him.

DAY 165

Is anyone among you sick? Then he must call for the elders of the church and they are to pray over him, anointing him with oil in the name of the Lord.
—JAMES 5:14

When we dig deeper into the meaning of a particular word, like the word *sick*, it is useful to first look to the Greek to discover its original meaning, then to look at other scriptures that use the same Greek word to explore its semantic range. Yesterday we looked at *Romans 14:1* for this purpose. Today, we'll look at two more verses that use the same word. The first is *1 Corinthians 8:9-10*, *"But take care that this liberty of yours does not somehow become a stumbling **block to the weak**. ¹⁰For if someone sees you, who have knowledge, dining in an idol's temple, **will not his conscience, if he is weak,** be strengthened to eat things sacrificed to idols?"* Paul is again referring to being *weak* in our understanding (or knowledge) of spiritual truth, not some form of physical sickness.

The second verse is *Romans 6:19a*, *"I am speaking in human terms because of the **weakness of your flesh."*** Once again, Paul is referring to a spiritual weakness, not a physical illness.

To be clear, reading these related verses still does not affirm with certainty what James is referring to (whether a spiritual or physical weakness) in *James 5:14*. However, these verses do give us greater insight to how the Greek word itself is most often used in all of Paul's letters (referring to a lack of understanding of spiritual truth or God's word). Tomorrow we will consider the immediate context of verse fourteen within *James 5*.

A JOYOUS THOUGHT FOR TODAY:

*Just as a father has compassion on his children
[referring to all believers], so the LORD has compassion
on those who fear [revere, worship] Him. ¹⁴For He
Himself knows our frame; **He is mindful that we
are but dust.*** —PSALM 103:13-14

For Today, take great joy in this: God's compassion for you will overcome every weakness you have (or don't yet know you have) and bring you to such great joy, you cannot help but praise Him!

Day 166

Is anyone among you suffering? Then he must pray. **Is anyone cheerful?** *He is to sing praises.* ¹⁴*Is anyone among you sick?*

—James 5:13-14a

Notice that in the immediate context of verse fourteen James is describing various spiritual conditions. Take, for example, the word *suffering* in verse thirteen, which refers to hardships or trouble of any kind. In fact, some translations (like the *NIV*) translate the verse, *"Is any one of you in trouble?"* Likewise, the word *cheerful* means to keep up courage or to be encouraged.

Expanding the context to the rest of chapter five, we recall from verse one through twelve that James has been talking about Christians who are becoming impatient and weary because of the financial hardships and continuing injustices imposed on them by unbelievers. Also in verse sixteen James says, *"Therefore [which is a word that summarizes what has gone before], confess your **sins** to one another."* The word *sins* refers to *spiritual shortcomings*—things like discouragement, lack in trusting the Lord, worry, fear, selfishness, etc.—which any believer can experience during their life of hardships and troubles. Finally, verse nineteen refers to *"straying from **the truth,**"* which carries the meaning of *spiritual truth,* not physical illness.

When we study the Greek word, consider other scriptural uses of that same word, and review the immediate context, it becomes clear that the word "sick" in *James 5:14* refers to those who have *a lesser understanding of spiritual truth,* or who have been *temporarily overcome by their flesh [by anger, fear, pride, or fighting hard to trust the Lord].* How many of us have ever thought: *I'm trying to trust the Lord, but it's really hard right now!* That is exactly what I believe James is referring to here by the term "sick."

A Joyous Thought for Today:

He has not dealt with us according to our sins, *nor rewarded us according to our iniquities.* —Psalms 103:10

For Today, be of good cheer, knowing that none of the hardships you are going through are punishment from God, but that He is using them *all* for your good: to manifest His greater power to glorify Himself, to grow your trust in Him, *and to give you peace!*

DAY 167

*Is anyone among you sick? Then he must **call for the elders** of the church and they are to pray over him, **anointing him** with oil in the name of the Lord; ¹⁵and the prayer offered in faith will restore the **one who is sick,** and the Lord will raise him up.*
—JAMES 5:14-15A

A careful study of the word *anointing* can also avoid another misunderstanding. *Aleipsantes* is the Greek word for *anointing* used by James and it means to *bestow honor and refreshment* on someone. The woman who poured perfume on Jesus' feet was performing this same act of honoring and refreshing Him. By contrast, a different Greek word (*chrio*), is used for the *anointing* associated with divine healing.

When James encourages those with a spiritual sickness to *"call for the elders"* to pray, he means to call for those who are entrusted with the church's welfare to come and pray with them. It does not mean that these men have special powers in their prayer, but only that they should be involved whenever there is a special need in the church. It also means that a spiritual needy person will be encouraged by the elders praying for them.

In verse fifteen the phrase *"the one who is sick"* comes from yet another Greek word than the *"sick"* in verse fourteen. In verse fifteen it means *to be weary or worn down by difficulty,* which relates back to how James began his letter: *Consider it all joy when you encounter **various trials.*** In context, we see that James' final words of encouragement to his readers is this: Whatever suffering, hardships, or spiritual weaknesses you are bearing (even physical illness), you can turn it all to God in prayer and *receive relief!*

A JOYOUS THOUGHT FOR TODAY:

*Be anxious for nothing, but in **everything by prayer**
and supplication **with thanksgiving** let your requests
be made known to God. ⁷And the peace of God, which
surpasses all comprehension, will guard your hearts and
your minds in Christ Jesus.* —PHILIPPIANS 4:6-7

For Today, take James' final words to heart; recognize that whatever your trials may be, you can take them all *TO GOD IN PRAYER,* with a grateful heart of thanksgiving because He will bring you into His peace and heartfelt joy. He promises to do that!

A PERSONAL TESTIMONY

James 5:14-15 reads, *"**Is anyone among you sick?** Then he must call for the elders of the church and they are to pray over him, anointing him with oil in the name of the Lord;* ¹⁵*and the prayer **offered in faith** will restore the one who is sick, and the Lord will raise him up, and if he has committed sins, they will be forgiven him."* Before God brought me the understanding I have today, I would pray for healing of the physically sick. When they did not get better, I would think to myself: *Don't I have enough "faith"? Or maybe the "sick" person is ill because of something they did, and they are being punished for it by God.* Today, however, I understand that this is *not at all* what James is talking about.

Unfortunately, my earlier confusion is not unique. These verses are heavily cited as scriptural authority for numerous "health and welfare" ministries that preach a "gospel" which promises the listener will be healed from any physical illness:

- *IF* they *just* give to that particular ministry "X" amount of money; or

- *IF* they *simply* buy a special "prayer cloth" from that ministry; or

- *IF* they pray a *certain* prayer; or

- *IF* they have *ENOUGH* faith!

While God certainly does heal the physically sick *according to His will,* we must take care to understand whether that is, in fact, what James is referring to here in his letter.

It is always worth remembering this: When we understand scripture properly, it never places us under condemnation, stress, negative burden, or harmful doubt; *but always produces joyous freedom in Christ (John 8:32)!*

DAY 168

*And the **prayer offered in faith** will restore the one who is sick, and the **Lord will raise him up**, and **if he has committed sins**, they will be **forgiven** him.*
—JAMES 5:15

The phrase *"if he has committed sins"* refers to our human shortcomings, which are ungodly attributes of our flesh like discouragement, fear, impatience, selfishness, worry, and things like that. The word *forgiven* is best understood from the *Berkeley Translation:* "... *in case he has committed sin, it will be **removed** from him.*" James is not referencing Christ's ***once and for all forgiveness*** according to *Hebrews 10:10-23, Colossians 2:13-14,* and *1 John 2:12,* to name a few references to this truth; but he is referring to a weary believer's discouragement, sense of defeat, anger, or loneliness that can (and will) be removed (or *lifted off* of them) *through prayer.* Praise the Lord!

I think we have all experienced what James is meaning in the phrase, "the Lord will raise him up." How many of us have prayed with someone over a current difficulty they have, and after doing so we see a smile begin to appear on their face as they say, "I feel much better now." That is exactly what I believe James is referring to when he says that the *Lord will raise them up.* He is referring to the *renewed strength and encouragement* that God brings to someone's life through the power of prayer *(Isaiah 40:29-31).*

So, without understanding anything more about prayer, how much does this increase our desire to pray for one another—if it lifts them up? How much more can we minister to those we care about—by just praying for them? *That is the mighty power of prayer!*

A JOYOUS THOUGHT FOR TODAY:

Pray without ceasing. —1 THESSALONIANS 5:17

For Today, as you go through your day, pray for others. As you do—realize that *God is lifting them up through your prayers.* Pray that the Lord will make this a regular part of *your* daily life. This will yield great peace and joy to you and to others. *God promises to do all of this for you!*

PRAYER

Dear Lord, teach me to appreciate how powerful and important prayer is for my own spiritual life and for the spiritual and physical welfare of those around me. For those I know who are struggling with health issues, bring them comfort and physical healing according to Your will. I also pray for those I know who are struggling with painful family issues. I pray that You will bring them patience, peace, and wisdom to deal with their difficulties. Dear God, continue throughout my day to bring others to my mind that I may pray for them. **Teach me**—*what it truly means to* **pray without ceasing.** *Amen.*

DAY 169

*Therefore, confess your sins to one another, and pray for one another so that you may be healed. **The effective prayer of a righteous man can accomplish much.***
—JAMES 5:16

What is *"the effective prayer of a righteous man"* that *"can accomplish much?"* Let's begin by understanding who James is referring to as *righteous*. Most of us immediately think: *Well, that leaves me out ... I'm far from righteous.* But think again! The *righteous man* James identifies in this verse refers to *all believers!* This is confirmed in *Genesis 15:6*, *"Then he (referring to Abraham) **believed in the Lord;** and He (the Lord) reckoned it to him as **righteousness.**"* So, all those who *believe in Christ* are righteous in the sight of God!

James is telling us that *any believer's* prayer can accomplish much! When we pray, God uses our prayer powerfully in the lives of others. But scripture points out one condition for our prayers to be powerful and accomplish much. We see this in *1 John 5:14-15, "This is the confidence which we have before Him, that, if **we ask anything** [or pray for anything] **according to His will**, He hears us. And if we know that He hears us in whatever we ask, we know that **we have** the requests which we have asked from Him."*

Tomorrow, we will see what praying according to *"God's will"* means. For now, simply understand that this one condition is *not* burdensome. God has provided an easy way for us to *always* pray according to His will.

A JOYOUS THOUGHT FOR TODAY:

*Then you will call upon Me and **come and pray to Me,** and I will listen to you. [13]You will seek Me and find Me when you search for Me with all your heart.*
—JEREMIAH 29:12-13

For Today, put every thought aside that God is distant and not listening to you. Just pray to Him, and you will discover that He is listening. *Seek, and you will find Him (Matthew 7:7)!* He will make Himself known afresh to you! Your joy will grow and grow, and increasingly have no bounds.

DAY 170

*Therefore, confess your sins to one another, and pray for one another so that you may be healed. The **effective prayer of a righteous man can accomplish much.***

—JAMES 5:16

The *effective prayer* of a righteous person is a prayer prayed according to God's will. When we pray for all things according to God's will, which includes His timing, we are never disappointed at the outcome. We give up our expectations and trust the Holy Spirit to touch our hearts and write on them how to pray as He desires us to pray. He will guide our steps and our prayers. We can rest in the fact that God has heard us and is working the outcome for our best *(Romans 8:28).*

Another way to know with certainty that we are praying according to God's will is to pray what scripture says. For example, *1 Thessalonians 5:14* tells us, *"be patient with everyone."* Since all of God's word reflects the will of God, we have confidence that we are praying according to His will when we pray *for patience* for ourselves or for someone else in the midst of a particular hardship. We need not ever doubt that we have prayed according to God's will, but need only wait upon Him for His timing.

Finally, here is perhaps the most comforting truth about *effective prayer.* In both of the examples above, what is the source of our *effective prayer? First,* it is the Holy Spirit's leading. *Second,* it is the word of God. You need not worry or stress over how to pray—just talk to God honestly about your feelings and worries. In the midst of that prayer Christ is interceding for you *(Hebrews 7:25),* the Holy Spirit is praying for you *(Romans 8:26)* and writing on your heart *(2 Corinthians 3:3),* and the Father is working out His will and good pleasure in your life *(Philippians 2:13).* It is not your responsibility to figure out and compose the *effective prayer* to God. He *initiates it and carries it out!*

A JOYOUS THOUGHT FOR TODAY:

In the morning, O LORD, You will hear my voice;
*in the morning **I will order my prayer to You***
and eagerly watch. —PSALM 5:3

For Today, be assured that your prayer, for anyone, is the most powerful way you can help them. Pray to God with new boldness, and experience great joy!

A PERSONAL TESTIMONY
Praying According to God's Will

If you are like me, we can pray about something, yet nothing appears to happen. We can get obsessed with a particular problem and then anguish over it for hours, praying for *specific outcomes* within *specific timeframes* of our choosing, as though God is our personal servant whenever we call on Him. This can lead to disappointment when we don't see our specific prayers answered *precisely* as we prayed them, and *exactly* when we wanted them answered. We may end up confused, discouraged, and questioning whether God is listening at all.

When this happened to me in my earlier years as a Christian, I would pester the Lord unmercifully, based on *Mark 7:25-30* and *Luke 11:5-13*, with my prayer requests for specific outcomes by *definite* deadlines. After all, I was a businessman and needed to hire people, make payrolls, and pay bills; all according to externally imposed deadlines. When I didn't receive the request, I eventually hardened my heart to believe that God was distant and didn't care for me in practical ways. It was enormously freeing when God brought me to see the pattern Jesus used when praying for a specific thing. In *Matthew 26:39* we read, *"And He went a little beyond them, and fell on His face and prayed, saying, 'My Father, if it is possible, let this cup [His pending death by crucifixion] pass from Me; **yet not as I will, but as You will.'"***

Here is where many Christians get intimidated. They freeze-up in their prayers to God, fearing that what they are about to pray for is not according to God's will. That is nothing but a lie from the enemy! *Philippians 4:6* tells us to *"Be anxious for nothing, **but in everything by prayer** and supplication with thanksgiving **let your requests be made known to God."*** God wants you to talk to Him about *everything,* and He is leading you to do so. He has also promised to answer your prayers according to His will.

This is an enormous freedom when you think about it. As we pray, we make our specific requests subordinate to God's will as Jesus did. In this way, we will never be disappointed in whatever form and timing God's answer comes. We may not "see" the answer until glory, yet we know that He has answered our prayers for our good and His glory!

Day 171

Therefore, confess your sins to one another, and pray for one another so that you may be healed. The effective prayer of a righteous man can accomplish much. ¹⁷Elijah was a man with a nature like ours, and he prayed earnestly that it would not rain, and it did not rain on the earth for three years and six months. ¹⁸Then he prayed again, and the sky poured rain and the earth produced its fruit.

—JAMES 5:16-18

Another misunderstanding we may have concerning prayer is this: if we have a problem, like a physical illness or bringing a loved one to the Lord, we sometimes think we can increase our chances of our prayers being answered *if* we get *more people* to pray. Of course, there is absolutely nothing wrong with more people praying because every person who prays receives the glorious benefit of prayer themselves. But James assures us in verse sixteen that this is not necessary.

James says the *"prayer of a righteous man can accomplish much."* James refers to the person praying in the singular. It is one person, not a large group of people. He then illustrates this truth in verses seventeen and eighteen by reminding us of what Elijah's prayer accomplished. Just *one* man praying turned "off" and "on" the rain on the entire earth! James points out that Elijah was a man just like us. He was *one* person praying, yet his prayer had an enormous effect.

Scripture is full of examples of *one* person praying. Praise the Lord that none of us need to feel disadvantaged because we have fewer friends praying for us in our time of need.

A JOYOUS THOUGHT FOR TODAY:

I pray [singular] that the eyes of your heart may be enlightened, so that you will know what is the hope of His calling, what are the riches of the glory of His inheritance in the saints." —EPHESIANS 1:18

For Today, know that as a believer in the Lord *you are righteous* in God's sight and *"can accomplish much"* in the lives of others (and yourself) with *just your* effective prayers. And don't forget, every *effective prayer* is initiated by God in you *(Philippians 2:13).*

DAY 172

*Therefore, **confess your sins** to one another, and pray for one another so that you may be healed. The effective **prayer** of a righteous man **can accomplish much.***

—JAMES 5:16

What is the *much* that is being accomplished, according to James? He begins this verse with the word *therefore* to connect what he has stated before. He has been discussing the various spiritual conditions that many in the church were experiencing. He concludes by sharing a process to gain healing from all of these spiritual ailments: *"confess your sins to one another, and pray for one another so that you may be healed."* This is not a small thing. Praying for one another is a powerful thing that can accomplish *much!*

To *confess* means to acknowledge and *sins* refer to any act, thought, or feeling that does not come from God; things we are struggling with, like anger, worry, and selfishness, to name a few. In simple terms, James is telling us to *share* our struggles with each other; so we can *pray* for one another; so we can be healed from our spiritual ailments and experience again God's *peace* and *joy* in our lives!

Paul shows us an example of this in *Ephesians 6:18-19, "With all prayer and petition **pray at all times in the Spirit,** and with this in view, be on the alert with all perseverance and petition **for all the saints,** [19]and **pray on my behalf,** that utterance may be given to me in the opening of my mouth, to make known with boldness the mystery of the gospel."* Paul encouraged the Galatians to be alert and pray for one another at all times. And he was not ashamed to ask for prayer for himself.

A JOYOUS THOUGHT FOR TODAY:

*First of all, then, I urge that entreaties and **prayers,** petitions and thanksgivings, **be made on behalf of all men,** [2]for kings and all who are in authority, **so that we may lead a tranquil and quiet life** in all godliness and dignity.* —1 TIMOTHY 2:1-2

For Today, expand your prayers to God for *all* men and women. Pray for Christians everywhere who are struggling, knowing God will quiet their life through your prayer.

DAY 173

*My brethren, **if any among you strays from the truth** and one turns him back,
²⁰let him know that he who turns a sinner from the error of his way will save his
soul from death and will cover a multitude of sins.*

—JAMES 5:19-20

There are two prevailing interpretations of these two concluding verses. The *first* suggests that James is speaking of individuals among the believers who were *not* truly saved. If any believer shares the gospel with a "straying" unbeliever (and they become a believer), then God has used this Christian messenger to save a person from *hellish death*.

The *second* interpretation (which I prefer because it best fits the context) suggests that the straying person refers to a believer who has "strayed" from the truth of God's word being *fresh in their lives*. These are the suffering and weak that James has been referring to throughout this final chapter. The *NIV* actually reads, *"My brothers, if one of you should wander from the truth."* The *Living Bible* reads, *"Dear brothers, if anyone no longer trusts the Lord."* Both translations suggest that the person who is straying is one of the believers who once trusted in God but is struggling to do so currently. I found it helpful to read *Walvoord & Zuck's Commentary* on *James 5:19-20,* "James referred here not to evangelism but to *restoration.* Revival, not redemption, is in view."

Christ, Himself, gives us a good word picture of this dynamic in *Matthew 18:12,* *"What do you think? If any man has a hundred sheep, and one of them has gone astray, does he not leave the ninety-nine on the mountains and go and search for the one that is straying?"* The terms *straying* and *astray* are the same Greek word used in *James 5:19.* Just because a sheep has strayed doesn't turn it into a goat. Our Great Shepherd, the Guardian of our souls, knows each and every one of His sheep by name and *He will always care for them.*

A JOYOUS THOUGHT FOR TODAY:

*For you were **continually straying like sheep,**
but now you have returned to the **Shepherd** and
Guardian of your souls.* —1 PETER 2:25

For Today, pray earnestly for those you know that have strayed from the truth of God's word and are now suffering because of it. God will renew their peace and joy in Him through your prayers for them, in His time. Praise the Lord!

Day 174

My brethren, if any among you strays from the truth and one turns him back,
*²⁰let him know that he who turns a sinner from the error of his way **will save his**
soul from death and will **cover a multitude of sins.***

—James 5:19-20

What does James mean when he says that a believer's soul will be saved *from death?* Since scripture repeatedly assures us that we can never lose our salvation, this is best understood to mean that the believer's life is saved from the deathly consequences of their sins (distrust in God, discouragement, selfishness, worry, etc.).

- They are *"saved"* from becoming physically or mentally ill from all of the worry and stress they suffer by trying to do things in their own effort;

- They are *"saved"* from the deathly consequences of wrong decisions taken when not trusting God regarding important life decisions;

- They are *"saved"* from the *"multitude of sins"* James has been talking about throughout his letter—impatience, anger, fear—and blaming God for it!

James concludes by saying that as this believer is restored, all of these sins are *"covered."* The term *"covered"* is best understood—*NOT* that the believer needs to be forgiven *again*—but that he is delivered from these painful, fleshly ailments, *back to joy in Christ!*

A Joyous Thought for Today:

My sheep hear My voice, and I know them, and they
follow Me; ²⁸and I give eternal life to them, and they
*will never perish; and **no one will snatch them out of***
***My hand.** ²⁹My Father, who has given them to Me, is*
*greater than all; and **no one is able to snatch them***
out of the Father's hand. —John 10:27-29

For Today, worship God with a thankful heart that He sent His Son to be *your* faithful Shepherd. Thank Him for loving *you* enough to *put you* on the hearts of other believers to pray for. Take comfort that *you* are in God's hands, *the safest place in the universe to be!*

DAY 175

*And the **prayer offered in faith** will restore the one who is sick, and the **Lord will raise him up,** and if he has committed sins, they will be forgiven him. [16]Therefore, confess your sins to one another, and **pray for one another** so that you may be healed. The **effective prayer** of a righteous man **can accomplish much.** [17]Elijah was a man with a nature like ours, and **he prayed earnestly** that it would not rain, and it did not rain on the earth for three years and six months. [18]Then he **prayed again,** and the sky poured rain and the earth produced its fruit.*

—JAMES 5:15-18

So, how powerful is prayer in the believer's life! We have seen that our individual prayer for another weary Christian can restore them to God's peace, comfort, and joy regardless of the difficulties they may be facing.

We have seen that our individual prayer contains the same power that turned *off* and *on* the rain from the earth. James tells us that Elijah was a man *just like us.* If God is putting something on our heart to pray for, then there is *nothing* too big for Him to accomplish.

Finally, we have seen God's promise in verse fifteen to *restore* another hurting believer and *raise them up.* It all begins with the Lord leading us to pray.

We now have a better understanding of what James meant when he said that "*the **effective prayer** of a righteous man **can accomplish much.**"* Every believer is that "righteous" person, whose prayers can accomplish *much more* than we can possibly comprehend. I simply do not have words to express how *"MUCH"* this term quantifies. For James, prayer is *the* most powerful thing we can do as Christians.

A JOYOUS THOUGHT FOR TODAY:

Blessed be the God and Father of our Lord Jesus Christ,
***who has blessed us with every spiritual blessing** in*
*the heavenly places **in Christ.*** —EPHESIANS 1:3

For Today, turn your earnest prayers and thanksgiving to God again and again, who has blessed you with every spiritual blessing in Christ; realizing that one of those blessings is His promised power *through your prayer.*

WISDOMS FROM GOD THAT PRODUCE JOY

JAMES 1:5

But if any of you lacks wisdom, let him ask of God, who gives to all generously and without reproach, and it will be given to him.

We have now journeyed with James, verse by verse, through his entire letter. Many think of James' letter as loosely equivalent to a New Testament *Proverbs*, a compilation of wise sayings, but not necessarily connected to each other. In our journey with James we have seen something quite different. James is sharing a cohesive message, with interconnected themes of wisdom-truths about God, for a specific purpose and goal: to bring understanding and clarification from scripture to give us genuine joy and peace in our lives regardless of our circumstances.

This is why James "hooks us" with his initial provocative pronouncement: *Be overjoyed when you have lots of problems (James 1:2)*. The whole notion of joy in the midst of trials seems wildly paradoxical. What kind of outlandish statement is James making? Yet it does force us to ask ourselves: *Am I joyous in the midst of the hassles I experience every day?* Most of us, I believe, would answer "no" to this personal inquiry. We reason logically to a wrong conclusion, that we are happy (or unhappy) because of our circumstances (as though we are neutral observers—or perhaps even innocent victims—of these external events). Since we perceive them to be outside of us, we conclude that *we* cannot possibly be the cause of the unhappiness we feel. When we employ this flawed logic, we are deceived into thinking that *if* our circumstances would only change for the better, we would be happier.

When this does not happen, we begin to question whether God is punishing us for something, which is a subtle way of *blaming God* for our problems and unhappiness. James tells us not to blame God for anything because *all* of our unhappiness is sourced from *inside of us (James 1:13-14)*. God is not responsible for our problems. *There is no unrighteousness in God!* He cannot do evil. He cannot tempt us to do bad things. He absolutely is not the source of any of the negative problems we are inclined to blame Him for. He doesn't take our jobs away, or give us cancer. He isn't punishing us. All of this evil comes from the broken world we live in. James powerfully emphasizes this wisdom-truth: God is *all* good! He is *always* good, there is *nothing but goodness* in Him, and *everything that is good is from* Him *(James 1:17)*.

James goes on to tell us that *all* our unhappiness is sourced in the lust of our fleshly "self," wanting what it wants when it wants it without any thought for God; which is what makes us miserable *(James 1:14)*. Our flesh is the declared enemy of God's peace. It clamors for self-sufficiency, strives to be right, and easily falls prey to growing bitterness and the urge to "get even" through retaliation or retribution. The flesh tempts us to worry about things that don't matter, and makes every situation seem urgent and critical. Its motivations are insidious and never pure, always egocentric, and stealthily deceitful. It stands ready at every moment to plunge us into the abyss of anxiety, panic, anger, and fear; and to strip us from the liberating experiences of God's abiding peace.

When James tells us that all our unhappiness is sourced in this fleshly abyss, it is a powerful insight from God. It is an essential step on a journey into God's wisdom that progressively yields more and more joy in our hearts regardless of our circumstances. James tells us that we often see every circumstance in terms of problems and trials. *Oh, NO! Not another problem! Why do I have to deal with another one? This is the fifth one this week!* Our flesh looks at it from the perspective of trying to reduce our five problems down to two—which would make us happier.

But here is how scripture describes it. In the midst of all these problems (no matter how many), God is gently strengthening within you and me (His children) the habit of increasingly *"faithing"* in Him—which, in turn, grows us more and more in His grace and joy, comfort, and wisdom. God tells us to *trust* His word: that He is taking *every* hurt that this evil world dishes out, *every* difficulty, *every* struggle, *every* injustice, and He is transforming it *all* into the good He promises us in *Romans 8:28*.

For James, recognizing how the flesh works is not a negative or discouraging thing. This understanding (wisdom) gives us a greater sense of what it means to be blessed, what it means to be saved, and what it means to live in the joy of our salvation. As we consider the actions of the "flesh trap" (Days 46-47), we are reminded that the flesh can *never* put down and defeat the flesh. This is often a source of great frustration for many Christians. They are painfully aware of their personal struggle with worry, selfishness, or lust for material things, yet they remain hopeful that *they* can (or should) make *themselves* better in *their* own effort (or with God's help).

But here is the glorious truth: God is *NOT* trying to improve your flesh; He is *replacing* every manifestation of it with *HIS SON*. God has taken us just as we are, full of fleshly anger, worry, impatience, impure thoughts, selfish desires, discouragement, etc. Then, by His mighty power, yet gently over the course of our entire life, God unveils a *true* knowledge of His Son's glorious life in us, which transforms us from glory to glory *(2 Corinthians 3:18)*. He replaces our fleshly attitudes with His own peace, joy, contentment, unconditional love, compassion, to name but a few; and produces in us a profound change that we could *never* accomplish on our own no matter how hard we tried. As *Ephesians 2:10* declares: *"For we are **His workmanship,** created in Christ Jesus ...."*

Think of it this way: Because God loves us, He chose you and me—to put our "clay" (which has no power to do anything for itself) on His potter's wheel—in order to shape us according to His will in a way that makes us increasingly joyful and happy in any circumstance. He progressively, day after day, over the course of our lives, defeats the fleshly ugliness in us. There is nothing for us to boast in after all. Our boast is *only* in God and His mercy for us. Many Christians think as I did for decades, that salvation is a "ticket to get into heaven," without realizing the incredible *salvation process* going on *every day of their lives* through the circumstances affecting them. This is how we are being saved *every day!*

James cuts through all of our self-deception and declares the truth: There is *only* good and evil in life. Evil is everything apart from God and since God is *all* good, it is everything contrary to what is truly good. Evil is contrary to *true* peace, *true* joy, and *true* happiness. Our flesh is saturated with evil, but God's Spirit *in us* is all good. This means, in practical terms, that the *more of* God *we experience, the less of our flesh we experience.* The more God draws us to pray, the more He sensitizes us to His Spirit's leading within us; and the more He leads us to read His word, the more of His "good" we experience instead of our flesh.

Dear reader, James' letter is all about sharing vital truths about God that will revolutionize your life in practical ways and infuse God's joy and peace into your daily experience. James cuts right to the chase—if you lack joy in your life, especially in the midst of trials, this is a "red flag" indicating you lack at that moment, or have temporarily forgotten, a vital wisdom-truth about God. Are you obsessing about some problem and lack peace and joy right now? Ask yourself, *what wisdom about God am I forgetting?* James' letter will lead you sequentially through this process. It is my prayer that the Lord will lead you to read and reread James' letter regularly as He grows these wisdom-truths within you for His glory and your daily peace, joy, and happiness.

PRAYER

Dear Lord, imprint on my mind and heart,
the life-giving wisdoms from this letter of James
that yield "joy" in every difficulty. I no longer
ask You to remove problems in my life, but only
that I might experience more and more of You
through each difficulty. Search me, like You did
David in Psalm 139:23-24, to find any
hurtful way in me. Grant me a deeper hunger
for Your word as You commanded in Joshua
1:8. For Your word, according to John 4:14, is
the spring of living water within me. Finally,
dear God, teach me to pray for others and lift
them up according to James 5:16. Guard my
mouth consistent with Ephesians 4:29,
that I would pray for others rather
than criticize them. Amen.

Now may the God of hope fill you with all joy
and peace in believing, so that you will abound in hope
by the power of the Holy Spirit.

—ROMANS 15:13

If the Lord leads,
go to the Grace Upon Grace Foundation
website (www.gugf.org) for more of
Daryl Kraft's Bible Studies.